The Economics of Rights, Co-operation and Welfare

The Economics of Rights, Co-operation and Welfare

Robert Sugden
University of East Anglia
UK

First edition published in 1986 by
Blackwell Publishers Ltd; second edition published 2004 by
PALGRAVE MACMILLAN
Houndmills, Basingstoke, Hampshire RG21 6XS and
175 Fifth Avenue, New York, N.Y. 10010
Companies and representatives throughout the world

PALGRAVE MACMILLAN is the global academic imprint of the Palgrave Macmillan division of St. Martin's Press, LLC and of Palgrave Macmillan Ltd. Macmillan® is a registered trademark in the United States, United Kingdom and other countries. Palgrave is a registered trademark in the European Union and other countries.

ISBN 0–333–68239–4

This book is printed on paper suitable for recycling and made from fully managed and sustained forest sources.

A catalogue record for this book is available from the British Library.

Library of Congress Cataloging-in-Publication Data
Sugden, Robert.
    The economics of rights, co-operation, and welfare /
Robert Sugden.–2nd ed.
        p. cm.
    Includes bibliographical references and index.
    ISBN 0–333–68239–4 (cloth)
        1. Free enterprise. 2. Liberty. 3. Property. 4. Welfare economics.
    5. Social choice. I. Title.

HB95.S84 2005
330.1–dc22   2004051675

10   9   8   7   6   5   4   3   2   1
13   12   11   10   09   08   07   06   05   04

Printed and bound in Great Britain by
Antony Rowe Ltd, Chippenham and Eastbourne

Contents

Introduction to the Second Edition

The Economics of Rights, Co-operation and Welfare is an attempt to understand social order and morality as conventions. It uses a theoretical method which, when the book was published in 1986, was virtually untried in the social sciences: evolutionary game theory. *ERCW* (as I shall call the book from now on) was modestly successful. It was read by quite a few economists, political theorists and philosophers. A scattering of people whose judgement I respected liked it, and used some of its ideas in their own work. But it went out of print before the evolutionary approach to social theory became fashionable.

Over the last fifteen years there has been a surge of interest in this approach, and a reaction against the rationalism that used to characterize economic theory, social choice theory and game theory. The idea that social order is grounded on convention, and that the emergence and persistence of conventions can be explained by evolutionary forms of game theory, is now widely espoused. Three prominent theorists have presented their own versions of these ideas: Ken Binmore in the two volumes of *Game Theory and the Social Contract* (1994, 1998), Brian Skyrms in *Evolution of the Social Contract* (1996), and Peyton Young in *Individual Strategy and Social Structure* (1998). These books clearly belong to the same genre as *ERCW*. But the approach I took is, I think, significantly different from, and more radically naturalistic than, most recent work in evolutionary game theory. In the belief that *ERCW* can make a contribution to current discussions, I have compiled this new edition.

Rather than revising the text, I have taken the stance of an editor – an editor who is sympathetic towards the original text, but who does not necessarily agree with every word in it. Apart from correcting a few errors, I have kept the text as it appeared in 1986, but I have added two sections of commentary: the Introduction you are now reading, and a longer Afterword. Most of what I want to say in commentary will make sense only to someone who has already read the relevant sections of the original book, and so is best written as an Afterword. But here is the right place for some general reflections on how the book came to be written and on why this new edition takes the form it does.

vii

Of all the things I have written, *ERCW* is the one of which I am most proud. I began work on the book in 1982, and finished it at the end of 1985. During this time, my mental picture of what I was writing changed enormously; the manuscript I finally sent to the publishers had little in common with the plan on which I had started out. Putting my ideas down on paper, I had experienced a growing sense of excitement. I felt as if I had found a new viewpoint on the old theoretical problem of explaining the nature of social order. I use the word *viewpoint* deliberately: I didn't feel that I was constructing a new theory, but rather that I was seeing things in a new perspective. Sometimes, looking back over what I had written, I feared that my readers would see in it only a collection of fairly obvious reflections on well-known pieces of theory; but I retained the sense – a sense that I still find hard to articulate – that the ideas I was struggling to express were true and significant. Perhaps all this is just a normal illusion of authorship. Still, in nothing else that I have written have I had quite the same sense of working with ideas that had a life of their own.

The origins of *ERCW* are explained in the Preface. I had started out intending to write a book about social contract theory, developing ideas from two books that had strongly influenced me: John Rawls's *A Theory of Justice* (1972) and James Buchanan's *The Limits of Liberty* (1975). My idea had been to dispense with Rawls's veil of ignorance and to look for principles that would command the rational assent of individuals drawing up a social contract in a Hobbesian state of nature. But the more I thought about the problem of finding unique rational solutions to bargaining games, the less confident I became that such solutions existed. It seemed to me that, in resolving bargaining problems, people typically draw on shared and tacit understandings which have evolved out of a history of previous interactions. I began to think that principles of justice might themselves emerge out of such tacit understandings. I found that this idea had been explored by David Hume in his *Treatise of Human Nature* (1740) and by Adam Smith in his *Theory of Moral Sentiments* (1759). In the work of these Scottish writers, I discovered an understanding of social life as a spontaneous order, in which what we take to be principles of morality and justice are conventions that have developed out of natural human sentiments through processes of recurrent social interaction.

I realized that these ideas could be developed by thinking of social interactions as games. However, the game theory of the early 1980s concerned itself only with the actions of perfectly rational players. 'Rationality' was defined extremely narrowly. A rational player, it was stipulated, could take account only of those features of a game (strategies, payoffs, information sets and so on) that are recognized by mathematical game theory. In forming expectations about what other players might do, a rational player makes deductive inferences from the premise that the rationality of all players is common knowledge. I soon discovered that this kind of modelling strategy could not represent evolutionary processes. To try to solve the problems I faced, I drew on ideas from three sources outside mainstream game theory.

First, there was the analysis of coordination problems in Thomas Schelling's *Strategy of Conflict* (1960). Schelling's idea that people solve coordination problems by drawing on common conceptions of prominence was widely known; but, because of the difficulties of explaining why prominence would matter for ideally rational agents, it had never been integrated into economics or game theory. Second, there was David Lewis's *Convention* (1969). Although this book had been applauded for presenting one of the first formal definitions of common knowledge, few economists had noticed its game-theoretic analysis of conventions. I was particularly influenced by Lewis's treatment of the role of precedent in the reproduction of conventions, and by his analysis of how conventions can become norms. My third source was the work of a group of theoretical biologists, led by John Maynard Smith, who were adapting game theory to explain the evolution of animal behaviour. At the time, this work had made little impact on economics; the idea that economics might learn something from biology had hardly been broached. In different ways, these three lines of analysis showed how there could be a theory of games which did not presuppose that players were ideally rational agents, abstracted from history and social context. My book became an attempt to understand social order as convention, in the spirit of Hume and Adam Smith, using a non-rationalistic approach to game theory inspired by Schelling, Lewis and Maynard Smith. It is because *ERCW* integrates ideas from these disparate but classic sources, and because it relies surprisingly little on the mainstream economics and game theory of the 1980s, that it has (as I believe) aged gracefully, and still has something to contribute to the understanding of social order and morality.

In trying to decide how best to re-introduce it into the current literature, I have been torn between conflicting sets of thoughts. Some aspects of the book have undoubtedly dated. This is most obviously true of some of the examples, such as the references to 33 rpm record players or to the significance of the line along which the Soviet army met the British and American armies in 1945. But that should not be a problem for a sympathetic reader: theories of social conventions are intended to apply to all human societies at all times, and so evidence from one period of history is just as valid as evidence from another.

It is a more serious problem that evolutionary game theory has advanced enormously since the 1980s. When I wrote *ERCW*, evolutionary game theory was almost wholly the preserve of biologists. In adapting this body of theory so that it could be used in social science, I started from scratch. I approached this task from the standpoint of a social theorist, trying to find ways of understanding certain aspects of the social world, rather than that of a game theorist, predisposed towards particular ways of modelling the interactions of rational agents. In truth (as will become obvious to many modern readers) my knowledge of mathematical game theory was quite limited. That was true of most economists in the early 1980s. In constructing evolutionary models, my template was the evolutionary game theory of biology, not the mathematical game theory of ideal rationality. Since I wrote the book, a whole genre of evolutionary game theory has been developed by economists and game theorists. Although this literature has been influenced by biology too, it is much more rooted in mathematical game theory than *ERCW* is. In fact, most of the formal analysis in *ERCW* can easily be re-expressed in the terms of modern evolutionary game theory; but the language of *ERCW* is not quite the same as the modern one.

ERCW often uses highly specific models to express hunches about what might be shown to be true in a more general framework. In some cases, more general results are now known. In addition, a huge amount of experimental research has been carried out since 1986, throwing new light on issues discussed in *ERCW*. If I were to rewrite the book, I would need to integrate these new ideas into an intricate argument that had been constructed many years ago. When I began to think about how this might be done, I found myself reluctant to change the original text.

I thought of my intellectual hero David Hume. Hume was in his mid-twenties when he wrote his masterpiece, the *Treatise of Human Nature*. On his account, it 'fell dead-born from the press'. In later life, having established his reputation as a writer and scholar, he rewrote the *Treatise* as the *Enquiries concerning Human Understanding and concerning the Principles of Morals* (1759). The *Enquiries* is a much more polished work than its predecessor. Plain Scottish language has been replaced by elegant literary English. Its pages are full of the classical allusions that, for eighteenth century readers, were an essential feature of any serious book. But much of the brilliance and originality of the *Treatise* – including some fascinating passages which, to a modern reader, anticipate ideas developed in game theory two centuries later – has been edited out. The moral I draw from this story is that, just as the nature of an author's contributions may not be appreciated by his first readers, so also it may not be appreciated by his older self. *ERCW* is probably the best book I will ever write, and I don't want to spoil it.

So, for this edition, I have allowed myself only the role of editor. In that role, in the Afterword, I explain how the arguments of *ERCW* relate to subsequent work on the evolution of conventions and norms, and how I think they stand up against objections that have been made by critical readers. I shall argue that, for the most part, they stand up well.

I am grateful for all the comments that have been given to me – in publications, in seminars and conferences, in correspondence and in private discussions – in response to the arguments in *ERCW*. Whether these responses have been supportive or sceptical, they have helped me to develop my ideas. Among the many people who have helped me in this way are Federica Alberti, Luciano Andreozzi, Michael Bacharach, Nicholas Bardsley, Ken Binmore, Robin Cubitt, Peter Hammerstein, Jean Hampton, Wade Hands, Shaun Hargreaves Heap, Govert den Hartogh, Martin Hollis, Maarten Janssen, Edward McClennen, Jane Mansbridge, Peter Marks, Judith Mehta, Shepley Orr, Mozaffar Qizilbash, Amartya Sen, Brian Skyrms, Chris Starmer, Peter Vanderschraaf, Yanis Varoufakis, Bruno Verbeek, and Jung-Sic Yang. I am also grateful to Peter Newman, who persuaded Palgrave Macmillan to publish a second edition of *ERCW*, and to my wife Christine who, when I was on the point of concluding that the second edition would never be written, encouraged me to change my mind and to set aside the time to finish the work.

Preface to the First Edition

The idea for this book started to take shape in the summer of 1982. I was enjoying the hospitality of the Center for Study of Public Choice, just before its move from Virginia Polytechnic Institute to George Mason University. Taking up a suggestion of Jim Buchanan's, I read David Hume's *Treatise of Human Nature*.

For some years I had been interested in social contract theory and, as readers of my last book will know, I had worked in the 'ideal contract' tradition of John Harsanyi and John Rawls. I was beginning to become dissatisfied with this kind of contractarianism. One thing that worried me was the great weight placed on particular principles of rational choice – principles that I began to realize were not at all self-evident. Another problem was that my inclinations were much more towards Rawls's view, in which justice is connected with ideas of co-operation and mutual advantage, than towards Harsanyi's utilitarianism; but, given the logic of choice behind a 'veil of ignorance', I found myself forced to side with Harsanyi. I wondered if the way out of these difficulties might be to abandon the veil of ignorance and to think (as Buchanan had done in *The Limits of Liberty*) of people drawing up a contract in a Hobbesian state of nature. But then the problem was that each individual could try to hold out for terms favourable to himself; there seemed no determinate answer to the question: 'On what terms would the contracting parties settle?'

Hume's account 'of the origin of justice and property' pointed me in a new direction. I began to think that the notion of a social contract was an artificial device and that it was much more natural to conceive of principles of justice gradually evolving out of the interactions of individuals pursuing conflicting interests. I realized too that Hume's insights could be developed by using the ideas of game theory. I soon found that many of the components I needed for a game-theoretic analysis of the evolution of rules of justice already existed, scattered through the literature of economics, political science, philosophy and (which may seem surprising) biology. In many ways I learned most from the biological literature, since it provided a theoretical framework for analysing evolutionary processes – a framework that neoclassical economics, with its emphasis on rational maximizing in a static environment, is ill-equipped to supply.

In the first seven chapters of this book I bring this work together and extend it in various ways. My object is to show that if individuals pursue their own interests in a state of anarchy, order – in the form of conventions of behaviour that it is in each individual's interest to follow – can arise spontaneously. In the final two chapters I argue that, although these conventions need not maximize social welfare in any meaningful sense, they will tend to become norms: people will come to believe that their behaviour *ought* to be regulated by convention. I argue that such beliefs represent a genuine and coherent system of morality, towards which most of us have some leanings, and for which none of us needs to apologize.

I have presented the main ideas in this book, and particularly the controversial ideas of the final chapters, to numerous seminars and conferences. I do not think that I have yet convinced many people, but I am grateful for all the comments and criticisms I have received from (usually sceptical) listeners. They have helped me sort out my thoughts and sharpen my arguments.

1
Spontaneous Order

In Britain, drivers almost always keep to the left-hand side of the road. Why? It is tempting to answer: 'Because that is the law in Britain.' Certainly someone who drove on the right would be in danger of prosecution for dangerous driving. But British drivers don't keep slavishly to *all* the laws governing the use of the roads. It is a criminal offence for a driver not to wear a seat belt, to drive a vehicle whose windscreen wipers are not in working order, or to sound a horn at night in a built-up area; but these laws are often broken. Even people who cheerfully break the law against drunken driving – a very serious offence, carrying heavy penalties – usually keep left.

The answer to the original question, surely, is: 'Because everyone else drives on the left.' To drive on the right in a country in which people normally drive on the left is to choose a quick route to the hospital or the cemetery. The rule that we should drive on the left is self-enforcing.

So we do not always need the machinery of the law to maintain order in social affairs; such order as we observe is not always the creation of governments and police forces. Anarchy in the literal sense ('absence of government') cannot be equated with anarchy in the pejorative sense ('disorder; political or social confusion'). The notion of spontaneous order – to use Friedrich Hayek's phrase[1] – or orderly anarchy – to use James Buchanan's (1975, pp. 4–6) – is not a contradiction in terms. Perhaps driving on the left is a rare example of spontaneous order, and in most cases the absence of government does lead to disorder and confusion; but this is not a self-evident truth. The possibilities of spontaneous order deserve to be looked into.

In this book I shall investigate the extent to which people can coordinate their behaviour – can maintain some sort of social order – without relying on the formal machinery of law and government. In short, I shall

1

study human behaviour in a state of anarchy. I shall begin by explaining why I believe such a study to be worthwhile, and in particular, since I am an economist, why I believe it has something to contribute to economics.

1.1   Economics and spontaneous order

It might be objected that economics is, and always has been, primarily a study of spontaneous order. The idea that the market is a self-regulating system has been one of the main themes of the discipline ever since Adam Smith. As Smith put it in one of the most famous sentences in economics, the individual who intends only his own gain is led by the institutions of the market to promote the public interest: he is 'led by an invisible hand to promote an end which was no part of his intention' (Smith, 1776, Book 4, Ch. 2). But in modern economics, the market is seen as a complex and imperfect system which has to be carefully looked after by the government: property rights have to be defined and protected, contracts have to be enforced, 'market failures' have to be corrected and income has to be redistributed to ensure social justice. The markets that are represented in economic theory are not states of anarchy.

It is certainly true that economists take a great deal of professional pride in the theory of the workings of an ideal competitive economy. Although this theory has been progressively refined by mathematical economists from Walras in the nineteenth century to Arrow and Debreu (1954) in the twentieth, it is in a direct line of descent from Smith's analysis of the invisible hand. Arrow is speaking for many fellow economists when he writes that the price system 'is certainly one of the most remarkable of social institutions and the analysis of its working is, in my judgement, one of the more significant intellectual achievements of mankind' (Arrow, 1967, p. 221). Nevertheless, the Walrasian (or Arrow–Debreu) theory of competitive equilibrium is not usually taken seriously at the practical as opposed to the theoretical level. Few economists are brave enough to claim that a modern industrial economy organized on *laissez-faire* principles would work much like the Walrasian model. It is more usual to say that the Walrasian model serves as a benchmark or limiting case; it provides a framework for thought. Thus economists tend to view the realities of economic life as divergences from an ideal Walrasian model. (That is why we use such expressions as 'market failure' and 'government intervention': the theoretical norm is a perfect market system and a *laissez-faire* government.) But the prevailing view is that these divergences are many and significant: market failure occurs in most areas of economic life, and so government intervention is required. When Arrow writes about the economics of medical care, for example, he presents a long list of ways in which reality diverges from the ideal model for which, as a theoretician, he has such admiration; he concludes by remarking that a study of these divergences 'force[s] us to recognize the incomplete description of reality supplied by the impersonal price system' and by endorsing the 'general social consensus... that the *laissez-faire* solution for medicine is intolerable' (Arrow, 1963, p. 967). The medical-care industry is perhaps an extreme case, but there can be few real world markets in which economists have not diagnosed some kind of market failure and prescribed some kind of government intervention.

Most modern economic theory describes a world presided over by *a government* (not, significantly, by governments), and sees this world through the government's eyes. The government is supposed to have the responsibility, the will and the power to restructure society in whatever way maximizes social welfare; like the US Cavalry in a good Western, the government stands ready to rush to the rescue whenever the market 'fails', and the economist's job is to advise it on when and how to do so. Private individuals, in contrast, are credited with little or no ability to solve collective problems among themselves. This makes for a distorted view of some important economic and political issues.

1.2   The problem of public goods

In one important respect economists are very pessimistic about the chances of promoting the public interest through the self-interested actions of individuals. The market, it is conventional to say, cannot solve the problem of supplying public goods. A public good is one that is consumed jointly by a number of individuals, so that the benefit each person derives from the good depends not on how much *he* buys or supplies, but on how much *everyone* does. (For example, suppose that a community of ten households is connected to the outside world by a single road. If one household spends time or money repairing the road, all the others benefit; so the activity of repairing the road is a public good to the community.) Conventional economic theory predicts that public goods will be seriously under-supplied unless the government intervenes (the US Cavalry again). If the supply of public goods is left to private individuals, it is said, everyone will try to take a free ride at the expense of everyone else; the result will be one that *no one* wants. Everyone ends up trapped in a situation in which everyone would prefer it if everyone contributed towards the supply of the public good; but each person finds it in his interest not to contribute. This problem is known variously as the 'problem of public goods', the 'problem of collective action', the 'prisoner's dilemma problem' and the 'tragedy of the commons'.

In reality, however, some public goods *are* supplied through the voluntary contributions of private individuals, without any pressure from the government. In Britain, for example, the lifeboat service is paid for in this way. If you are in danger at sea, the boats of the Royal National Lifeboat Institution will come to your rescue, even if you have never contributed a penny towards their costs; and you will be charged nothing. So the existence of the lifeboat service is a public good to everyone who might have to call on its services. The same applies to blood banks. If you need a blood transfusion in Britain, the National Blood Transfusion Service will supply the blood without charge; so the existence of a blood bank is a public good to everyone who might some day need a transfusion. This public good is supplied by unpaid donors. Countless more examples could be given. Works of art, great houses and stretches of countryside are bought for the nation through fund-raising appeals; the work of the churches in many countries is almost entirely financed by private gifts; and so on, and so on.

Economics has found it extremely difficult to explain this sort of activity, which runs counter to the theoretical prediction of free-riding behaviour.[2] It seems that economics underestimates the ability of individuals to coordinate their behaviour to solve common problems: it is unduly pessimistic about the possibility of spontaneous order.

1.3   The limits of government

The power of governments is not unlimited: some laws have proved almost impossible to enforce. The most famous example is probably the American experience of Prohibition. Prostitution, too, is notoriously resistant to the laws of puritanical governments. In centrally planned economies, black markets are similarly resistant to the forces of law. The attempts of successive British governments to regulate trade union activity have had, at best, mixed success.

Wise governments do not risk losing credibility by passing laws that cannot be enforced; and when such laws are passed, wise police forces turn a blind eye to violations of them. British policy towards speed limits on roads provides an interesting example. The speed at which most people actually drive on a particular road is used to help determine the level at which the speed limit is set. If the vast majority of drivers are observed to break a speed limit on a particular stretch of road, this is taken to be evidence in favour of raising the limit.

One implication of this is that governments must, if only as a matter of prudence, take some account of the possibility that the laws they might wish to pass may be unenforceable. The willingness or unwillingness of individuals to obey the law is a constraint on the government's freedom of action. Obviously, for any law, there will always be some people who will not obey it except under threat of punishment; but the system of policing and punishment is liable to break down if everyone is in this position. In other words, if a law is to work it must not go too much against the grain of the forces of spontaneous order. Adam Smith put this point well in *The Theory of Moral Sentiments*:

> The man of system . . . is often so enamoured with the supposed beauty of his own ideal plan of government, that he cannot suffer the smallest deviation from any part of it. . . . He seems to imagine that he can arrange the different members of a great society with as much ease as the hand arranges the different pieces upon a chess-board. He does not consider that the pieces upon the chess-board have no other principle of motion besides that which the hand impresses upon them; but that, in the great chess-board of human society, every single piece has a principle of motion of its own, altogether different from that which the legislature might chuse to impress upon it. If those two principles coincide and act in the same direction, the game of human society will go on easily and harmoniously, and is very likely to be happy and successful. If they are opposite or different, the game will go on miserably, and the society must be at all times in the highest degree of disorder. (1759, Part 6, Section 2, Ch. 2)

A more fundamental implication is that it may sometimes be misleading to think of the law as the creation of the government, imposed on its citizens. This characteristically utilitarian view is the one economists usually take; the law, for most economists, is a 'policy instrument' to be controlled by a benevolent social-welfare maximizing government. (Economists often recommend that the government 'corrects' a market failure by means of some change in the law – for example that monopoly power should be limited by anti-trust law, or that the law of property should be changed so as to 'internalize' external effects.) But it may be that some important aspects of the law merely formalize and codify conventions of behaviour that have evolved out of essentially anarchic situations; as in the case of the speed limits, the law may reflect codes of behaviour that most individuals impose on themselves.

The British rule of driving on the left provides another example. If you were caught driving on the right-hand side of the road you would normally be charged, not under any law specifically requiring you to drive on the left, but with the catch-all offence of 'dangerous driving'. Clearly it *is* dangerous to drive on the right, but only because everyone else drives on the left. In other words, driving on the right is illegal *because* it is contrary to convention: the law follows the regularity in behaviour, and not the other way round. To admit this possibility is to say that if we are to understand why the law is as it is, and how it works, we must study anarchy as well as government.

There is another way in which the power of governments is limited: every government inhabits a world that contains other governments. The difficulties that this creates are often swept under the carpet in theoretical economics, where the typical model is of a self-contained society presided over by a single government. As I mentioned earlier, economists tend to talk about 'the government' rather than 'governments'.

Writing in the seventeenth century, Thomas Hobbes noted that international affairs provided one of the best examples of pure anarchy (Hobbes, 1651, Ch. 13). Three hundred years later, that insight remains true; we are no nearer to the prospect of a world government with the power to enforce its rulings on recalcitrant states. In the meanwhile, unfortunately, the dangers of international anarchy have increased immeasurably. Quite apart from the continuous increase in the destructive power of military weapons, there is a growing tendency for the peacetime activities of one nation to impinge on the citizens of others. Consider the problems of acid rain, pollution of the sea, over-fishing and deforestation. In all these cases – and there are many others – conservation is a public good on an international scale. Each nation has an incentive to take a free ride on the conservation efforts of other nations.

In cases like these, the economist's traditional recommendation of 'government intervention' is useless; there is no government to intervene in the affairs of nations. The institutions and conventions of anarchy are the only ones we have within which to find solutions for some of the most pressing problems of our time. This alone would be sufficient reason for studying spontaneous order.

1.4 Moral viewpoints

Practical economists are expected to draw 'policy conclusions' from their studies of human behaviour. A policy conclusion, as every economist knows, is a recommendation about what the government ought to do. The economist's job, it seems, is to observe and explain the behaviour of private individuals – workers, consumers and entrepreneurs – and then to advise the government. It is a curious fact that academic economists rarely think of doing things the other way round – observing the behaviour of governments and then using their findings to advise private individuals. Such work *is* done, but only in response to a demand, and for pay: it is 'consultancy'. In contrast, advice to governments – unasked for and unheeded – can be found in any economics journal.

In a sense, the usual stance of the economist is to pretend he *is* the government, and free to implement any policy he wishes. Applied economics is largely about predicting the consequences of alternative policies that the government might adopt. In order to make these predictions, the economist has to try to model the behaviour of private individuals as accurately as possible; he has to understand how they actually behave. But there is no need to do the same for the government; the concern is not with how governments actually behave, but with what would happen if particular policies were adopted. In the jargon of economics, the behaviour of governments is exogenous to the theory. This is part of what I have called the 'US Cavalry' model in which the government is an unexplained institution, always on call to implement whatever solutions to social problems the economist can devise.

This government's-eye view of the world has led economists to take a rather one-sided view of moral questions. The normative branch of economics – called, significantly, 'welfare economics' or 'social choice theory' – is concerned with questions of the kind: 'What is best for society?' or 'What would generate most welfare for society?' or 'What ought society to choose?' Notice that these are the sort of moral questions that would be faced by a benevolent and all-powerful government of the kind that the economist imagines himself to be advising.

This, however, is only one aspect of morality, and one that is rather remote from the concerns of the ordinary individual. For most of us, 'What ought *I* to choose?' is a much more pressing moral question than 'What ought *society* to choose?' Economists have had very little to say about the morality of individual behaviour. The prevailing view, I think, is that we should take individual morality as we find it, and treat it as a kind of preference. There is even a tendency to restrict the words 'moral' and 'ethical' to judgements about the good of society as a whole. Many economists (including myself, I must confess) have made use of Harsanyi's (1955) distinction between 'subjective preferences' and 'ethical preferences'. A person's subjective preferences, which by implication are non-ethical, are those that govern his private choices, while his ethical preferences are his disinterested judgements about the welfare of society as a whole. Harsanyi argues that in order to arrive at ethical preferences, a person must try to imagine himself in a position where he doesn't know his own identity, and has an equal chance of becoming anyone in society. The logic of this approach is that the proper viewpoint from which to make moral judgements is that of an impartially benevolent observer, looking on society from above; in a literal sense we can never take this viewpoint, but when we think morally we must try our best to imagine how things would look to us if we were impartial observers. This conception of moral thinking is not, of course, peculiar to modern economics; it is the view characteristically taken by writers in the utilitarian tradition and can be traced back at least as far as Smith (1759) and Hume (1740).

One of the main themes of this book is that there is another viewpoint from which an individual can make moral judgements: his own viewpoint. Individuals living together in a state of anarchy, I shall argue, tend to evolve conventions or codes of conduct that reduce the extent of interpersonal conflict: this is spontaneous order. The origin of these conventions is in the interest that each individual has in living his own life without coming into conflict with others. But such conventions can become a basic component of our sense of morality. We come to believe that we are entitled to expect that other people respect these conventions in their dealings with us; when we suffer from other people's breaches of conventions we complain of injustice.

So, I shall argue, some of our ideas of rights, entitlements and justice may be rooted in conventions that have never been consciously designed by anyone. They have merely evolved. A society that conducts its affairs in accordance with such standards of justice may not maximize its welfare in any sense that would be recognized by an impartial observer. To put this the other way round, a benevolent government may find that it cannot maximize social welfare, evaluated from some impartial viewpoint, without violating conventions that its citizens regard as principles of justice.

It is, of course, open to the utilitarian or the welfare economist to say, 'Too bad about the citizens' ideas of justice: our duty is to maximize social welfare.' But to say this is to take a viewpoint something like that of a colonial administrator benevolently trying to advance the welfare of a native population.[3] Or, as Buchanan (1975, p. 1) puts it, there is a suggestion of playing God. In a democratic and open society, public morality cannot be something separate from the morality that guides private individuals in the conduct of their own affairs. A good deal of our private morality, I shall be arguing, has nothing to do with the rational reflections of an impartial observer. To understand it we must understand the forces of spontaneous order.

2
Games

2.1 The idea of a game

The notion of spontaneous order can, I shall argue, best be understood by using the theory of games. In this chapter I shall explain how I intend to use this theory, illustrating my argument with a very simple game which provides a useful model of how social conventions might evolve.

A game is a situation in which a number of individuals or players interact, and in which the outcome for each of them depends not only on what he or she chooses to do, but also on what the others choose to do. Here is a simple example, which I shall call the 'banknote game'. Two people, A and B, are taken to different rooms, and are not allowed to communicate with one another. The organizer of the game then tells each player: 'I have donated a £5 note and a £10 note to enable this game to be played. You must say which of the two notes you want to claim. If you claim the same note as the other player, neither of you will get anything; but if you claim different notes, you will each get the note you claim.' Notice that both players have an interest in the existence of some convention about who takes which note, even though they would not agree but about which convention was best.

I have deliberately chosen a game that could be played in a controlled experiment, so as to exclude the complications that would be bound to arise in any discussion of real social relationships. For the present, my purpose is only to set out the logic of game theory. However, there are many real problems whose structure is similar to that of the banknote game; some of these will be discussed in Chapter 3.

In the banknote game, each player has to choose one of two strategies. A can claim the £5 note (which may be called strategy A_1) or the £10 note (strategy A_2). B too can claim either the £5 note (B_1) or the £10

B's strategy

		B_1	B_2
A's strategy	A_1	A wins nothing B wins nothing	A wins £5 B wins £10
	A_2	A wins £10 B wins £5	A wins nothing B wins nothing

Figure 2.1   The game form of the asymmetrical banknote game

note (B_2). For every possible combination of strategies there is a clearly defined outcome. To have a list of possible strategies for each player and an outcome for every possible combination of strategies, is to have what is known technically as a game form.[1] For ease of exposition, however, I shall usually speak of a game form simply as a 'game'.

The game form for the banknote game is described by the matrix in Figure 2.1. Notice that this matrix has the following property of symmetry. Let $Q(A_i, B_j)$ stand for the outcome that occurs if A plays strategy A_i and B plays strategy B_j. Then for any values of i and j, the descriptions of the two outcomes $Q(A_i, B_j)$ and $Q(A_j, B_i)$ are identical except for the transposition of 'A' and 'B'. This general property of a two-person game form – or, more loosely, of a game – will be called outcome symmetry. In essence, a game has outcome symmetry if it provides the same possibilities for both players.

The banknote game has two special features that may seem atypical of social interaction in real life: the players choose their strategies simultaneously, and there is no communication between the players. In most board games, players move in turn. In chess, for example, Black does not have to choose his first move until he has seen White's. The same is true in many real-life games of social interaction. Suppose Arthur would like Bert to help him with some job on Monday, and Bert would like Arthur to help him with a different job on Tuesday. Arthur can wait to see whether Bert helps him before deciding whether to help Bert. At first sight, these games look very different from the banknote game. The truth, however, is that games that involve a sequence of moves can be represented as though each player independently chooses a single strategy, covering every possible contingency. Part of Black's strategy for a chess game might be: 'If White opens with P-K4, reply with P-QB4.' Arthur's strategy might be: 'If Bert helps on Monday, help him on Tuesday; if he doesn't help on Monday, don't help him on Tuesday.'

It must be admitted that the list of strategies open to a player can be very long indeed, even in quite simple games. (If every chess game came to an end after Black's first move, White would have 20 possible strategies and Black would have 20^{20} – that is, more than 100 million billion billion!) Obviously, then, there are many games for which it is impractical to list strategies. There may be other reasons for choosing to represent games in ways that make more explicit the order in which the players move. None the less, lists of strategies are always theoretically possible: the idea of such a list always makes sense. In other words, there is nothing logically contradictory about representing a game of sequential moves in terms of simultaneously-chosen strategies.

In the banknote game the players are not allowed to communicate with one another. This makes it impossible for them to co-operate when choosing their strategies. There are certainly some interactions between people in which explicit co-operation is impossible. (Suppose two cars are approaching one another at speed on collision courses. The drivers cannot negotiate a solution to their problem.) There are also cases in which co-operation, although possible, is pointless. (This is true of any two-person game in which each player's sole object is to beat the other: it is logically impossible to make any arrangement that benefits both players.) But in many game-like situations, deals between players are both possible and mutually beneficial – indeed the game may be all about making deals. This is most obviously true of market transactions: I want to buy, you want to sell, and the problem is to settle on a price. But deals, agreements, treaties or contracts feature in just about every aspect of social life. Even in war – perhaps the closest analogue to the game in which each player's sole object is to beat the other – there is always room for mutually beneficial arrangements, for example over the treatment of prisoners.

It is however, quite possible to represent these kinds of game in a framework of simultaneously chosen strategies. Suppose that Charlie puts his car up for sale, and invites offers. Deborah wants to buy it. Charlie's strategy, which he might choose before communicating with Deborah at all, might be: 'If Deborah offers £1500 or more, accept; if she offers less, refuse to trade.' Deborah's strategy might be 'Offer £1300. If Charlie refuses to sell, offer £1400. If he still refuses to sell, don't trade.'

So the idea that a game can be described in terms of strategies, and that players choose their strategies independently and simultaneously, is a theoretical one. It represents a way of thinking about interactions between people, and not a particular and narrowly defined type of interaction. I hope to be able to show that it is also a useful way of thinking about social life.

2.2 Repeated games

Consider the banknote game again, and suppose we carry out the following experiment. We form a large group of people. Then we choose two individuals at random and set them to play the banknote game against each other. The two players are not allowed to meet or to communicate or even to know who their opponents are. Each player chooses his strategy, is told which strategy his opponent has chosen, and collects his winnings (if any). Then two more people are chosen at random to play against one another. (They are chosen from the whole group, and so it is possible that one or both of the original players may be chosen again.) We repeat this process many times, so that each person in the experiment plays many games, and watch to see if the way the game is played eventually settles down in any sort of pattern. In this book I shall be mainly concerned with repeated games of this kind.

There are two alternative ways of setting up this experiment. The difference may seem tiny, but it turns out to be very important. One way would be to describe the game to each player as one between 'you' and 'your opponent'; then the two players in any game would receive identical descriptions of the kind shown in Figure 2.2. Each player has to choose between two strategies, S_1 and S_2, knowing that his opponent faces the same choice. Notice that this presentation of the game is possible only because the banknote game has the property of outcome symmetry. In this version of the experiment the positions of the two players are completely symmetrical; I shall call a game of this kind a symmetrical game.

A different way of setting up the experiment would be as follows. Suppose that after two individuals have been chosen at random to play the

	Your opponent's strategy	
	S_1	S_2
S_1	You win nothing Your opponent wins nothing	You win £5 Your opponent wins £10
S_2	You win £10 Your opponent wins £5	You win nothing Your opponent wins nothing

Figure 2.2 The game form of the symmetrical banknote game

banknote game against one another, one of them (chosen at random) is told he is playing the role of A and the other is told he is playing the role of B. Then the game is described to the players in the form shown in Figure 2.1 – as a game between A and B. This matrix has the property of outcome symmetry, but it has what I shall call a labelling asymmetry. The game does not look exactly the same from the viewpoints of the two players, since one has been told he has been labelled 'A' while the other has been told he has been labelled 'B'. Any game which contains an element of asymmetry – whether outcome asymmetry or merely labelling asymmetry – will be called an asymmetrical game.

If we are to say anything about the strategies people will choose, we need to know what they are trying to achieve. It is a fundamental assumption of the theory of games that players are concerned only with outcomes. Strategies have no value in themselves: they are the means, and outcomes are the ends. Each player, it is assumed, can attach some subjective value to every outcome, and chooses his strategy so as to do the best he can in terms of this scale of value. The value of an outcome to an individual is measured by a utility index. Exactly what 'utility' means will be discussed in Section 2.3; for the present it is sufficient to say that the utility of an outcome to a player is a measure of how much that player wants it to come about.

Consider any one individual playing a particular symmetrical game repeatedly. If there are n alternative strategies for each of the two players in any one game there are n^2 possible outcomes and hence n^2 utility indices for the individual in question. Figure 2.3 presents illustrative utility indices for an individual playing the symmetrical banknote game. Matrices of this kind will be used throughout as a standard notation for describing symmetrical games.

Now consider any one individual playing an asymmetrical game repeatedly. If there are m alternative strategies for player A and n for player B, there are $2mn$ possible outcomes for each individual, since he can play the game either as A or B. Thus there are $2mn$ utility indices

		Opponent's strategy	
		S_1	S_2
Player's strategy	S_1	0	1
	S_2	2	0

Figure 2.3   The symmetrical banknote game

		B's strategy	
		B_1	B_2
A's strategy	A_1	0, 0	1, 2
	A_2	2, 1	0, 0

Figure 2.4   The asymmetrical banknote game

for any individual. Figure 2.4 presents illustrative utility indices for the asymmetrical banknote game. (Notice that I am assuming that the asymmetry in the banknote game is one of labelling and nothing else; a player's utility depends only on how much he wins and is independent of whether he is playing as A or B.) Each cell in the matrix represents a pair of strategies that might be chosen by the two players in any game. The first entry in the cell is the utility derived by the individual in question if this pair of strategies is played when he is A; the second entry is the utility derived by the same individual if this pair of strategies is chosen when he is B. It is important to notice that a matrix like Figure 2.4 presents the utility indices of one individual and not two: A and B are different roles that a given individual might play, and not different individuals. I shall use matrices of this kind as a standard notation for describing asymmetrical games.

2.3   Utility

What does 'utility' mean? Essentially, the utility of an outcome to an individual is a measure of how much it is wanted by that individual. For the purposes of game theory it does not matter why an outcome is wanted. In particular, there is no need to equate utility with self-interest. The players in a game may be trying to achieve many things, not all of which can be reduced to self-interest; and their unselfish aims may come into conflict just as much as their selfish ones.

Suppose Frank and Gertrude are negotiating the price of some good that Frank is selling to Gertrude, that Frank wants to receive the highest possible price and that Gertrude wants to pay the lowest possible one. Perhaps Frank wants money to spend on drink and Gertrude wants to save money so she has more to spend on cigarettes. Or perhaps Frank wants money to support his aged parents and Gertrude wants to save money so she can give more to charity. The logic of the game is essentially the same in either case: Frank's wants and Gertrude's wants conflict.

Not all games are about conflict. Suppose Frank and Gertrude accidentally lose one another while walking in a busy city. They have made no plans for this contingency. Where should each person go in the hope of finding the other? (This is an example of a coordination game: see Section 3.3.) If each person's sole concern is to go to the place where the other person is most likely to be, there is no conflict of interest; but each of them faces a real problem of choice among strategies. The logic of this game is quite independent of the reasons why Frank and Gertrude are trying to regain contact: they may be organizing a charitable venture or plotting a robbery. The point of all this is that the concepts of conflict and co-operation – the central concerns of game theory – are quite distinct from those of selfishness and selflessness.

Economists and game theorists have usually defined utility in ways that presuppose that individuals have 'consistent' preferences and choose 'rationally'. The rational-choice conception of utility was first fully formulated by two of the pioneers of game theory, von Neumann and Morgenstern, in their classic book *Theory of Games and Economic Behaviour* (1947). They showed that if an individual's preferences over gambles satisfied a number of axioms, it was in principle possible to assign a utility index to every conceivable outcome. Faced with any choice under uncertainty, an individual would choose the course of action that maximized 'expected utility'. (The expected utility of an action is a weighted average of the utilities of all the outcomes to which the action might lead; the weight assigned to each outcome is the probability of that outcome's occurrence.)

Much of the theory of games has been built on this conception of utility. Unfortunately, this has proved to be a rather shaky foundation. There is a large and growing body of evidence to show that, in reality, most people do not behave in accordance with von Neumann and Morgenstern's axioms. The problem is not that observed behaviour deviates from the axioms in a random fashion; there are some quite systematic patterns in human behaviour that cannot be reconciled with the theory of expected utility (see, for example, Allais, 1953; Kahneman and Tversky, 1979; Schoemaker, 1982).

Some expected-utility theorists, including Morgenstern (1979, p. 180) himself, have fought a rearguard action by arguing that their axioms are necessary properties of rational choice, even if many people do not in fact behave as rationality requires. According to Morgenstern, 'if people deviate from the theory, an explanation of the theory and of their deviation will cause them to re-adjust their behaviour.' As a statement of fact, this proposition is questionable, as there is some evidence that people continue to want to behave contrary to the theory even after their supposed irrationality has been pointed out to them (cf. Slovic and Tversky, 1974). It is also debatable whether it really is irrational to deviate from expected utility theory. (That such deviations need not be irrational has been argued strongly by Allais (1953); Loomes and Sugden (1982) have made the same point.) But even if we were to agree with Morgenstern, the evidence about how people behave would remain. We should have to decide whether the theory of games was to be a theory of how people actually play games, or a theory of how they would play them, were they fully rational.

Many game theorists would choose the second alternative. Indeed, the theory of games is often defined as the theory of how games would be played by totally rational individuals. According to one theorist, 'game theory is concerned with the behaviour of absolutely rational decision makers whose capabilities of reasoning and memorizing are unlimited' (Selten, 1975, p. 27). According to another, the definition of a game for the purposes of game theory 'is restrictive [in the following sense]: *the players are perfect*. Perfect, that is, in reasoning [and] in mental skills...'(Bacharach, 1976, p. 1). It is here that my approach to games diverges from the conventional one. Indeed, on a strict interpretation of these definitions, the present book is not about game theory at all.

My ultimate objective is to explain how social conventions can emerge out of anarchic interactions between individuals. I shall be concerned with conventions like promises, property and mutual aid – conventions that are found in a wide range of societies and cultures and that are as old as recorded history. If I am to explain these phenomena as the product of game-playing behaviour, I need a theory of how people *actually* play games. Any assumptions I make about behaviour must be ones that most human beings act on, and have acted on, in almost all places and times. I can make no use of a concept of rationality that is so sophisticated that ordinary people do not act on it unless it has been carefully explained to them.

However, I do not necessarily need a complete theory of choice – one that applies to every game that a person could possibly play. I shall be looking at a limited number of simple games of human interaction. These games share two important common properties: they are played for fairly small stakes, and they are played repeatedly. It is sufficient for my purposes to have a theory of how people play games of this kind. The crucial feature of this sort of game is that players can learn by experience. My analysis will rest on a very simple notion of what it is to learn by experience: I shall assume that individuals tend to adopt those strategies that have proved most successful over a long sequence of games.

In the banknote game there is no particular problem in defining 'success' since we can assume that over a sequence of games each player wants to win the largest possible sum of money. Thus the success of a strategy over a sequence of games can be measured by the total amount of money it wins. But, in general, the values of the outcomes of games are measured in utility rather than money. I shall assume that the success of a strategy over a sequence of games is measured by the sum of the utilities it generates in the games that make up the sequence.

This assumption is not quite as innocuous as it looks, since it rules out many possible patterns of preference over sequences of outcomes. For example, consider an individual playing a game which has just two possible outcomes, x and y. Suppose he plays the game twice. Thus there are four possible sequences of outcomes: (x, x), (x, y), (y, x) and (y, y). At the level of the individual game there are only three possibilities: either x has a higher utility than y, or y has a higher utility than x, or they both have the same utility. The first possibility entails that (x, x) is the sequence with the largest total utility, followed by (x, y) and (y, x) which have the same total utility as one another, followed by (y, y) which has the smallest total utility. The second possibility entails that (y, y) is the best sequence, (x, x) is the worst, and (x, y) and (y, x) are equally good. The third possibility entails that all four sequences are equally good. Notice that it is impossible for (x, y) to be better than (y, x) or vice versa. In other words, my assumption rules out the possibility than an individual might care about the order in which outcomes are experienced. Notice also that it is impossible for (x, y) or (y, x) to be better than both (x, x) and (y, y): there can be no preference for variety over sameness. Nor is it possible for (x, y) or (y, x) to be worse than both (x, x) and (y, y); a preference for sameness over variety is also ruled out.

Is it plausible to rule out all these possibilities? It is easy enough to think of cases in which my assumption would not hold. (Think of a game in which x stands for 'the player eats a hamburger' and y stands for 'the player eats an ice cream'.) So the assumption certainly cannot be defended as an axiom of rationality. But it may be defensible as a simplifying device when analysing certain kinds of game. The essence of the assumption is that outcomes can be evaluated independently of one another; we can talk about how much a player wants a particular outcome without asking which game in a sequence is being played, or what outcomes have occurred in previous games, or what outcomes are likely to occur in future games. I believe that this assumption is reasonable enough for the sort of games I shall be discussing in this book; I shall therefore adopt it as a working rule.[2]

This rule has important implications for the way utility numbers are assigned to the outcomes of a game. Consider the utility indices presented in Figure 2.3 for an individual playing the symmetrical banknote game; he derives a utility of 0 if he wins nothing, a utility of 1 if he wins £5, and a utility of 2 if he wins £10. These indices imply more than that the individual prefers winning £10 to winning £5, and winning £5 to winning nothing. They also imply, for example, that he will be indifferent between (on the one hand) winning the £5 note in every game he plays and (on the other) winning the £10 note in half his games and winning nothing in the others. More generally, they imply that in any sequence of games the individual seeks to win as much money as possible in total. We might say that the relative size of the differences between these utility indices represent the player's relative strength of preference between the outcomes: his preference for winning the £10 note rather than nothing is twice as strong as his preference for winning the £5 note rather than nothing. If we say this, however, we must understand that we are defining strength of preference in terms of preferences over sequences of outcomes.

For my purposes, *all* that matters is that the utility numbers assigned to the outcomes of a game accurately represent the player's preferences over sequences of outcomes. Thus in the banknote game we could, if we wished, assign a utility of 10 to the outcome in which the player wins nothing, 12 to the outcome in which he wins £5, and 14 to the outcome in which he wins £10. Or we could assign the utilities 6.2, 6.3 and 6.4. All of these sets of numbers convey the same information. Mathematically, the measurement of a player's utility is unique up to a positive linear transformation. (That is, we can add any constant to a set of utility numbers, or multiply each utility number by any positive constant, without distorting the information they convey.)

It is often convenient to assume that all the individuals who might play a particular game have the same preferences over sequences of outcomes. In the banknote game, for example, it would be natural enough to assume that every individual who played a long sequence of games would want to win as much money as possible in total. In other words, each individual can be assumed to rank alternative possible sequences of outcomes in terms of the total winnings they generate. Given this assumption, the utility indices presented in Figure 2.3 apply to every individual and not just to one particular individual.

Notice, however, that this does not amount to making any comparisons of utility across persons. Suppose that of two individuals playing the banknote game, one is vastly richer than the other. We might be inclined to say that the richer person's want for extra money is less intense than the poorer person's – that each extra £1 received by the poorer person would satisfy a more intense want than each £1 received by the richer person. Nevertheless, provided that each person wants to win as much money as possible, the utility indices in Figure 2.3 can be applied to both of them. Utility indices, as I shall interpret them, are intended only to represent each individual's preferences over sequences of outcomes; they are not to be understood as conveying any judgements about the relative intensity of different individuals' wants.

When I am analysing games I shall not make any comparisons between the utility levels of different individuals. I shall not consider questions such as 'Is such-and-such an outcome better for individual A than for individual B?' or 'Is A's preference for *x* over *y* stronger than B's preference for *w* over *z*?' Such questions would be important to a disinterested observer who was making judgements about the welfare of society as a whole, since such an observer would need to balance one person's wants against another's. But I am concerned with the viewpoints of individuals. To each player in a game, what matters are his own wants. Whether his own wants are more or less intense than other people's is immaterial to him, since he is not trying to balance his wants against other people's. He is trying to satisfy his own wants – full stop.

2.4   Equilibrium in a symmetrical game

If a game is played repeatedly, I have argued, players will tend to gravitate towards those strategies that are most successful in the long run. But which strategy is most successful for one player may depend on which strategies are chosen most frequently by his opponents. Thus if one player switches from a less successful strategy to a more successful one, he may make another player's chosen strategy less successful. In general, therefore, it is by no means certain that a settled pattern will ever emerge; there might be an endless process in which players switch back and forth between strategies.

It is possible, however, that the community of players will eventually settle down in a state in which each person has adopted his own strategy for playing the game. Given the strategies other people play, each person's own strategy does better (or at least as well) as any other he could follow; individuals may occasionally experiment with other strategies, but these experiments never lead them to change their customary patterns of behaviour. Such a state is a stable equilibrium. I shall illustrate the concepts of equilibrium and stability by using the two versions of the banknote game, and then I shall define these concepts more generally in Sections 2.6 and 2.7.

Consider the experiment described in Section 2.2, in which the symmetrical banknote game is played repeatedly within a large group of individuals. I shall assume that the matrix of utility indices in Figure 2.3 represents the preferences of every individual in the experiment: in other words, everyone wants to win as much money as possible.

Consider the position of someone who is taking part in the experiment and who is about to play his first game. Since he has no experience of the game, all he has to rely on is forward-looking reasoning. But this does not seem to provide him with any particularly compelling argument for choosing one strategy rather than the other. It is clear that *if* his opponent is going to choose the £5 note, his own best strategy is to choose the £10 note, and vice versa; but this hardly helps, since he has no way of knowing what his opponent will do. If he tries to put himself in his opponent's position, and asks himself what it would be rational for his opponent to do, he will see that his opponent faces exactly the same problem as he does; deductive reasoning leads round in a circle.

Nevertheless, the person who is playing his first game must choose *some* strategy, whether rationally or not. Suppose he chooses the £10 note. He then discovers that his opponent has also chosen the £10 note, and so he has won nothing. Had he chosen the other strategy, he would have won £5. Of course, that was only one game; he may decide to try for the £10 note again in his next game. But the more games he plays, the more experience he accumulates. Suppose that the strategy of choosing the £5 note is consistently more successful than the other strategy. If our player is capable of learning from experience, he will sooner or later spot this pattern, and recognize the good sense of choosing the £5 note in future games. Some players may notice the differential success of strategies very quickly; others may be much slower. But the general tendency seems clear enough: players will gravitate towards successful strategies.

This allows us to define a notion of equilibrium. Consider the experiment at any point in time. Let p be the probability that if a person is selected at random to play the banknote game, he will claim the £5 note. This probability reflects the strategies that the various people in the experiment are following at the time. If, for example, 30 per cent of them invariably claim the £5 note and the other 70 per cent invariably claim the £10 note, p is equal to 0.3. Alternatively, some people may adopt mixed strategies, claiming the £5 note in some games and the £10 note in others. (To play the same strategy in every game is to adopt a pure strategy.) Suppose that 50 per cent of the people in the experiment invariably claim the £10 note, 20 per cent invariably claim the £5 note, and the remaining 30 per cent claim the £10 note in two-thirds of the games they play and the £5 note in the other games. Then again p is equal to 0.3.

Given any value of p, we can ask whether it could perpetuate itself in the long run, or whether it would tend to change over time. To answer this question we must consider how successful each strategy would be, given p. Recall that each player derives a utility of 0, 1 or 2 according to whether he wins nothing, £5 or £10 in any game (see Figure 2.3). If a player claims the £5 note, there is a probability of p that he will win nothing (because his opponent claims the £5 note too); and there is a probability of $1 - p$ that he will win £5 (because his opponent claims the £10 note). Thus the expected utility from claiming the £5 note is $1 - p$. If a player claims the £10 note, there is a probability of p that he will win £10 and a probability of $1 - p$ that he will win nothing. So the expected utility from claiming the £10 note is $2p$.

Whichever strategy generates the larger expected utility will tend to be more successful in the long run. That is, over a sufficiently long sequence of games, the strategy with the larger *expected* utility will normally generate the larger *total* utility. Thus we should expect players to tend to gravitate towards whichever strategy has the larger expected utility – not necessarily as the result of any sophisticated forward-looking calculations, but merely because they learn from experience which strategy is more successful.

In the present case it is clear that claiming the £5 note is more successful than, just as successful as, or less successful than claiming the £10 note according to whether p is less than, equal to, or greater than $\frac{1}{3}$. (That is, whether $1 - p$ is greater than, equal to, or less than $2p$.) Thus if p is less than $\frac{1}{3}$, there will be a tendency for players to switch to the strategy of claiming the £5 note, which will cause p to increase. Conversely, if p is greater than $\frac{1}{3}$, there will be a tendency for p to fall. But if p is exactly equal to $\frac{1}{3}$, all strategies (pure and mixed) are equally successful in the long run, and so there is no particular tendency for p to change. The value $p = \frac{1}{3}$ is self-perpetuating: it is an equilibrium.

Notice also that whatever the initial value of p, there is a tendency for it to move towards $\frac{1}{3}$. I shall say that the zone of attraction of the equilibrium $p = \frac{1}{3}$ includes all possible values of p. This implies that this equilibrium is highly stable: it will tend to restore itself if it is disturbed. For example, suppose the experiment has settled down at the equilibrium point. Perhaps a third of the people in the experiment always claim the £5 note and two-thirds always claim the £10 note. These two strategies do equally well, each yielding an expected utility of $\frac{2}{3}$ per game. No one has anything to gain or lose by switching strategies. What if, by chance, many people simultaneously switch strategies in the same direction? Suppose the switch is towards claiming the £5 note. Then p will increase, making the strategy of claiming the £5 note less successful than that of claiming the £10 note; and this will induce people to switch back to the latter strategy. So any deviations from $p = \frac{1}{3}$, however they are caused, will be self-correcting.

For this particular experiment, then, we can predict the eventual outcome with some confidence: it will tend to settle down in a state in which the £5 note is claimed in a third of all cases and the £10 note in the rest. From the viewpoint of the players, this outcome is not particularly desirable. In five games out of every nine, both players claim the same note, and so neither wins anything. Each player derives an expected utility of $\frac{2}{3}$ from each game, which is less even than the utility of the £5 note. (This is not a peculiarity of the money values or utility indices I happened to choose. In equilibrium, players must do equally well whichever strategy they adopt. Those players who claim the lesser prize cannot win it in every game, since in some games they meet each other. So every player must derive an expected utility that is less than the utility of the lesser prize.) From every individual's point of view, it would be preferable if every individual played each strategy in half his games. This would ensure that each individual derived an expected utility of $\frac{3}{4}$ per game, the highest expected utility that players can achieve if they all play the same (pure or mixed) strategy. Nevertheless, a state of affairs in which $p = \frac{1}{2}$ cannot be sustained, while one in which $p = \frac{1}{3}$ can. The equilibrium of a repeated game need not be a state of affairs that anyone would choose; it is simply the unintended outcome of the independent choices of many individuals, each of whom is seeking to satisfy his own wants.

2.5 Equilibrium in an asymmetrical game

I shall now analyse the asymmetrical version of the banknote game. Recall the nature of the experiment. From a large group of people, pairs are selected at random to play the banknote game against one another. No communication between the players is allowed, and complete anonymity is maintained. However, in every game, one of the players (picked at random) is told he is A and the other is told he is B.

In this version of the game it is possible for players to distinguish between the results they have experienced when playing as A and the results they have experienced when playing as B. If a player does evaluate his experience in the light of this distinction, and if he discovers that his experience as A has been different from his experience as B, he has the opportunity to play the game differently according to whether he is A or B. Admittedly there seems to be no reason to expect any systematic difference between the way A-players approach the game and the way B-players approach it; but nevertheless the distinction between A and B exists for players to make use of as they choose.

Suppose that the players recognize that this distinction might possibly be significant. When they look back on their experience of the game, they distinguish between their experiences in the two roles. Then if players learn by experience, there will be a tendency for A-players to gravitate towards the most successful A-strategies and for B-players to gravitate towards the most successful B-strategies. This means that A-strategies and B-strategies may evolve in different directions.

Consider the experiment at any point in time. Let p be the probability that if a person is selected at random to play as A he will choose strategy A_1 (claim the £5 note). Let q be the corresponding probability for B-players. The state of the experiment can then be described by the pair of probabilities (p, q). Given any state, we may ask whether it could perpetuate itself in the long run, or, if not, in which directions the two probabilities would tend to change.

Assuming that every individual wants to win as much money as possible over a long sequence of games, the matrix of utilities shown in Figure 2.4 applies to all individuals. Then it is easy to calculate that, for A-players, the expected utility of playing A_1 is greater than, equal to, or less than that of playing A_2 according to whether q is less than, equal to, or greater than $\frac{1}{3}$. Thus, if q is less than $\frac{1}{3}$ there will be a long-run tendency for A-players to switch to A_1, and thus for p to rise towards 1. Conversely, if q is greater than $\frac{1}{3}$ there will be a long-run tendency for A-players to switch to A_2, and hence for p to fall towards 0. If q happens to be exactly equal to $\frac{1}{3}$, all A-strategies (pure or mixed) are equally successful, and so there is no particular tendency for p to change. By the same argument, q will tend to rise, fall or stay constant according to whether p is less than, greater than, or equal to $\frac{1}{3}$.

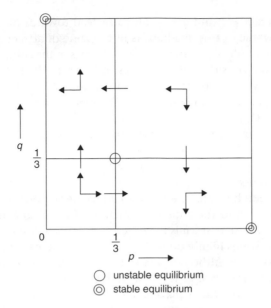

Figure 2.5   A phase diagram for the asymmetrical banknote game

These conclusions can be presented in a phase diagram (see Figure 2.5).
Each state of the experiment corresponds with a point in the diagram.
The implied directions of movement from each state are shown by the
arrows. By linking these directions of movement together it is possible
to trace out the path along which the experiment will move from any
given initial state.

There are three states from which there is no tendency for movement.
These states, circled in Figure 2.5, are $(0, 1)$, $(1, 0)$ and $(\frac{1}{3}, \frac{1}{3})$. The first
of these points – the north-west corner of the diagram – represents the
state in which A-players invariably claim the £10 note and B-players
invariably claim the £5 note. Clearly each individual player of either type
is playing the best possible strategy, given the predictable behaviour of
his opponents. The second of these points – the south-east corner of the
diagram – is the mirror image of the first: A-players invariably claim the
£5 note and B-players the £10 note. The third point represents the state
in which both A-players and B-players, on average, claim the £5 note in
one game in every three.

Whatever the initial state of the experiment, it will tend to move to one
or other of these three points. In the north-west quadrant of the diagram

(that is, where $p < \frac{1}{3}$ and $q > \frac{1}{3}$) all paths lead towards (0, 1). In other words, the whole of this quadrant is in the zone of attraction of (0, 1). Similarly, the whole of the south-east quadrant is in the zone of attraction of (1, 0). Now consider the north-east quadrant. Here all movement is south and west. Such movement must lead eventually either to the north-west quadrant, and hence to (0, 1), or to the south-east quadrant, and hence to (1, 0), or to the central point $(\frac{1}{3}, \frac{1}{3})$.

Any small movements away from (0, 1) are self-correcting, since all points in the neighbourhood of (0, 1) are in the zone of attraction of (0, 1). Similarly, small moves away from (1, 0) are self-correcting. These two points, then represent stable equilibria. In contrast $(\frac{1}{3}, \frac{1}{3})$ is an unstable equilibrium: the slightest movement north or west from this point leads into the zone of attraction of (0, 1) and the slightest movement south or east leads into the zone of attraction of (1, 0).

It therefore seems highly unlikely that the state $(\frac{1}{3}, \frac{1}{3})$ could persist for any length of time. Although this state implies no *particular* tendency for change in either p or q, it is vulnerable to any chance variation in the frequency with which players adopt the two strategies. It is even vulnerable to rumour. For example, suppose that some of the B-players come to believe that A-players are claiming the £5 note in more than a third of all games. Initially this belief may be quite false, but it will tend to make itself true. Acting on this belief, B-players will tend to switch to strategy B_2, thus pushing q below $\frac{1}{3}$; this will make A_1 the more successful strategy for A-players, with the result that p will rise, validating what originally was a false belief. As more A-players switch to A_1 the incentive for B-players to switch to B_2 increases, and so on. The obvious end to this self-reinforcing process is a state in which A-players always play A_1 and B-players always play B_2. Eventually, then, we should expect the experiment to settle down at one or other of the two stable equilibria.

Each of these equilibria can be described as a convention. (The concept of a convention will be discussed further in Section 2.8.) The structure of the asymmetrical banknote game is such that sooner or later one of two possible conventions will evolve spontaneously: either that the A-player always takes the £5 note and the B-player the £10 note, or vice versa.

2.6   Evolutionarily stable strategies in symmetrical games

The concept of equilibrium which has been used here is one that was first developed by biologists, and in particular by John Maynard Smith and his collaborators,[3] but it is now beginning to be used by social scientists.

The biologists have been primarily concerned with explaining animal behaviour.

To take one example that has been much analysed by biologists, consider the behaviour of two animals of the same species when they come into conflict, say over a single piece of food or territory. What determines which animal wins? Do they fight, and if so, how seriously? If we were dealing with human beings we could analyse the situation as a game. (This will be considered in Chapters 4 and 5.) There are various strategies open to each individual, some of which are more aggressive than others. Aggressive individuals are likely to do well when they come into conflict with unaggressive ones: the unaggressive ones back down, and the aggressive ones take whatever resources were in dispute. However, two aggressive individuals will do much more damage to one another than two unaggressive ones. Thus which sort of strategy is best for any one individual depends on which strategies are played by other individuals. There is an obvious analogy here with the banknote game.

In my analysis of the banknote game, I assumed a limited degree of rationality on the part of the players: they were capable of choosing between strategies in the light of experience. For many non-human animals, this kind of rationality is too much to expect. It seems that birds, for example, do not learn from experience how to handle disputes with one another – when it is better to stand their ground and when it is better to fly away. Their inclinations or drives to particular kinds of behaviour are part of their nature; they are genetically determined or 'preprogrammed'. Nevertheless, the ideas of game theory are still applicable. This is because the genetic constitution of any species is not arbitrary; it is the product of evolution.

In the world of biological evolution, value is measured in terms of survival and replication. A pattern of behaviour – in game-theoretic language, a strategy – is successful to the extent that it fosters the survival and replication of the genes that give rise to it. Different strategies, like 'fight' and 'run away', have value on this scale of success or 'fitness'. Over time we should expect the more successful strategies to be played more frequently, not through any process of choice or learning, but because the genes that predispose animals to successful strategies will tend to spread through the 'gene pool'. The gene pool is in a state of equilibrium when there is no systematic tendency for its composition to change. At the behavioural level, this is a state in which animals are predisposed to play best-reply strategies against one another – 'best' being interpreted in terms of biological fitness. *In a purely formal sense*, this concept of equilibrium is essentially the same as the one invoked in Section 2.4

when the symmetrical banknote game was analysed. I emphasize 'in a purely formal sense' because my concept of utility is quite different from the Darwinian concept of fitness, and because learning by experience is quite different from natural selection. I am concerned with social evolution and not with genetic evolution, with economics and not with sociobiology.

Maynard Smith (1982, pp. 10–14) formulates his concept of equilibrium in the following way. Consider any symmetrical two-person game in which there are m pure strategies, $S_1, \ldots, S_m$, for each player. Then for any individual there is an $m \times m$ matrix of utility indices, on the model of Figure 2.3. For Maynard Smith these indices are measures of gains and losses of biological fitness, but the formal logic of his analysis does not require this interpretation; we may if we wish interpret utility in terms of the preferences of human players. Assume that the same matrix of utility indices applies to all players. Assume also that the game is played repeatedly within some community, individuals being paired at random and playing the game anonymously.

In general a strategy is a list or vector of probabilities $(p_1, \ldots, p_{m-1})$ where for any i, p_i is the probability that the relevant individual will play the pure strategy S_i in a random game. (Since the probabilities associated with the m pure strategies sum to 1, there is no need to specify the probability that the mth strategy will be played.) This notation allows the concept of a strategy to encompass both pure and mixed strategies.

We may now define $E(I, J)$ as the expected utility derived by any player from a game in which he plays strategy I and his opponent plays strategy J. We may say that I is a best reply to J if, for all strategies, $K, E(I, J) \geqslant E(K, J)$ – that is, if no strategy is any more successful than I against players who follow strategy J. Now consider the following property that might be possessed by strategy I:

For all strategies J (pure or mixed),

$$E(I, I) \geqslant E(J, I) \tag{2.1}$$

This condition states that I is a best reply to itself. If this condition holds, then in a community in which every individual plays strategy, I, no single individual can gain by switching to a different strategy.

Notice that this condition does not exclude the possibility that there may be some strategy J for which $E(J, I) = E(I, I)$ – in other words, that I may not be the only best reply to itself. Suppose that J and I are both best replies to I. Then in a community in which initially everyone played strategy I, any individual who switched to strategy J would suffer no loss. In biological terms, suppose that the genetic make-up of some animal population is such that individuals always play strategy I. Then some mutant individual appears who plays J instead. Unless $E(I, I)$, is strictly greater than $E(J, I)$ the forces of natural selection will not immediately come into play to eradicate J-playing behaviour. Analogously in the human case, if initially everyone plays I, an individual who experiments with J will not find that the latter strategy is any less successful than the former; so the process of learning by experience will not immediately come into play to discourage him from repeating the experiment. It is possible, therefore, that an I-playing population might begin to be invaded by J-playing individuals.

In order to see whether such an invasion could be successful, consider a game in which $E(J, I) = E(I, I)$ and consider a situation in which a small proportion of a large population have begun to play J. Everyone else is still playing I. For any player, I and J are equally successful, provided that his opponent plays I. However, there is some small probability that his opponent will play J. Thus which of the two strategies is more successful overall will depend on the relative values of $E(I, J)$ and $E(J, J)$. If $E(I, J)$ is greater than $E(J, J)$ – that is, if I is a better reply than J to J – the J-playing deviants will be less successful in the long run than the rest of the population. If this is the case, an invasion by J-players will not succeed. Thus we may say that I is an uninvadable strategy if, in addition to (2.1), the following condition holds:

For all strategies J (pure or mixed) where $J \neq I$,

$$\textit{either} \quad E(I, I) > E(J, I) \quad \textit{or} \quad E(I, J) > E(J, J) \qquad (2.2)$$

In the biological literature a strategy that satisfies (2.1) and (2.2) is called an evolutionarily stable strategy or ESS. Some writers have proposed different names – such as 'developmentally stable strategy' (Dawkins, 1980) or 'collectively stable strategy' (Axelrod, 1981)[4] – for this concept when it is applied to cases in which individuals (whether human or animal) learn by experience rather than behave in genetically preprogrammed ways. It is probably simpler to retain the better-known term 'evolutionarily stable strategy' and to recognize that there can be social as well as genetic evolution. Following Selten (1980) I shall say that a strategy that satisfies (2.1) is an equilibrium strategy; a strategy that also satisfies (2.2) is a stable equilibrium. Thus the terms 'ESS' and 'stable equilibrium' are to be understood as synonyms.

Now consider how this characterization of stable equilibrium applies to the symmetrical banknote game. In this game there are two pure strategies, S_1 (claim the £5 note) and S_2 (claim the £10 note). Any probability mix of these two strategies is itself a strategy, so we may write any strategy as p where p is the probability that the pure strategy S_1 will be played.

Given the utility indices presented in Figure 2.3, it is clear that the strategy $p = 1$ is the unique best reply to any strategy with $p < \frac{1}{3}$; that $p = 0$ is the unique best reply to any strategy with $p > \frac{1}{3}$; and that every strategy is a best reply to the strategy $p = \frac{1}{3}$. (Compare the discussion in Section 2.4.) Thus $p = \frac{1}{3}$ is the only strategy that is a best reply to itself – that is, the only equilibrium strategy.

We may ask now whether $p = \frac{1}{3}$ is a stable equilibrium or ESS. Let I be the strategy $p = \frac{1}{3}$ and let J be any strategy $p = p^*$. We know that every strategy is a best reply to I, so $E(I, I) = E(J, I)$ for all J. Thus, using (2.2), I is a stable equilibrium only if $E(I, J) > E(J, J)$ for all $J \neq I$. It is easy to calculate that

$$E(I, J) = \frac{3p^* + 1}{3} \tag{2.3}$$

and $E(J, J) = 3p^*(1 - p^*)$ \hfill (2.4)

From these equations it follows that $E(I, J) > E(J, J)$ is true for all $p^* \neq \frac{1}{3}$. This establishes that $p = \frac{1}{3}$ is a stable equilibrium or ESS – a result that reproduces the conclusion of Section 2.4.

2.7   Evolutionarily stable strategies in asymmetrical games

The concept of an ESS can be extended quite easily so that it applies to asymmetrical games. Consider any asymmetrical game between players in two distinct roles, A and B. Let the pure strategies available to A be $A_1, \ldots, A_m$ and let those available to B be $B_1, \ldots, B_n$. Then for any individual there is an $m \times n$ matrix of pairs of utility indices, on the model of Figure 2.4. Assume that the same matrix of utility indices applies to all players. And assume that the game is played repeatedly within some community, individuals being paired at random and playing the game anonymously. Which of the two individuals is A and which B is also determined by a random process; each individual has an equal probability of being A or B in any randomly selected game in which he is involved.[5]

For any given individual we may define an A-strategy and a B-strategy. An A-strategy is represented by a vector $(p_1, \ldots, p_{m-1})$ where for any i, p_i is the probability that the individual in question will play the pure strategy A_i in games in which he is A. Similarly, a B-strategy is represented by a vector $(q_1, \ldots, q_{n-1})$ where for any j, q_j is the probability that the same individual will play B_j in games in which he is B. The conjunction of an A-strategy and a B-strategy is a strategy of the form 'If A, do ...; if B, do ...'. I shall call such a strategy a universal strategy.

Now consider any pair of universal strategies I and J. We may ask how successful I will be against J or, more precisely, what expected utility is derived from playing I against an opponent who is playing J. We may evaluate this expected utility for a randomly selected game between an I-playing individual and a J-playing individual. If this game is selected at random there is a probability of 0.5 that the I-playing individual is A and the same probability that he is B. Thus $E(I, J)$, the expected utility derived from playing I against J, is the arithmetic mean of two values – the expected utility of playing I's A-strategy against J's B-strategy, and the expected utility of playing I's B-strategy against J's A-strategy.

Given this definition of $E(I, J)$ we may invoke conditions (2.1) and (2.2) again. A universal strategy I is an equilibrium strategy if it satisfies (2.1) – that is, if it is a best reply to itself. I represents a stable equilibrium or ESS if it also satisfies the non-invadability condition (2.2).

Consider what it means to say that a universal strategy is a best reply to itself. Suppose that I is the conjunction of the A-strategy $(p_1, \ldots, p_{m-1})$ and the B-strategy $(q_1, \ldots, q_{n-1})$. Then I is a best reply to itself if and only if $(p_1, \ldots, p_{m-1})$ is a best reply to $(q_1, \ldots, q_{n-1})$ *and* $(q_1, \ldots, q_{n-1})$ is a best reply to $(p_1, \ldots, p_{m-1})$. This implies that in asymmetrical games there is a one-to-one correspondence between the concept of equilibrium embedded in condition (2.1) and the concept of Nash equilibrium used in traditional game theory. At the level of a one-off game between two players, a Nash equilibrium is a pair of strategies, one for each player, such that each strategy is a best reply to the other. So in an asymmetrical game between players labelled 'A' and 'B', a Nash equilibrium consists of an A-strategy and a B-strategy, each of which is a best reply to the other. If the game is played repeatedly, the conjunction of these two strategies is clearly a universal strategy that is a best reply to itself.

Notice, however, that this equivalence between condition (2.1) and the definition of Nash equilibrium holds *only* for asymmetrical games. For symmetrical games, (2.1) requires that both players follow *the same* strategy, while there can be a Nash equilibrium when they play different strategies, so long as each strategy is a best reply to the other. This difference reflects the difference between one-off and repeated games. In a one-off symmetrical game it is perfectly possible for the two players to adopt different strategies. In a single play of the symmetrical bank-note game, for example, it is perfectly possible that one player will claim the £5 note and that the other will claim the £10 note – a Nash equilibrium. This is a case in which the two players adopt non-identical strategies that mesh together in a favourable way. But if the game is played repeatedly, with random pairings of anonymous individuals, such meshing can occur only by chance: there can be no *systematic* meshing of non-identical strategies in repeated symmetrical games.

Now consider how this concept of stable equilibrium can be applied to the asymmetrical banknote game. In this game each player has a choice of two strategies, so a universal strategy is fully described by the pair of probabilities (p, q) where p is the probability that the relevant individual will claim the £5 note if he is A and q is the probability that he will claim the same note if he is B. It follows immediately from the discussion in Section 2.5 that three – and only three – universal strategies satisfy the equilibrium condition (2.1); these are $(0, 1)$, $(1, 0)$ and $(\frac{1}{3}, \frac{1}{3})$.

The first two of these universal strategies are clearly stable, since each is the unique best reply to itself. (If you are convinced that your opponents will always claim the £5 note when they have one particular role and the £10 note when they have the other, it is obviously best for you to follow the same rule yourself.) However, the stability of $(\frac{1}{3}, \frac{1}{3})$ is more doubtful, since *every* universal strategy is a best reply to $(\frac{1}{3}, \frac{1}{3})$. (If you are convinced that there is a probability of exactly $\frac{1}{3}$ that your opponent will claim the £5 note, it doesn't matter which note you claim.) To test the stability of this equilibrium we must ask whether it could be invaded. Let $I = (\frac{1}{3}, \frac{1}{3})$ and let J be any universal strategy (p^*, q^*). Since every universal strategy is a best reply to I, we know that $E(I, I) = E(I, J)$. It is easy to calculate that

$$E(I, J) - E(J, J) = 3(p^* - \tfrac{1}{3})(q^* - \tfrac{1}{3}) \tag{2.5}$$

So whether I or J is the best reply to J depends on whether the right-hand side of (2.5) is positive or negative. If $p^* > \frac{1}{3}$ and $q^* < \frac{1}{3}$, *or* if $p^* < \frac{1}{3}$ and $q^* > \frac{1}{3}$, then the right-hand side of (2.5) is negative and $E(I, J) < E(J, J)$. This implies that I fails to satisfy the stability condition (2.2): it can be invaded successfully by any one of a whole set of universal strategies, each of which has the property that A-players claim one note more frequently than in I and that B-players claim the other note more frequently than in I. The only stable equilibria or ESSs then are $(0, 1)$ and $(1, 0)$. These correspond with the two possible conventions – that A takes the £10 note and B the £5 note, and the converse. This result reproduces the conclusion of Section 2.5.

2.8 Conventions

So far I have spoken of 'conventions' fairly loosely; I have assumed that we all know what a convention is. I need not apologize for this: the word 'convention' is an ordinary English word with an ordinary meaning. (What the word 'convention' ordinarily means is itself a convention.) Nevertheless, I shall from now on use the word in a special sense – but one which, I suggest, is reasonably close to at least one ordinary meaning of the word.

Consider what we mean when we say that some practice is a convention among some group of people. When we say this, we usually mean that everyone, or almost everyone, in the group follows the practice. But we mean more than this. Everyone eats and sleeps, but these are not conventions. When we say that a practice is a convention, we imply that at least part of the answer to the question 'Why does everyone do X?' is 'Because everyone else does X.' We also imply that things might have been otherwise: everyone does X because everyone else does X, but it might have been the case that everyone did Y because everyone else did Y. If asked 'Why does everyone do X and not Y?', we may find it hard to give any answer at all. Why do British drivers drive on the left rather than the right? No doubt there is some historical reason why this practice grew up, but most British drivers neither know nor care what it is. It seems sufficient to say that this is the established convention.

I shall define a convention as: any stable equilibrium in a game that has two or more stable equilibria. To see the point of this definition, recall that a stable equilibrium (or ESS) is defined for a community of individuals who play some game repeatedly against one another. To say that some strategy I is a stable equilibrium in some such game is to say the following: it is in each individual's interest to follow strategy I provided that everyone else, or almost everyone else, does the same. Thus a stable equilibrium may be understood as a self-enforcing rule. But not all self-enforcing rules are ones that would ordinarily be called conventions. A self-enforcing rule, I suggest, should be regarded as a convention if and only if we can conceive of some *different* rule that could also be self-enforcing, provided it once became established. Thus 'always drive on the left' is a convention because not only is 'always drive on the left' a self-enforcing rule, but so also is 'always drive on the right'. Or, to put this more formally, because we can model driving behaviour as a game in which 'always drive on the left' and 'always drive on the right' are both stable equilibria. On this definition, the stable equilibrium strategy for the symmetrical banknote game ('claim the £5 note with probability $\frac{1}{3}$')

is not a convention, even though it is a self-enforcing rule. In contrast, the two stable equilibrium strategies for the asymmetrical game ('if A, claim the £10 note; if B, claim the £5 note' and 'if A, claim the £5 note; if B, claim the £10 note') *are* conventions.

In one respect my definition may seem to depart from common usage. On my definition a practice can be called a convention irrespective of whether or not everyone actually follows it. Thus 'always drive on the left' and 'always drive on the right' are *both* called conventions, even though in any one country only one of these strategies is in fact followed. In ordinary speech we should probably say that 'always drive on the left' was *the* convention in Britain. Unfortunately there does not seem to be any simple expression for 'a rule that could have been the convention but in fact isn't'; rather than invent a new expression, I shall simply use the term convention. If there is any risk of confusion I shall call the convention that everyone actually follows the established convention.

In another respect my definition differs from one that has gained some currency among philosophers, following the publication of Lewis's deservedly famous book, *Convention: A Philosophical Study* (1969). Lewis begins by defining a class of games which he calls 'coordination problems'. A coordination problem, essentially, is a game that has at least two stable equilibria,[6] each of which has a special property. This special property is that 'no one would have been better off had *any one* agent acted otherwise, either himself or someone else'; equilibria of this kind are 'coordination equilibria'. Then Lewis defines a 'convention' as follows:

A regularity R in the behaviour of members of a population P when they are agents in a recurrent situation S is a *convention* if and only if it is true that, and it is common knowledge in P that, in any instance of S among members of P,

(1) everyone conforms to R;
(2) everyone expects everyone else to conform to R;
(3) everyone prefers to conform to R on condition that the others do, since R is a coordination problem and uniform conformity to R is a coordination equilibrium in S. (1969, p. 58)

This definition is essentially the same as my definition of an 'established convention' – except for Lewis's final clause, stipulating that 'uniform conformity to R is a coordination equilibrium'. For Lewis it is part of the definition of a convention that each individual wants every other individual to follow it; my definition does not require this.

In Chapter 3 I shall be discussing games of the kind that Lewis would call coordination problems; these are games in which there is little conflict of interest between the players. These games have stable equilibria that are conventions both by Lewis's definition and mine. But in Chapters 4–7 I shall be examining other kinds of games, in which there is more conflict of interest; I shall show that in some of these games practices can evolve that are conventions on my definition, but not on Lewis's. If I am charged with using the term 'convention' in an eccentric way, I can appeal to the precedent of David Hume, who – I shall argue – used it in much the same way as I do.

3
Coordination

3.1 The crossroads game

Suppose that two drivers are approaching a crossroads. Each has a choice of two strategies: he can either slow down or maintain speed. If one slows down and the other maintains speed, both get safely through the crossroads and there is a slight delay to the driver who has slowed down. If they both slow down they reach the crossroads with the problem of priority still to be settled; I take it that this outcome is worse for both drivers than the one in which only one driver slows down. Worst of all, of course, is the outcome in which they both maintain speed. This game is a close relative of the banknote game of Chapter 2; games with this structure are sometimes called leader games (Rapoport, 1967).

As in my analysis of the banknote game, I shall assume that there is some large community of drivers who play against one another repeatedly. Each individual plays many games and, in any game, each of the other drivers in the community is equally likely to be his opponent. I shall also assume that the game is played anonymously: players do not remember one another as individuals. Thus when Jane Smith and Joe Soap find themselves approaching one another at a crossroads, they cannot search through their memories for previous occasions when they met one another like this. All they can remember is their general experience of playing the game. One implication of this is that a driver cannot build up any sort of personal reputation – say as someone who never slows down. An individual may, in fact, never slow down; but his opponents will not know this.

For many kinds of social interaction the assumption of anonymity seems reasonable enough. The interactions of road users provide one obvious example. More generally, the interactions of strangers in public

		Opponent's strategy	
		Slow down	Maintain speed
Player's strategy	Slow down	0	2
	Maintain speed	3	−10

Figure 3.1   The symmetrical crossroads game

places – on the streets, in public transport, at theatres and cinemas and sporting events – are anonymous in my sense. Many forms of trade are also anonymous – consider private sales of second-hand cars. For the present I shall concentrate on anonymous games. (Some of the special properties of non-anonymous games will be discussed in Sections 4.8 and 4.9.)

Figure 3.1 presents illustrative utility indices for the crossroads game. I shall assume that these utility indices represent the preferences of every individual in the community. The precise numbers are not important; what matters for the structure of the game is the ranking of the four possible outcomes.

What happens in this community – initially at least – depends on how the game is perceived by individuals. One possibility is that everyone thinks every crossroads is like every other, and can think of no general way of distinguishing between the two drivers in the game. Then each individual thinks of each game simply as one between 'me' and 'my opponent': this is the case of a symmetrical game. Another possibility is that there is some labelling asymmetry between the roles of the players in any game, so that one may be called 'A' and the other 'B', and that this asymmetry is recognized by everyone. (A might be the driver whose opponent approaches from the left, or the driver on the more important of the two roads, or the driver of the larger vehicle.) This gives rise to an asymmetrical game. This second possibility may seem to be an extreme case, since it requires not only that *everyone* recognizes an asymmetry in the game, but also that everyone recognizes the *same* one. Nevertheless, I shall argue, there is a long-run tendency for the game to be played in this way – for everyone to recognize a single asymmetry. First, however, I shall analyse the symmetrical version of the game.

The symmetrical crossroads game

This version of the game can be analysed in much the same way as the symmetrical version of the banknote game (Section 2.4). It is easy to work out that there is just one equilibrium. If p is the probability that a randomly selected player in a randomly selected game plays 'slow down', equilibrium occurs where $p = 0.8$. (To check that this is an equilibrium notice that when $p = 0.8$, 'slow down' and 'maintain speed' both yield the same expected utility, namely 0.4.) This equilibrium is stable: if the proportion of drivers who slow down rises above 0.8, maintaining speed becomes the more successful strategy, while if it falls below 0.8, slowing down becomes more successful.

In this state of affairs there is no convention to assign priority at crossroads, and the consequences are rather inconvenient. Sometimes (to be exact, in 32 per cent of cases) one driver gives way to the other; sometimes (64 per cent of cases) they both slow down; and sometimes (the remaining 4 per cent of cases) they both maintain speed. Needless to say, these particular percentages reflect the particular utility indices I assigned to the outcomes of the game and have no special significance. The important point is that there are some cases in which both drivers slow down and some cases in which they both maintain speed; in these cases, the outcome is worse for both drivers than it would have been if either one of them had given way to the other.

The asymmetrical crossroads game

Suppose instead that everyone in the community thinks of the game as asymmetrical, and that they all focus on the same asymmetry, say that between left and right. Then we may define A as the driver who finds his opponent approaching from the left and B as the driver who finds his opponent approaching from the right. When anyone remembers a game, he classifies it according to the direction from which his opponent approached; thus he can distinguish between his experience as an A-player and his experience as a B-player. Using the same utility indices as before, the game can now be described by the matrix shown in Figure 3.2.

		B's strategy	
		Slow down	Maintain speed
A's strategy	Slow down	0, 0	2, 3
	Maintain speed	3, 2	−10, −10

Figure 3.2   The asymmetrical crossroads game

This game can be analysed in much the same way as the asymmetrical version of the banknote game (Section 2.5). Let p and q be the probabilities that randomly selected A-players and B-players will play 'slow down' in a randomly selected game. As far as A-players are concerned, 'slow down' is more successful than, just as successful as, or less successful than 'maintain speed' according to whether q is less than, equal to, or greater than 0.8. Thus if A-players learn by experience, p will tend to rise towards 1 if $q < 0.8$, and will tend to fall towards 0 if $q > 0.8$. Similarly, q will tend to rise towards 1 if $p < 0.8$, and will tend to fall towards 0 if $p > 0.8$. These tendencies are shown in the form of a phase diagram in Figure 3.3.

There are three (p, q) combinations at which there is no tendency for change; these are $(0, 1)$, $(1, 0)$ and $(0.8, 0.8)$. Each of these combinations is a universal strategy that is a best reply to itself (compare Section 2.7) and therefore represents an equilibrium.

The first two of these equilibria are stable. Take $(0, 1)$. This represents a state of affairs in which A-drivers always maintain speed and B-drivers always slow down. In such a state of affairs, the best universal strategy

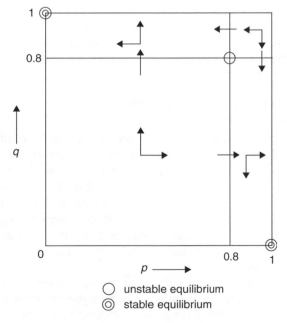

Figure 3.3   A phase diagram for the asymmetrical crossroads game

for any individual is clearly: 'If A, maintain speed; if B, slow down.' In other words, the universal strategy (0, 1) is the unique best reply to itself, satisfying the stability condition (2.1) explained in Section 2.6. Or in terms of the phase diagram, any small movement away from (0, 1) leads to a point that is in the zone of attraction of (0, 1). A similar argument establishes that (1, 0) is also a stable equilibrium.

In contrast, the equilibrium (0.8, 0.8) is unstable. In this state of affairs 80 per cent of all drivers – whether A or B – slow down; then for any individual, every universal strategy is just as successful as every other. So (0.8, 0.8) is not the *unique* best reply to itself; indeed, every universal strategy is a best reply to (0.8, 0.8). It is easy to show that (0.8, 0.8) can be invaded by any universal strategy (p, q) such that *either* $p > 0.8$ and $q < 0.8$ *or* $p < 0.8$ and $q > 0.8$. In terms of the phase diagram, any movement north or west from (0.8, 0.8) leads to a point in the zone of attraction of (0, 1) and any movement south or east from (0.8, 0.8) leads to a point in the zone of attraction of (1, 0).

So there are only two stable equilibria or evolutionarily stable strategies for the asymmetrical crossroads game; in the long run, we should expect the game to settle down in one or other of these states. In other words, some rule of priority – either 'give way to drivers approaching from the right' or 'give way to drivers approaching from the left' – will evolve, and once it has evolved it will be self-enforcing. This is a convention. Such a convention is not invented by anyone; it is not negotiated; no one consents to it. It simply evolves. The asymmetrical crossroads game is a model of spontaneous order.

The crossroads game when only some players recognize an asymmetry

For a player to recognize an asymmetry in a game, he must make an imaginative leap. In the case of the left–right asymmetry, for example, a driver must realize that his experiences at crossroads can be grouped into two distinct classes – those where the other driver approached from the left, and those where he approached from the right. He must also realize that this apparently irrelevant asymmetry might have some significance. At first sight it seems arbitrary to assume that *everyone* will recognize some asymmetry, and even more arbitrary to assume that everyone will recognize the *same* asymmetry.

I shall now consider, therefore, what would happen if only some of the players in the crossroads game recognized the left–right asymmetry, while the others thought of the game as symmetrical. I shall call the first set of players smart (they are smart enough to spot the asymmetry) and the second set dumb. I shall assume that no one can recognize in advance whether his opponent is smart or dumb. What would equilibrium look like in this version of the game?

One kind of equilibrium occurs if *none* of the players behaves differently according to whether he is A or B. In this case, equilibrium occurs when a randomly selected player – whether A or B – has a probability of 0.8 of playing 'slow down'. (For example, smart and dumb players might both be split 80–20 between those who invariably play 'slow down' and those who invariably play 'maintain speed'.) Then the two strategies are exactly as successful as one another from each of three points of view: that of smart players choosing between strategies to play as A, that of smart players choosing between strategies to play as B, and that of dumb players (who do not differentiate between A and B). Since there is no particular tendency for anyone to change strategies, this is clearly an equilibrium. However, it is unstable. Recall that in the case in which *all* players recognized the asymmetry in the game, it was possible to have a mixed-strategy equilibrium but that such an equilibrium was unstable: any slight tendency for A-players to behave differently from B-players would magnify itself until a convention was established. In the present case, exactly the same forces are at work, but they bear only on the smart players. Thus in the long run, we should expect one or other of the two possible conventions – 'give way to drivers approaching from the right' or 'give way to drivers approaching from the left' – to establish itself amongst those players smart enough to recognize the left–right asymmetry.

As the smart players begin to adopt a convention, the dumb players will notice a change in the frequency with which their opponents play 'slow down'. For example, suppose that initially both smart and dumb players are split 80–20 between those who invariably play 'slow down' and those who invariably play 'maintain speed'. When a smart player adopts a convention, he plays each strategy in 50 per cent of the games he plays (since in 50 per cent of his games he is A and in 50 per cent he is B). Thus as a convention spreads among smart players, the overall frequency with which 'slow down' is played will start to fall below 80 per cent. From the viewpoint of the dumb players, who cannot spot the asymmetrical pattern in the behaviour of their opponents, this implies that 'slow down' is now the more successful strategy. Thus dumb players will tend to switch to 'slow down'.

Equilibrium is reached when all the smart players are following a convention, and when (depending on the proportion of dumb players) *either* the dumb players divide between 'slow down' and 'maintain speed' in such a way that the probability of any dumb player's opponent play-ing 'slow down' is 0.8 *or* all the dumb players play 'slow down' and the probability that a dumb player's opponent will slow down is less than 0.8. (In either case, dumb players are following the most successful strategies they can find, given their inability to recognize the asymmet-rical convention.) It is not difficult to check that this kind of equilibrium is stable.

Needless to say, the smart players are more successful than the dumb ones. For example, suppose that 20 per cent of the players are smart and that the convention among the smart players is to maintain speed as A and to slow down as B. Then there is a stable equilibrium if seven-eighths of the dumb players (i.e. 70 per cent of the total number of players) slow down in every game while the remaining one-eighth of them (10 per cent of all players) maintain speed in every game. Then each dumb player meets an opponent who slows down in 80 per cent of the games he plays. (In 70 per cent of his games he meets a dumb player who slows down; in 10 per cent of his games he meets a smart player who is slowing down because he is B.) Thus for a dumb player the expected utility of either strategy is the same (0.4). Smart players, however, can differentiate between the games they play as A and the games they play as B. When a smart player is A, his opponent slows down in 90 per cent of cases. (In 70 per cent of cases, the opponent is a dumb player who slows down; in 20 per cent of cases, the opponent is a smart player who knows he is B.) If the A-player maintains speed (the better strategy) he has an expected utility of 1.7. When a smart player is B, his opponent slows down in only 70 per cent of cases; if the B-player slows down (the better strategy) he has an expected utility of 0.6. Thus in a randomly selected game a smart player has an expected utility of 1.15 (the average of 1.7 and 0.6) in comparison with a dumb player's 0.4.

In a theoretical sense, such a situation is a stable equilibrium. It seems unlikely, however, that this would really be the end of the story. No doubt some people are quicker than others at recognizing patterns in their experience and at learning how to profit from this knowledge; but if a pattern exists, and if there are benefits to be had from recognizing it, we should expect a tendency over time for more and more people to recognize it. Once the smart players have evolved a convention, there is a clear pattern to be observed: drivers in general are more likely to slow down if they are approaching from (say) the left than if they are approaching from the right. Anyone who can spot this pattern can gain the same benefits as the smart players are already gaining. So we should expect more and more people to join the smart players in recognizing and following the convention. The more people follow the convention, the plainer it becomes, and the easier for any remaining dumb players to recognize. The long-run tendency of this process is towards a state in which everyone follows the convention.

Because I wished to show that the growth of conventions can be genuinely spontaneous, I have assumed that the players do not communicate with one another. Communication is likely to speed up the process by which a convention, once established among some players, spreads to the rest. Notice that in the crossroads game, once someone has started following a convention, he wants other people – in particular, his opponents – to follow it too. (Once a convention is established, the expected utility that a smart player derives from a game increases with the proportion of smart players – from just above 0.4 when there are very few smart players to 2.5 when everyone is smart.) So even if a dumb player cannot infer the nature of the convention from his own experience, he will probably find plenty of smart players eager to explain it to him.

The crossroads game with several asymmetries

Up to now, I have supposed that the players in the crossroads game can recognize only one asymmetry – that between left and right. This is the asymmetry that provided the basis for the convention that once was generally recognized at road junctions in continental Europe and the United States: priority to the right. However, there are many other asymmetries. For example, the players might focus on the relative status of the two roads that cross one another, classifying them as 'more important' and 'less important'. (This was the basis of the traditional British convention of giving priority to the vehicle on the more important road. Older British drivers will recall the problems of interpreting this convention at unmarked crossroads.) Or the players might focus on the vehicles, classifying them in relation to some scale of importance. Or they might focus on the speed at which the vehicles are travelling. ('Slow vehicles give way to fast ones' is a workable if dangerous convention.) Presumably some players will be particularly inclined to recognize one asymmetry, and some another. How, then, does one asymmetry get singled out?

Consider two independent asymmetries, say that between left and right and that between major and minor roads. (I shall suppose that at every crossroads it is quite clear which road is more important.) Now suppose that one group of drivers recognizes the left–right asymmetry but not the major–minor one; for another group it is the other way round. Then two conventions could evolve simultaneously: perhaps the first group of drivers gives priority to the right and the second group gives priority to the major road. At first, each group believes that its own convention is the only one in existence, and that its own members are smart while all the other players are dumb. Which group will be more successful? Clearly, whichever is larger. (Recall that in the case in which some players are smart and some are dumb, the smart players are more successful, the greater the proportion of smart players.) Sooner or later, however, some players will become aware that there are two asymmetries and two conventions, rather than just one; and *all* such players will be attracted to the convention that is followed by more players. Success breeds success; the more popular convention will grow still more popular at the expense of the other. The same argument applies if three or more conventions start to evolve side by side. Since everyone wants to find and follow the convention that most other people are following, there is an inevitable long-run tendency for one convention to establish itself at the expense of the rest.

3.2 Which convention?

If the crossroads game is played repeatedly for a long enough period, it seems that some convention will evolve. So long as *some* players share a common recognition of *some* asymmetry, there is scope for these players to evolve a convention among themselves; and any situation in which they lack such a convention is fundamentally unstable. Once this kind of convention has become established among some players, everyone has an incentive to follow it, so it will tend to spread through the community. There are many possible conventions – perhaps an unlimited number – but eventually one of them will establish itself in any particular community. An interesting question remains: Are some kinds of convention more likely to establish themselves than others?

The analysis in Section 3.1 provides some clues as to how this question might be answered. First of all, it is clear that a convention cannot evolve until some players come to recognize that they are playing an asymmetrical game, and come to focus on the same asymmetry. Second, there must be some asymmetry in behaviour – or at least in beliefs about behaviour – in order to set in motion the process that leads to one of the corners of the phase diagram. Suppose that initially no one has thought of the crossroads game as asymmetrical, and so it has settled down in the symmetrical equilibrium (in which 'slow down' is played in 80 per cent of all games). Then some players come to recognize the left–right asymmetry. This, in itself, is not enough to generate a convention based on the distinction between left and right. There must also be some initial tendency, observed or credited or suspected, for people to behave differently according to whether their opponents approach from the left or from the right. This initial tendency might be quite slight, and still set in motion the process by which it magnifies itself into a convention; but the tendency must exist.

If we were concerned only with the question, 'Will *some* convention eventually evolve?', we might rely on chance. Sooner or later, we might say, some slight asymmetry of behaviour will occur by chance; some players will think that something more than chance is involved, and expect the asymmetry to continue. Even though this expectation has no foundation, it is self-fulfilling. When, however, we ask the question '*Which* convention will evolve?', we cannot rely on arguments about what will happen sooner or later. In a sense, alternative conventions are in competition with one another to establish themselves as *the* convention for a community. Remember that once a convention begins to evolve, everyone is attracted to it; and that if several conventions start to evolve side by side, the most popular convention is the most attractive. So the relationship between conventions in this competition is rather like that between seedlings in a crowded plot of ground: whichever is the first to show vigorous growth can stifle the others. Conventions that are capable of establishing themselves are ones that exploit asymmetries that are recognized quickly. We must ask, therefore, whether certain kinds of asymmetry are likely to be recognized more quickly than others.

Asymmetries are particularly likely to be recognized quickly if they are embedded in the structure of the game itself. Let me give an example. In my presentation of the crossroads game so far, I have assumed that 'left' and 'right', 'major' and 'minor' and so on are nothing but labels: there is no difference between being the player on the major road and being the player on the minor road except that one road is *called* 'major' and the other 'minor'. But suppose that there *is* some other difference, even though slight.

Here is one possibility. Drivers occasionally fail to notice crossroads. A driver who does not notice that he is converging on another vehicle at a crossroads does not know he is playing the crossroads game; he maintains his speed, not as a consciously chosen strategy, but merely by default. Now suppose that it is harder to notice a crossroads when you are on the major road. To simplify the analysis I shall suppose that some proportion – I shall assume 5 per cent – of major-road drivers fail to spot crossroads, while this mistake is *never* made by minor-road drivers. To be more precise, 5 per cent of major-road drivers fail to spot crossroads until it is too late to slow down. They play these games unconsciously in the sense that they do not choose their strategies; they unavoidably play the strategy of maintaining speed. However, they are aware, after the event, of their carelessness: they know that they have played the crossroads game, and with what result.

First suppose that no one realizes the significance of the major–minor asymmetry: everyone thinks of the game as asymmetrical. Each driver knows from experience that he occasionally fails to notice crossroads as he approaches them, but it never occurs to him that these mistakes have the particular pattern that they do. What would equilibrium look like?

I shall assume that each driver is on the major road in 50 per cent of the games he plays. So he plays 2.5 per cent of all his games unconsciously; his scope for choice extends only to the remaining 97.5 per cent of games that he plays consciously. Equilibrium occurs when 80 per cent of all players slow down. (Recall that this makes both strategies equally successful in the long run for a player who does not perceive the asymmetry in the game. Remember too that each player's memory ranges over all the games he has played, consciously or unconsciously.) This requires that 82.1 per cent of *conscious* players slow down. As long as the asymmetry remains unrecognized, this is a stable equilibrium; if conscious players choose 'slow down' in more than 82.1 per cent of games, 'maintain speed' becomes the more successful strategy, and vice versa.

Now suppose that one player realizes that the major–minor asymmetry might be significant. How will things look to him? He will discover that drivers on minor roads are more likely to slow down. Minor-road drivers slow down in 82.1 per cent of cases, since they are all conscious players; major-road drivers, in contrast, slow down in only 77.9 per cent of cases (i.e. 95 per cent of 82.1 per cent). Since minor-road drivers slow down in more than 80 per cent of cases, the best strategy for a major-road driver is to maintain speed. Conversely, since major-road drivers slow down in less than 80 per cent of cases, the best strategy for a minor-road driver is to slow down. From our player's point of view, it is *as if* a convention of giving priority to the major road had already started to evolve – although in reality, he is the first person to be conscious of the distinction between major and minor roads. Clearly, he will do best if he adopts this convention. By doing so, he makes the asymmetry in the behaviour of major-road and minor-road drivers slightly more marked.

It is not difficult to work out that, as more players become aware of the asymmetry (which, of course, is becoming increasingly hard to miss), the

B's strategy

		Slow down	Maintain speed
A's strategy	Slow down	0, 0	2, 3
	Maintain speed	3, 2	−9, −11

Figure 3.4 A variant of the asymmetrical crossroads game

convention of 'priority to the major road' will establish itself by a self-reinforcing process. Eventually a stable equilibrium will be reached in which all conscious players follow this convention. (In this particular example, all players behave as though following the convention, since the unconscious players are all on major roads. If I had assumed only that major-road drivers were more likely not to notice crossroads, the final equilibrium would have been one in which the convention was occasionally broken by absent-minded minor-road drivers.)

Here is another example of essentially the same phenomenon. Consider the variant of the asymmetrical crossroads game shown in Figure 3.4. As before, I shall assume that each individual plays half his games as A and half as B. In this game the asymmetry is more than a matter of labelling, because the utility a player derives from the outcome in which both players maintain speed depends on his role: this outcome is worse for B-players than for A-players. Nevertheless, this asymmetry is relatively minor and might for some time pass unnoticed.

Suppose that players rely on past experience to guide their choices between strategies. Then if a player does not spot the asymmetry between the roles of A and B, his experience will tell him only that in those cases in which he and his opponent maintain speed, the outcome is a utility of −9 in 50 per cent of games and −11 in the other 50 per cent. The average utility of these outcomes is −10. So as long as he fails to recognize the pattern in these outcomes – that one outcome occurs when he is A and the other when he is B – he will behave just as if he were playing the original crossroads game (in which both players derive a utility of −10 if they both maintain speed: see Figures 3.1 and 3.2). If everyone fails to spot the asymmetry, a stable equilibrium will occur where 80 per cent of players slow down. (Compare the analysis of the symmetrical crossroads game in Section 3.1.)

Now suppose, however, that one player realizes that the outcomes he experiences as A are slightly different from those he experiences as B. Since in either case 80 per cent of his opponents slow down, he will discover that 'maintain speed' is the more successful strategy when he is

| | | B's strategy | |
		Slow down	Maintain speed
A's strategy	Slow down	0, 0	2.2, 3
	Maintain speed	3, 1.8	−9, −11

Figure 3.5   Another variant of the asymmetrical crossroads game

A and 'slow down' is the more successful strategy when he is B. ('Maintain speed' is more successful for A-players so long as more than 78.6 per cent of B-players slow down; 'slow down' is more successful for B-players so long as less than 81.3 per cent of A-players slow down.) So the player who spots the asymmetry will have an immediate incentive to adopt – or initiate – the convention 'B gives way to A'. As more players adopt this convention, the proportion of A-players slowing down falls from 80 per cent and the proportion of B-players slowing down rises above 80 per cent. This makes the A–B asymmetry more visible and the incentive to follow the convention becomes greater. Again, a self-reinforcing process is set in motion.

Interestingly, the convention that is embedded in the structure of a game – the one that will tend to evolve if players gradually become aware of an asymmetry – is not necessarily the one that is in the best interests of the players. Figure 3.5 shows yet another variant of the crossroads game. As in the previous example, there are slight asymmetries in the outcomes of an otherwise symmetrical game. If this case is analysed in the same way as the previous one, it turns out that the convention that will evolve is again 'B gives way to A'. Yet it is easy to see that the opposite convention would yield better results. If everyone follows the convention 'B gives way to A', the average utility derived by each player is 2.4 (i.e. 3 when he is A and 1.8 when he is B). If, instead, everyone followed the opposite convention, the average utility derived by each player would be 2.6. The former convention evolves because it is the better one for a player to follow in a situation in which no one else – or hardly anyone else – follows any convention at all.

The essential point is this: if we are to explain why a particular convention has evolved, we must ask why individuals have been attracted to it, and not what purpose it serves for the community as a whole. Once a convention has become established, there is no puzzle about why individuals are attracted to it: each person wants to follow it because everyone else does. It is of no direct concern to any individual whether a different convention would be better for everyone, since no one has the power to change what everyone else does. So the vital stage in the evolution of a convention is the initial one. To explain why a convention has evolved, we must explain why it first attracted players.

3.3 Prominence

The analysis in Section 3.2 rests on the assumption that individuals learn by experience; conventions start to evolve when some individuals are able to infer from their past experience that one strategy is more success-ful for them when they are playing one role and that another is more successful when they are playing another role. The essential ideas behind this sort of explanation of the evolution of conventions were developed by biologists, in particular by Maynard Smith and Parker (1976); I have merely adapted them to a human context.

A very different but complementary approach can be traced to Schelling's fascinating book *The Strategy of Conflict* (1960). Consider the position of two individuals playing the crossroads game for the first time, with no knowledge of how the game is customarily played by other people. They can see which of them is approaching from the left, which is on the major road, which is in the larger vehicle and so on; but they do not know of any convention of priority based on any of these asymmetries. What is the best strategy for each player?

It seems clear that deductive reasoning, as employed in conventional game theory, would be of little help to these players. Each knows that it is best for him to slow down if his opponent is going to maintain speed, and that it is best for him to maintain speed if his opponent is going to slow down. But how can he possibly tell what his opponent is going to do? If he tries to put himself in his opponent's position, he will see that his opponent faces exactly the same problem as he does. Deductive reasoning seems to lead to an infinite regress: what it is rational for A to do depends on what B is going to do, but if A tries to predict B's behaviour by asking what it would be rational for B to do, he finds that this depends on what *he* is going to do. It is equally clear that the players cannot be guided by their experience of playing the game, since they have no such experience. On the face of it, their problem is incapable of solution; all they can do is choose one or other strategy and hope for the best.

Nevertheless, Schelling shows that people are often able to solve these sorts of problems very successfully. It seems that human beings have an ability to coordinate their behaviour, and that this ability is some-thing distinct from 'rationality' in the deductive sense. Here is one of Schelling's examples (1960, pp. 54–8). Two people are not allowed to communicate with one another. Each is asked to name either 'heads' or 'tails'. If both players give the same answer, they both win a prize; if they give different answers, they both win nothing. This is an example of a pure coordination game. (It is 'pure' because there is no conflict of interest between the players, who should be thought of as partners rather than opponents; compare the positions of partners in card games like bridge.) The logic of the game is transparent: each player wants to do whatever the other player does. But deductive reasoning seems to offer no help to a player. How can there be any reason for naming 'heads' rather than 'tails', or 'tails' rather than 'heads'? Rational analysis seems to suggest that it doesn't matter which the player names, and that he has only a 0.5 probability of winning the prize.

Schelling set this problem to 42 people. (Apparently he asked each of them the hypothetical question: 'What would you do if you were playing this game?') Thirty-six chose 'heads'. So if this sample is representative, a player who chooses 'heads' has a 0.86 probability of winning the prize; for the player who chooses tails, the probability is only 0.14. For each player – given the tendency for the others to name 'heads' – 'heads' is clearly the best strategy; and 86 per cent of Schelling's sample knew this. How?

In a variant of this problem, Schelling asked people to write down any positive number. Again, a prize would be awarded if two partners selected the same number. There is an infinity of positive numbers, and any one of them is just as good as any other, so long as both partners choose it. Rational analysis suggests that the probability of winning the prize is virtually zero. In fact, 40 per cent of people chose the number 1, thus achieving a 0.4 probability of winning the game when playing with a random partner. How did they know that 1 was the right answer?

A slightly more realistic game with the same logical structure is the rendezvous game (briefly mentioned in Section 2.3). You and your partner are unable to communicate with one another, but want to meet. The problem is to choose where (and perhaps when) to go in the hope of finding your partner there too. Schelling asked his sample to name a place somewhere in New York City. More than 50 per cent of them chose the same place: Grand Central Station (Schelling's respondents were all from New Haven, Connecticut, and presumably the question was asked in the late 1950s). When asked to name a time, almost everyone chose 12 noon.

All of these games are similar in structure to the crossroads game. (The difference is that the crossroads game is not a game of *pure* coordination. In a pure coordination game, all that matters to any player is that he coordinates his behaviour with that of his partner. In the crossroads game there is some conflict of interest, since if one player is to give way to the other, each would prefer not to be the one who gives way.) If these games were played repeatedly, conventions would eventually evolve – like 'Always choose "heads" ' and 'Always go to Grand Central Station.' But if everyone relied only on trial and error, it could take a very long time for a convention to begin to establish itself. (Think of how many places there are to go to in New York City, and how rarely anyone would meet his partner if he chose a place at random.) Schelling's respondents, however, didn't play these games repeatedly, and yet they showed a remarkable ability to converge on conventions straight away. Somehow they knew in advance which conventions were most likely to emerge. If people have some ability of this kind, even if imperfect, it may be very important in explaining how conventions first start to evolve – and hence which conventions establish themselves. (Remember that once *some* people adopt a convention, a self-reinforcing process is set in motion.)

What, then, lies behind this ability of people to coordinate their behaviour? Schelling's answer is that, of all the possible ways in which people could coordinate their behaviour, some are more prominent or conspicuous or salient than others. Prominence 'depends on time and place and who the people are'; in the final analysis, he says, 'we are dealing with imagination as much as with logic' (1960, p. 58). Nevertheless, people often have shared notions of prominence and can use these to solve coordination problems.

Prominence is sometimes a matter of unconscious ideas of *precedence*. Take the case of 'heads' and 'tails'. Most of us, I think, sense that 'heads' has some sort of priority over 'tails' – it is somehow more important. I certainly do, even though I cannot account for this belief. (As a child, I always called 'tails' when a coin was tossed, because I had some kind of feeling that in doing so I was supporting the underdog.) Schelling's respondents apparently felt the same. More to the point, they must have guessed (for how could they have known?) that others shared their sense that 'heads' ranked above 'tails'.

As Schelling points out, prominence is often linked with uniqueness. In the set of positive integers, 1 stands out because it is the smallest. No other property as important as 'being smallest' is unique to any of the positive integers. How can I prove that 'being smallest' is more important than 'being unlucky' or 'being the number of cents in a dollar'? I can't; but I feel that it is so. Remember that in this sort of game, there is no point in trying to be clever; the test of a good answer is that it agrees with other people's. If Schelling's respondents are typical, number 1 *is* the right answer, simply because it is the answer most people give. 'Being central' is another property that often assigns unique prominence to one thing in a set. This perhaps accounts for the prominence of 12 noon among all possible times of day.

Prominence may also be determined by analogy. Why does a railway station stand out as the place to meet someone? Not, surely, because railway stations are prominent in themselves. (Suppose Schelling's question had been: 'Name one landmark in New York City.' Would his respondents still have converged on Grand Central Station? I suspect not.) The explanation, I think, is an association of ideas. The particular problem Schelling set his respondents was one that, I take it, they had never faced before. However, it is related to a common problem, in which two people have to agree in advance on a time and place to meet one another. Such meetings are often planned for railway stations, partly because the railway station is often the outsider's first point of contact with a city, and partly because stations are designed to accommodate people who are waiting to meet other people. (The proverbial assignation in London is: 'Meet me under the clock at Charing Cross Station.') So there already is an understanding that arranged meetings take place at railway stations. Schelling's respondents, I suggest, used this piece of common knowledge to solve the problem of finding a location for an unarranged meeting.

Analogies of this kind are particularly important because they provide a means by which conventions can reproduce themselves in new situations. In a sense, of course, all conventions rest on analogies, since no two coordination problems are ever exactly the same. Consider the crossroads game again. Suppose I have driven round a certain country for several months, and I have observed a marked tendency for drivers at crossroads to give priority to the right. I am approaching a crossroads I have never used before. How do I know that 'priority to the right' is the appropriate convention for *this* crossroads? Or suppose that previously I have always driven by day, but now I am driving at night. How do I know that night-time conventions are the same as day-time ones? The truth is that I cannot know for certain; but it surely makes sense for me to look for the most obvious analogies between my present, necessarily unique, problem and those I have faced in the past.

Now imagine a community living in an area with many crossroads. Suppose that a convention begins to evolve at just one crossroads, and that this convention is that drivers on one road (say, running north–south) have priority over drivers on the other (running east–west). There are likely to be many other features distinguishing these two roads.

Perhaps the north–south road is wider and carries more traffic; the north–south road has a gradient while the east–west road is flat; and so on. Any of these features could be used to describe the convention: we might say that north–south drivers have priority over east–west drivers, or that drivers on the major road have priority, or that drivers going uphill or downhill have priority over drivers on the level. As long as the convention is specific to this particular crossroads, all of these descriptions are equivalent.

Now consider other crossroads in the same community. Drivers may now draw analogies with the first crossroads, for which a convention of priority has become established. A driver who has thought of the original convention in terms of major and minor roads will have some prior expectation that the same convention will apply, or will emerge, elsewhere. For him, this solution to the coordination problem has a special prominence. He will be inclined to adopt the strategy of giving way when on a minor road and maintaining speed when on a major road. Provided that a significant number of drivers think in this way, a general convention of 'priority to the major road' will begin to evolve, and a self-reinforcing process will be set in motion. Of course, other drivers may draw different analogies. Some may interpret the original convention in terms of north–south and east–west, and expect to find east–west traffic giving way to north–south, and so this convention may begin to spread too. Whichever interpretation of the convention is initially most popular will tend to supplant the others. Thus it is the analogies that strike most people most quickly that will provide the basis of the conventions that establish themselves.

Some conventions are more fertile than others, in the sense that they are better equipped to reproduce themselves by analogy. The rule 'drivers on the level give way to drivers on a gradient' can be applied only to a very special class of crossroads. The same is true of the rule 'east–west traffic gives way to north–south' (although it might spread throughout a city with a grid-iron plan). 'Give way to drivers on the major road' applies to many more crossroads, although there remain many cases where this convention would be ambiguous. 'Give way to traffic approaching from the right (or left)' is far more fertile, since it can be applied at any crossroads. Indeed, it can be applied whenever two vehicles or ships or planes or horses or people are on collision courses and are not meeting exactly head-on. It is thus capable of spreading by analogy from one context to many others. It might, for example, first evolve as a rule for ships in open water, and then spread to road traffic.

So general conventions – ones with a wide range of possible applications – are likely to come to predominate in the pool of established conventions. Specific conventions may survive in particular cases, just as rare plants and animals can survive in specialized habitats; but it is the most versatile conventions that will be most successful in spreading to new situations.

3.4   Conventions in social life

The crossroads game can serve as a model for many of the conventions that enable people to live with one another in a reasonably harmonious way. Consider, for example, the role of money in social life. In every modern society, intrinsically worthless pieces of paper and scraps of metal are accepted in exchange for goods and services of real value. In earlier times, it was more common to use gold and silver coins as money. These metals did have some intrinsic value, particularly for decoration, but the exchange value of gold and silver in terms of other goods would have been much less if these metals had not been used as money. (This is a simple matter of supply and demand. The demand for gold and silver was greater than it would have been, had they not been used as money; so the price of gold and silver relative to other goods was higher.) In this sense gold and silver had a purchasing power that probably far exceeded their intrinsic value.

That the value of money is fundamentally a convention – that each of us accepts that money has value because everyone else does – was recognized by Locke in the seventeenth century: 'Gold and Silver, being little useful to the Life of Man in proportion to Food, Rayment, and Carriage, has its *value* only from the consent of Men.' Men, he argues, 'had *agreed, that a little piece of yellow Metal*, which would keep without wasting or decay, should be worth a great piece of Flesh, or a whole heap of Corn'. How could such an agreement come into existence? Locke describes the process by which money had acquired value as one of 'tacit agreement'; this agreement had been reached 'without compact' (Locke, 1690, Second Treatise, Ch. 5). What he seems to have in mind is the gradual evolution of a convention.[1] Hume provided a similar explanation of the value of money half a century later. According to Hume, human recognition of rules of property is a convention that 'arises gradually, and acquires force by a slow progression, and by our repeated experience of the inconveniences of transgressing it'. And 'In like manner do gold and silver become the common measures of exchange, and are esteem'd sufficient payment for what is of a hundred times their value' (Hume, 1740,

Book 3, Part 2, Section 2). Whether, as Hume argues, rules of property are conventions will be the subject of Chapters 4 and 5.

What people use as money in any particular society is to a great extent arbitrary, in the same sense that it is arbitrary whether we give way to traffic approaching from the right or to traffic approaching from the left. Once established, however, a monetary convention can have enormous staying power. The convention that gold is money has lasted for thousands of years. At the time of writing there is no law to prevent British people from carrying out their transactions in Deutschmarks or French francs or US dollars. These currencies are freely available from banks and are not intrinsically unsuitable for use in Britain. Yet ordinary shops price their goods only in pounds sterling and do not accept other currencies, and ordinary people carry only British currency around with them. Why do we all continue to use pounds? The basic answer is: 'Because everyone else does.' We do not carry foreign currency because we know that shops will not accept it; shopkeepers do not incur the costs of handling foreign currency because they know that their customers will carry pounds. That trade in Britain is conducted in pounds sterling is a convention.

The standardization of complementary products provides many more examples of conventions. Take, for example, gramophone records and record-players. Manufacturers of records want their products to be compatible with as many record-players as possible; manufacturers of record-players want their products to be compatible with as many records as possible. So the answer to the question: 'Why do almost all record-player manufacturers design their products to be played at 33 rpm?' is basically: 'Because everyone else does.' The same principle seems to lie behind the evolution of market-places, market days and shopping hours: sellers wish to trade where and when buyers congregate, and buyers wish to go where and when sellers congregate.[2] Similarly, most communities have conventions about where and when particular kinds of classified adverts are placed; everyone knows, for example, that houses for sale are customarily advertised in the Saturday edition of a particular newspaper. These conventions work because sellers want their adverts to be seen by as many buyers as possible, and buyers want to read newspapers in which many sellers are advertising.

As Hume (1740, Book 3, Part 2, Section 2) recognized, language is a system of conventions. We all wish to speak and write in a form that is comprehensible to the people with whom we wish to communicate, and so there is a self-reinforcing tendency for communities to evolve common languages. For example, English seems to have established itself as the international language of economics. Economists whose first language is not English learn to read English because it is the language in which most economics is written; and they write in English because it is the language that can be read by most economists. In short, economists use English because that is what other economists do. The processes that lie behind the evolution of languages can also be seen at work in the evolution of ideograms, such as the picture of a cigarette with a line through it that signifies 'No smoking'. Anyone who wants to communicate a message by means of an ideogram will want that ideogram to be understood by as many people as possible, and so will want to use the one that is most widely recognized as carrying the relevant message. Thus there is a self-reinforcing tendency for ideograms to become standardized.

The exchange of Christmas cards provides a more homely example. I take it that, in most cases, people want to send cards to those people who send cards to them, and not to other people. In Britain, at least, the Christmas post is so slow that it is difficult to wait to see if someone sends you a card before you post a card to him; and to post a card very late is to signal that your original intention had been not to send a card at all. So each year pairs of individuals are playing a game with essentially the same structure as the crossroads game. In one respect, the Christmas card game is easier to play: it is not anonymous. Thus it is possible to adopt the cautious rule of sending cards to exactly those people who sent cards to you last year. But the real skill comes in trying to anticipate *changes* in the list of people who send you cards – guessing who is going to send you a card for the first time, and who will decide that this is the year to stop. Many people do seem to be quite successful at anticipating these changes. Their success is made possible, I suggest, by the existence of conventions about which kinds of relationships between people are associated with the exchange of Christmas cards. These conventions are subtle and ill-defined – which is why success at the Christmas card game requires skill and imagination – but they do exist.

These examples could be multiplied almost endlessly. A great deal of social organization depends on conventions like the ones I have described. These are rules that have never been consciously designed and that it is in everyone's interest to keep. It is easy to overlook the importance of such rules, precisely because they have not been designed and because it is in our interest to keep them. There is a strong temptation to associate social order with planning and with constraint – to suppose that order must be the product of human design and that it must require enforcement. As Hayek (1960, p. 159) puts it, there is a very widespread 'inability to conceive of an effective coordination of human activities without deliberate organization by a commanding intelligence'. Our sense of the rationality of the human species tends to blind us to the possibility that social order might be spontaneous.

4
Property

4.1 Hobbes's state of nature

In the previous chapter, I quoted Hume's claim that the law of property is, at root, a convention that has evolved spontaneously – that 'arises gradually, and acquires force by a slow progression, and by our repeated experience of the inconvenience of transgressing it' (Hume, 1740, Book 3, Part 2, Section 2; and Section 3.4 above). In this chapter and the next, I shall ask whether Hume could be right: I shall ask whether, in the absence of any formal system of law, self-enforcing rules of property could evolve out of the interactions of individuals concerned only with their own interests.

One starting point for answering this question is to consider a state of nature: a state in which human beings live together without any government or formal law. The classic account of the state of nature is given by Hobbes in *Leviathan* (1651), and in particular in his Chapter 13, 'Of the Natural Condition of Mankind as concerning their Felicity and Misery'.

Hobbes begins by arguing that men[1] are roughly equal in the natural endowments of skill, strength and cunning appropriate for survival in a state of nature:

> Nature hath made men so equal, in the faculties of the body, and mind; as that though there be found one man sometimes manifestly stronger in body, or of quicker mind than another; yet when all is reckoned together, the difference between man, and man, is not so considerable, as that one man can thereupon claim to himself any benefit, to which another may not pretend, as well as he. For as to the strength of body, the weakest has strength enough to kill the strongest, either by secret machination, or by confederacy with others, that are in the same danger with himself.

From this Hobbes deduces that in a state of nature, men would be permanently at war with one another:

> From this equality of ability, ariseth equality of hope in the attain-
> ing of our ends. And therefore if any two men desire the same thing,
> which nevertheless they cannot both enjoy, they become enemies;
> and in the way to their end, which is principally their own conserva-
> tion, and sometimes their delectation only, endeavour to destroy, or
> subdue one another. (Hobbes, 1651, Ch. 13)

Thus men fight for gain. And since each man knows that others will seek to deprive him of what he has, each man has another interest in subduing his fellows: even if he does not want to take what they have, he wants to reduce as far as possible their power to attack him. There is, Hobbes says, 'no way for any man to secure himself, so reasonable, as anticipation' (1651, Ch. 13). So men fight for safety. Hobbes adds a further argument, that men naturally want the respect of others, and are predisposed to believe that other people are undervaluing them; they resent and seek to avenge any slights on themselves. Thus men fight for reputation.

The results of all this are extremely unpleasant:

> Hereby it is manifest, that during the time men live without a com-
> mon power to keep them all in awe, they are in that condition which
> is called war; and such a war, as is of every man, against every man.
> For WAR, consisteth not in battle only, or the act of fighting; but in
> a tract of time, wherein the will to contend by battle is sufficiently
> known...
>
> In such condition, there is no place for industry; because the fruit
> thereof is uncertain: and consequently no culture of the earth; no
> navigation, nor use of the commodities that may be imported by sea;
> no commodious building; no instruments of moving, and removing,
> such things as require much force; no knowledge of the face of the
> earth; no account of time; no arts; no letters; no society; and which
> is worst of all, continual fear, and danger of violent death; and the
> life of man, solitary, poor, nasty, brutish, and short. (Hobbes, 1651,
> Ch. 13)

The central problem of life in the state of nature is that there are no settled rules of property; everyone seeks to take everything he can lay his hands on. Hobbes makes this point by asserting that in the state of nature 'every man has a right to every thing' (1651, Ch. 14). Each man has a natural right to do whatever he judges best to preserve his own life, and, in the insecurity of a war of all against all, anything he can get hold of is likely to be of some use in helping to preserve him against his enemies – that is, against everyone else. Thus, according to Hobbes, each man has a right to whatever he can grab or fight for.

As a model of the interactions that would occur in such a state of nature, we may take Hobbes's own illustration: the case where 'two men desire the same thing, which nevertheless they cannot both enjoy'. Perhaps one man has just gathered a pile of wood for a fire; a second man appears on the scene and wants the wood for his own fire. They must either come to some accommodation or fight. If one of the men had such superior strength that he could be sure of winning a fight *at no cost to himself*, the outcome would be obvious: the stronger man would take the wood. But this, according to Hobbes (and I agree with him), is not the typical case. Human beings are sufficiently equal in strength and cunning that most individuals have the power to inflict *some* harm on most other individuals. If two individuals fight, the fight itself is likely to harm both of them, even if (which need not be the case) the spoils of victory are sufficient to compensate the winner for the costs of the fight. Provided that each of the two men in the example has some power to hurt the other, their interaction has a game-like character. I shall investigate whether conventions of property could evolve from the repeated playing of this kind of game.

If such conventions could be expected to evolve, Hobbes's picture of the state of nature is unduly pessimistic. Admittedly, Hobbes's picture is not one in which everyone is fighting all the time; everyone merely stands ready to fight, making his 'will to contend by battle' known to everyone else. But in Hobbes's state of nature there seem to be no settled conventions about who has possession of what; no one has any confidence that, so long as he does not overstep certain recognized boundaries, he will be left in peace. For Hobbes the state of nature is a state of war, while a system of conventions would represent at least an armed truce.

As I argued in Chapter 1, the idea of the state of nature can be used as a model for some significant areas of human life. The case of the two men in conflict over the pile of wood has obvious parallels in international affairs, for example. When two nations are in dispute over the possession of some valuable resource – say, territory or fishing rights or navigation rights – it is usually the case that each has the power to inflict enormous harm on the other. If both nations press their claims to the limit, there will be all-out war, but such a war would be immensely costly to both winner and loser. (There may not even be any winner; between nuclear powers, all-out war means mutual extinction.) Conventions in international relations can allow unfriendly nations to live in a state of peaceful coexistence rather than total war.

On a much smaller scale, many of the human interactions that make up everyday life have an element of the state of nature about them. Take the homely case of disputes between neighbours. Where exactly is the boundary between A's garden and B's garden? How noisy may A's party be when B is trying to sleep? May A light a bonfire while B is sunbathing downwind? And so on. When two households live close to one another, there are all sorts of subtle (and not so subtle) ways in which each can harm the other; each therefore has the power to escalate the quarrel into a kind of limited warfare. In principle, of course, these sorts of disputes can usually be settled in the courts, but going to law in a dispute between neighbours is like going to war in an international dispute: it is available as a last resort, but (in relation to what is at stake) it is normally very costly for both parties. Both parties therefore have a strong interest in reaching some kind of accommodation before their quarrel escalates to the level of writs and injunctions. Here again conventions may be important in setting the terms on which individuals settle their differences.

4.2 The hawk–dove game

I shall begin by presenting a very simple game that seems to capture the main features of Hobbes's quarrel between the two men who 'desire the same thing, which nevertheless they cannot both enjoy'. This game has been used by two biologists, Maynard Smith and Price (1973), as a model of contests between animals; it is known to biologists as the 'hawk–dove game'. To most game theorists it is better known as 'chicken', after the game of bravado played by teenage boys[2] (cf. Rapoport, 1967). I shall use the biologists' name because my evolutionary analysis of this game draws heavily on their work.

Maynard Smith and Price are concerned with animal behaviour in cases where this is genetically predetermined. Thus in their model, individuals do not *choose* between strategies; instead, each individual has an inherited predisposition to follow a particular strategy. The success of a strategy is measured in terms of the Darwinian concept of 'fitness'; a strategy is successful to the extent that animals with a predisposition to follow it are successful at reproducing themselves. By a process of natural selection more successful strategies tend to supplant less successful ones. To avoid any misunderstanding, let me repeat what I said in

Section 2.6: I am concerned with *social* and not *biological* evolution. In adapting Maynard Smith and Price's game to a human context, I am substituting a subjective concept of utility for Darwinian fitness as the measure of success, and I am assuming that more successful strategies supplant less successful ones by a process of imitation and learning rather than by one of biological natural selection. Nevertheless, much of Maynard Smith and Price's analysis can be carried over to the human case.

Suppose that two individuals, A and B, come into conflict about which of them should take some valuable resource. Each has some power to hurt the other. This may be physical harm – each may be able to inflict pain or injury on the other – but it need not be. In international affairs – perhaps the closest modern analogy with the Hobbesian state of nature – war is available as a last resort, but there are many milder ways in which nations deliberately harm one another in the pursuit of their own ends. (Economic, sporting or diplomatic links may be severed, or obstacles may be put in the way of travel from one country to the other.) In the case of a quarrel between neighbours, even the last resort may be a lawsuit rather than physical warfare. What matters is that each individual has the power to do *something* that the other would prefer he didn't do. I shall use the word 'fight' to include all the ways in which A and B might set out to hurt each other. For the moment I shall assume that A and B are exactly equal both in their capacity to hurt and in their capacity to be hurt: if it comes to a fight, they are evenly matched.

Suppose that there are just two possible strategies an individual might adopt. One strategy is submissive; Maynard Smith and Price call it the dove strategy. In effect, a dove stakes a claim to only one-half of the resource. (Alternatively, in a contest between human beings, we might suppose that doves propose using some random device – like the toss of a coin – that would give each person the same chance of taking the resource.) Doves, however, are not prepared to fight in support of their claims; if their opponents show any inclination to fight, doves immediately concede defeat.

The other strategy – the hawk strategy – is aggressive: it is the strategy of trying to win the whole of the resource by fighting. If a hawk meets a dove, the hawk lays claim to the whole of the resource and signals his readiness to fight; the dove then immediately backs down, allowing the hawk to take the resource without having to fight for it. But if a hawk meets a hawk, they fight it out. Maynard Smith and Price assume that there is some recognized point in a fight at which a winner emerges; the loser accepts defeat and the winner takes the resource. By this stage the loser – and possibly also the winner – will have suffered some harm: this is what distinguishes a losing hawk from a dove. Since the two contestants are evenly matched, we must assume that which of them wins is a matter of chance. Thus an individual who engages in a long series of fights can expect to win half of them and to lose the other half.

Clearly the most desirable state of affairs for any individual is to meet a dove when playing 'hawk': this wins the whole of the resource at no cost. Next best is to meet a dove when playing 'dove'. This wins a half share of the resource (or a 50 per cent chance of winning it all) at no cost. In principle the other two states of affairs – meeting a hawk when playing 'dove' and meeting a hawk when playing 'hawk' – could be ranked either way, depending on whether the best response to a known hawk would be to fight or to concede defeat. If the best response was to fight, however, the game would be trivial, since then 'hawk' would be the best response to both strategies and there would be no reason for anyone ever to play 'dove'. It makes more sense to suppose that the risk of being hurt in a fight is sufficiently great, and the hurt sufficiently serious, to make 'dove' the best response to 'hawk'. In other words, the worst possible state of affairs is to get involved in a fight. Figure 4.1 shows a particular matrix of expected utilities that is consistent with these general suppositions. (Expected utilities are required because there is a random element: the outcome of any single contest between two hawks is determined by chance.)

The structure of this game has some similarities with that of the crossroads game, but the two games are different: there is more conflict of interest between the players in the hawk–dove game. In the crossroads game, drivers who slow down (the more submissive strategy) *want* their opponents to maintain speed; in the hawk–dove game, doves prefer to meet other doves.

As in my analysis of the crossroads game, I assume that there is a large community of individuals, each of whom has preferences that can be represented by the utility indices in Figure 4.1. Each individual plays the game many times; in any game, each of the other individuals is equally likely to be his opponent.

		Opponent's strategy	
		Dove	Hawk
Player's strategy	Dove	1	0
	Hawk	2	–2

Figure 4.1   The symmetrical hawk–dove game

For the moment I shall assume that this game, like the crossroads game, is played anonymously. Thus each individual remembers his *general* experience of the game but not how he has fared against particular opponents. This assumption seems appropriate for cases where the pool of players is large, and where any given pair of individuals play against one another very infrequently. Consider, for example, the case of two drivers disputing over which should take the last space in a car park, or the case of two people in a hurry at a railway station disputing over which should have the first use of a public telephone. These are instances of the hawk–dove game in which the players are unlikely to meet each other again (and probably would not recognize each other if they did). Admittedly, there are many other instances in which the hawk–dove game is played repeatedly between individuals who are well known to each other – for example, the case of quarrels between neighbours. I shall consider these cases later (Sections 4.8 and 4.9).

Suppose the players do not recognize any asymmetry in the game, interpreting each game as one between 'me' and 'my opponent'. Then this is a symmetrical game with a stable equilibrium. Let p be the probability that a randomly selected player plays 'dove' in a randomly selected game. Then 'dove' is more successful than, just as successful as, or less successful than 'hawk' according to whether p is less than, equal to, or greater than $\frac{2}{3}$. Thus there is equilibrium if and only if $p = \frac{2}{3}$. And this equilibrium is stable. If 'dove' is played in more than two-thirds of all cases, 'hawk' becomes the more successful strategy; and if 'hawk' is played in more than one-third of all cases, 'dove' becomes the more successful strategy. Thus, so long as the game is perceived to be symmetrical, any deviations from $p = \frac{2}{3}$ will be self-correcting.

This equilibrium has the look of a Hobbesian state of nature. Some conflicts, admittedly, are resolved peacefully: those in which doves meet doves. But all other conflicts – 56 per cent in my example – are resolved by force or by the threat of force. When hawks meet doves, the hawks win by threatening to fight, and the doves surrender. When hawks meet hawks, there is a damaging fight. Since no one knows which strategy his opponent is going to adopt, no one can ever be confident of being able to gain the disputed resource, or even to gain a share of it. In other words, there are no settled rules of property. If war 'consisteth not in battle only, or the act of fighting, but in a tract of time, wherein the will to contend by battle is sufficiently known', then this is a state of war 'of every man against every man' (cf. Section 4.1).

Everyone suffers from this state of war. In equilibrium every individual – whether he always plays 'dove', always plays 'hawk', or sometimes plays one and sometimes the other – gains an expected utility of $\frac{2}{3}$ from each game. If instead everyone played 'dove', everyone would gain a utility of 1 from each game. So, relative to this peaceful state of affairs, everyone loses by war. It is not a case of the strong exploiting the weak; recall that everyone has been assumed equal in fighting ability and that everyone has the option of being a hawk. Rather, everyone has the same incentive to fight if he expects that his opponent will not. Everyone would prefer a state of peace to a state of war; but in the state of peace, every individual has an incentive to fight.

So, in the absence of asymmetries, conflicts of the hawk–dove kind lead to a Hobbesian state of nature. It is natural to ask what would happen if, instead, the players recognized some asymmetry in the game. I shall postpone answering this question until Section 4.5, since first I wish to examine some more complicated, but more realistic, versions of Hobbes's game in which two men desire the same thing, which they cannot both enjoy.

4.3   The war of attrition

The hawk–dove game provides a neat and simple model of conflict between pairs of individuals, but it has serious limitations. One very obvious problem is that fighting is represented as an all-or-nothing affair from which a winner emerges by chance. In reality, many of the ways in which individuals fight one another involve a long-drawn-out process of mutual harm. One individual loses not by suffering some kind of random knock-out blow, but rather by choice: fighting continues until one person decides that enough is enough, and concedes defeat.

Take, for example, the case of a dispute between neighbours. Each can inflict continual minor irritation on the other; in the neighbourhood equivalent of a war, this process can continue – to the detriment of both sides – for as long as both keep it up. The end comes when one of the disputants lets the other have his way. Or take the case of two drivers who meet head-on in a lane that is too narrow to allow two vehicles to pass. One must reverse to the nearest passing-place; but which driver should do the reversing? Each driver has the option of refusing to reverse and sitting tight. If both do this there is a deadlock. The longer this continues, the more delay both drivers suffer. The contest comes to an end when one driver backs down and agrees to reverse. Notice that this example might be interpreted as a game about bargaining rather than fighting. The essence of the problem is that the two drivers must *agree* about which of them is to reverse; each can try to hold out for an agreement that favours his own interests, but the longer they both hold out, the more costly it is for both. The analogies with international relations and with labour disputes are obvious.

This type of problem can be formulated as a simple game in which two players each choose to incur costs in order to win some prize; the prize goes to the player who chooses to incur the greater cost, but neither player can retrieve the costs he has sunk in the contest. Possibly the earliest analysis of this type of game is due to Tullock (1967). A better-known version of the game was later presented by Shubik (1971) as the dollar auction game. As in the case of the chicken game, the evolutionary analysis of this kind of game has, for the most part, been carried out by biologists. Here the pioneering work was done by Maynard Smith (1974). Many variants of Maynard Smith's game have been studied in the literature of theoretical biology (e.g. Maynard Smith and Parker, 1976; Norman *et al.*, 1977; Bishop and Cannings, 1978; Bishop *et al.*, 1978). Here is a very simple version. As my analysis draws heavily on the work of biologists, I shall use their name for the game: the war of attrition.

Suppose that two players, A and B, are in dispute over some resource. As long as they remain in dispute, each incurs a loss of utility at some constant rate per unit of time.[3] At any time, each player has the option of surrendering, in which case the other player takes the resource. If both players happen to surrender simultaneously, the resource is shared (it will emerge that this event has a vanishingly small probability of occurring). For each player, the utility of winning the resource is v, the utility of sharing the resource is $v/2$, and the utility loss through fighting is c per unit of time.

If we analyse this game in terms of simultaneously-chosen strategies, each player must choose a persistence time – that is, a time limit at which, if his opponent has still not surrendered, he will surrender himself. The set of pure strategies open to each player can thus be interpreted as the set of all possible persistence times. Let l_A and l_B be the persistence times chosen by the two players. The length of the fight is given by whichever of l_A and l_B is the less; the fight is won by whichever player has the greater persistence time. Thus if $l_A > l_B$, A wins the fight and derives a utility of $v - cl_B$; B loses the fight and derives a utility of $-cl_B$. Conversely, if $l_A < l_B$, A derives $-cl_A$ and B derives $v - cl_A$. In the (infinitely unlikely) event that $l_A = l_B$, each player derives a utility of $v/2 - cl_A = v/2 - cl_B$.

As in my analysis of other games, I shall assume that the game is played anonymously. One implication of this is that no purpose can be served by communication between the players during the course of a game. At first sight it might seem that the players could avoid the need for a fight simply by telling each other their persistence times at the start of the game. But, of course, it is in each player's interest that his opponent should believe that his persistence time is very long, whatever his true intentions may be. Any player has the option of bluffing – of claiming to have a longer persistence time than he actually has. In an anonymous game there can be no penalty for having one's bluff called. If individuals cannot remember their experience of playing the game against particular other individuals, there is no way in which anyone can earn a reputation for telling the truth; so no individual has anything to lose by bluffing. However, each player remembers his experience of games in general. Thus if everyone bluffs, bluffs will cease to convince. It seems clear, therefore, that communication between the players can have no real significance for the outcome of the game.

In this section I shall analyse only the symmetrical form of the war of attrition; the asymmetrical form will be considered in Section 4.7. It is easy to see that, in the symmetrical game, no pure strategy can be an equilibrium strategy. Let I be the pure strategy of using the particular persistence time I^*, and let J be any pure strategy whose persistence time is greater than I^*. If an I-playing individual meets a J-playing one, the J-player is more successful; hence I cannot be a best reply to itself. This is common sense: if you could be sure that your opponent was going to surrender at a particular time, it would be stupid to choose exactly that moment to surrender yourself.

So if an equilibrium strategy exists, it must be a mixed strategy. One way of describing a mixed strategy is in terms of its surrender rate. Suppose that a war of attrition game has already gone on for some time, say 60 minutes, neither player having surrendered. We may then ask what the probability is that a particular player will surrender in the next very short interval of time, say in the next second. Suppose this probability is 0.001. Then this player's surrender rate at this point in the game is 0.001 per second, or 0.06 per minute. A mixed strategy can be described by stating its surrender rate at every possible stage in the game. Letting t stand for the time elapsed in a game, I shall write a player's surrender rate at time t as $S(t)$; a mixed strategy is fully described by a surrender function assigning a surrender rate $S(t)$ to every time t.[4]

It turns out that the symmetrical war of attrition has a unique and stable equilibrium. This is the mixed strategy for which the surrender rate is constant over time and equal to c/v. This result has been proved formally by Bishop and Cannings (1978). Here I shall give a simple account of why this strategy is an equilibrium one, but I shall not reproduce Bishop and Cannings's proofs of uniqueness and stability.

Consider any individual engaged in the symmetrical war of attrition, facing a random opponent. Consider two alternative pure strategies that the first player might adopt. The first strategy is to set $l = t$: the player will fight up to time t but then if his opponent has not surrendered, he will surrender himself. The second strategy is to set $l = t + \delta t$, where δt is a very short interval of time. Which of these two strategies will be more successful in the long run?

Whenever our player faces an opponent who surrenders before time t, the two strategies yield exactly the same result. So in comparing them, we may restrict our attention to those cases in which the opponent is still fighting at time t. Consider any fight that is still continuing at time t. If our player decides not to surrender until $t + \delta t$, rather than surrendering immediately, he incurs the additional costs of fighting beyond time t. Since the probability that his opponent will surrender during the interval δt is close to zero, the expected loss of utility from this additional fighting is approximately $c\delta t$. However, if the opponent *does* surrender during this interval, our player will gain a large amount of utility from winning the resource (large, that is, relative to $c\delta t$.) The probability that the opponent will surrender between t and $t + \delta t$ is approximately $S(t)\delta t$, where $S(t)$ is the opponent's surrender rate at time t. So the expected gain in utility attributable to this probability of victory is $vS(t)\delta t$. Thus the relative success of the two strategies depends on the relative size of $c\delta t$ and $vS(t)\delta t$, or (cancelling out δt) on the relative size of c and $vS(t)$. 'Surrender at time $t + \delta t$' is more successful than, just as successful as, or less successful than 'surrender at time t' according to whether $vS(t)$ is greater than, equal to, or less than c – or, equivalently, whether $S(t)$ is greater than, equal to, or less than c/v.[5]

Now consider the mixed strategy I for which $S(t) = c/v$ for all t – that is, the strategy that has a constant surrender rate of c/v. Against this strategy, *all* persistence times are equally successful. (At any time t, the options 'surrender immediately' and 'fight on' are equally attractive.) In other words, every strategy, pure or mixed and including I itself, is a best reply to I. This establishes that I is an equilibrium strategy.

This equilibrium, even more than the corresponding equilibrium in the hawk–dove game, is a state of war of every man against every man. *All* disputes are settled by fighting; there is nothing corresponding to the case in which doves meet doves. There are no settled rules of property – except that resources always go to whichever of the disputants is the more determined fighter. (Not the stronger: all individuals are equal in fighting ability.) Perhaps most disturbing of all: in the long run, no one gains anything from participating in the war of attrition. Everyone is no better off than he would have been if there had been no resources to fight over; it is just as if, instead of fighting, individuals settled their differences by destroying the resources that they all want.[6]

Why is this? In equilibrium, all persistence times are equally successful. One possible persistence time is zero: a player may surrender at the very beginning of the game. Such a player has a vanishingly small probability of winning any of the resource. (With a constant surrender rate, the probability that an opponent will choose *exactly* $t = 0$ as his time for surrendering is effectively zero.) However, he incurs no costs of fighting, since he never fights. The expected utility derived from a persistence time of zero is therefore zero. Since all persistence times are equally successful, the expected utility derived from *any* persistence time, and hence from the equilibrium strategy I, must be zero. Over many games, then, the benefit that any individual derives from his victories is exactly offset by the costs of fighting. This conclusion is independent of the value of the resource and of the cost of fighting per unit of time. The more valuable the resource, or the less costly it is to fight, the longer people are prepared to fight. The surrender rate always tends to a level at which the value of the resource is dissipated in fighting. This is a truly Hobbesian state of nature.

4.4 The division game

Both in the hawk–dove game and in the war of attrition, it is possible for the two players to share the resource equally, and without fighting. In the hawk–dove game this is the result if both players choose the 'dove' strategy; in the war of attrition this is the result if both players choose zero persistence times. But these peaceable solutions are not equilibria. If everyone else plays 'dove', it pays any individual to play 'hawk'; if everyone else surrenders at the beginning of the game, it pays any individual to fight a little longer. Social evolution does not favour rules of sharing – at least, not in these games.

Part of the reason for this is that the structure of the two games prevents players from reaching agreements of the form 'I shall do . . . if you do . . .'. Take the hawk–dove game. Two players might each be attracted by the idea of an arrangement that they should both play 'dove', thus sharing the resource. But the game is structured so that neither player has the option of playing 'dove' conditional on the other player doing the same. If the players are able to communicate with one another, they might each *promise* to play 'dove' in return for the same promise from the other; but there is nothing to prevent them from breaking their promises. If, as

I have assumed, the game is played anonymously, there is no way in which anyone can earn a reputation for keeping promises; so promises, like threats, will be worthless. The same argument applies to the war of attrition. Both players might be attracted by the idea of an arrangement that they should both surrender simultaneously, at the start of the game; but they are unable to make such an agreement, since neither can rely on the other's word.

This corresponds with a genuine problem in the anonymous games of real life. Consider the case of the two drivers meeting head-on in the narrow lane. If they agree to toss a coin to settle who is to reverse, how can either driver be satisfied that if the coin falls in his favour, the other driver will reverse? Or suppose that two factions in a civil war are each holding hostages. If neither side trusts the other, how is an exchange of hostages to be arranged? But, as the hostage example suggests, these problems are not always insurmountable. (If there are many hostages, the two sides may arrange to release them one at a time, the releases being simultaneous on the two sides.) Bargains are easier to strike when there is trust; but trust is not always an essential precondition for bargaining. It seems worthwhile, therefore, to consider a game in which two players are in dispute over a resource and in which agreements to share it *are* feasible.

The game I shall consider is a variant of one suggested by Schelling (1960, p. 61); I shall call it the division game. The essential idea is that two individuals are in dispute over a divisible resource. If they can reach agreement on how to divide the resource between them, there is a peaceful settlement. If they cannot agree, there is a fight which is damaging to both.

The formal structure of the game is as follows. There are two players. A strategy is a claim to some share of the resource; a player may make any claim between 0 (nothing) and 1 (the whole of the resource). If the two claims are compatible – that is, if they sum to no more than 1 – each player takes exactly what he has claimed, winning a unit of utility for each unit of the resource he takes.[7] If the two claims are incompatible, each player loses one unit of expected utility,[8] representing the net cost of fighting (i.e. after making allowance for the possibility of winning the fight and so taking the resource). As in my analysis of the hawk–dove game and the war of attrition, I shall assume that the game is played anonymously and that the players recognize no asymmetries. (The asymmetric form of the game will be analysed in Section 4.6.)

A strategy in this game may be either pure (i.e. a single claim) or mixed (i.e. two or more different claims, each with an associated probability).

I shall say that a strategy contains[9] all those claims to which it assigns a non-zero probability, and that two claims are complementary if they sum to exactly 1. Now consider any two strategies I and J, such that J is a best reply to I. It is easy to prove the following result, which will be central to my analysis of the division game: for every claim contained in J, there must be a complementary claim contained in I. I shall call this the complementarity result.

Why does this result hold? Suppose that I contains no claim in a certain range, say between 0.2 and 0.4. Suppose you are playing the division game and you know your opponent's strategy is I. Then you know he will not make a claim between 0.2 and 0.4. So if you are going to claim more than 0.6, you should clearly claim at least 0.8; within this range you have nothing to lose by claiming more rather than less. From this kind of argument it follows that when playing against any given strategy I, the only claims that can possibly be worth making are those that are complementary with claims contained in I – the complementarity result.

One implication of this result is that the only pure strategy that can be an equilibrium is the claim 0.5. (Consider any pure strategy I, and let c be the claim contained in I. If I is to be an equilibrium, it must be a best reply to itself; so, by the complementarity result, it must contain the claim $1 - c$. But if $c \neq 0.5$, this is incompatible with the assumption that I is a pure strategy.) It is easy to see that the pure strategy $c = 0.5$ is a stable equilibrium, since it is the unique best reply to itself. (If you know your opponent is going to claim exactly one-half of the resource, your best strategy must be to claim one-half as well.)

It is possible to construct a stable mixed-strategy equilibrium out of any two complementary claims c and $1 - c$, where $c < 0.5$. (Notice that the pure-strategy equilibrium $c = 0.5$ is the limiting case of this set of mixed-strategy equilibria.) Consider any claim c where $c < 0.5$; and consider the strategy that claims c with probability p and $1 - c$ with probability $1 - p$. Against an opponent playing this strategy, the only sensible claims to make are c and $1 - c$ (i.e. the complements of the claims contained in the original strategy). The expected utility from claiming c is c; that from claiming $1 - c$ is $p(1 - c) - (1 - p)$. These expected utilities will be equal if $p = (1 + c)/(2 - c)$. Notice that if c lies in the range $0 \leq c < 0.5$, p lies in the range $0.5 \leq p < 1$. Thus there must be some probability p that makes both claims equally successful. Let I be the strategy associated with this particular value of p. Against I, either claim, or any probability mix of them, is a best reply. Hence I (which is such a probability mix) is a best reply to itself – an equilibrium strategy.

Notice that the only strategies that are best replies to I are those that contain only the claims c and $1 - c$. (This is an implication of the complementarity result.) So to test the stability of I we need only consider whether it could be invaded by some other probability mix of the claims c and $1-c$. No such invasion can succeed. Let J be any strategy using a probability mix of the two claims different from that of I. It is easy to work out that, although J is a best reply to I, I is a better reply than J to J; hence J cannot invade I (cf. Section 2.6). Putting the same point another way, consider a community of players who invariably claim either c or $1 - c$. If the proportion of players claiming c rises above its equilibrium level, $1-c$ becomes the better claim to make, and vice versa; hence any deviations from the equilibrium mix of these two claims is self-correcting.

I shall now show that the equilibria I have described are the only stable equilibria for the game. Let I be any equilibrium strategy. Since, by assumption, I is a best reply to itself, the following must be true: if I contains any claim c, it must also contain the complementary claim $1 - c$. (This is another implication of the complementarity result.) If I contains only one claim, or only one pair of complementary claims, it is a member of the class of stable equilibria I have already described. So suppose it contains more pairs: say it contains the claims c, $1 - c$, d, $1 - d$ and perhaps other pairs too. Is I a stable equilibrium? Let J be the stable equilibrium strategy that contains just the two claims, c and $1 - c$. It is clear that J is a best reply to I. (Since J is an equilibrium strategy, all the claims it contains must be equally successful; and J is a probability mix of some of these claims.) Since J is an equilibrium strategy, J is a best reply to itself. But, by the complementarity result, I is *not* a best reply to J. (I contains claims that are not complementary with claims in J.) Thus J is a better reply than I to J. This establishes that I can be invaded by J. In other words, any equilibrium involving more than one pair of complementary claims is unstable.

So the division game has a family of stable equilibria, each involving a different pair of complementary claims c and $1 - c$ combined in a particular probability mix; there is an equilibrium for every value of c in the range $0 \leq c \leq 0.5$. In equilibrium the expected utility of making either claim must be c. So the utility that each player can derive from the game depends on the nature of the equilibrium. At one extreme is the equilibrium in which $c = 0.5$. This represents a self-enforcing rule – a convention – of equal division. In a community in which this convention is recognized, everyone knows what he can expect: a half-share of the resource in every dispute. Disputes are always resolved without fighting (although, of course, everyone stands ready to fight for his half-share: this is why the rule is self-enforcing). At the other extreme is the equilibrium in which $c = 0$. In this equilibrium the claims 0 and 1 are each made with a probability of 0.5. Fights are common (they occur in a quarter of all games). And, as in the war of attrition, no one gains anything from taking part in the game: the expected utility of making either claim is zero. A community in this kind of equilibrium is in something like a Hobbesian state of nature. Such a state of affairs, if once reached, is self-perpetuating. Everyone would prefer it if everyone would claim a half-share; but when no one else is doing so, any individual who does only makes himself worse off.

4.5   Property conventions in the hawk–dove game

I have now looked at three games which, in different ways, model Hobbes's problem of the two individuals in dispute over a resource. In each case I assumed that the players did not recognize any asymmetry between their roles. These games tend to generate stable equilibria with Hobbesian properties; they might be regarded as models of the allocation of resources in a Hobbesian state of nature. I shall now examine how these games would be played if asymmetries *were* recognized; I shall begin with the hawk–dove game. (The symmetrical form of this game is set out in Section 4.2.)

The analysis of the asymmetrical hawk–dove game turns out to be very similar to that of the asymmetrical crossroads game (Section 3.1). Suppose there is some labelling asymmetry between the roles of the players in each instance of the hawk–dove game, so that the game can be described as one between 'A' and 'B'. (Take, for example, the case in which two people are disputing over which of them should have first use of a public telephone. Then A might be the person who has waited longer.)

In this game a strategy is described by a pair of probabilities (p, q); this is shorthand for: 'If A, play "dove" with probability p; if B, play "dove" with probability q.' (In the language of Section 2.7, this is a universal strategy – a combination of an A-strategy and a B-strategy.) Using the utility indices set out in Table 4.1, it is easy to calculate that, for an A-player, 'dove' is more successful than, just as successful as, or less successful than 'hawk' depending on whether his opponent's value of q is less than, equal to, or greater than $\frac{2}{3}$; and that the relative success of the two strategies for a B-player depends similarly on *his* opponent's value of p. Thus there are three equilibrium strategies; $(0, 1)$, $(1, 0)$ and $(\frac{2}{3}, \frac{2}{3})$.

The first two of these equilibria are stable. Take the equilibrium $(0,1)$. This strategy is clearly the unique best reply to itself. If A-players are confident that their opponents will always play 'dove' – and this will be the case if $q = 1$ – it will pay A-players to play 'hawk'. If B-players are confident that *their* opponents will always play 'hawk' – and this will be the case if $p = 0$ – it will pay B-players to play 'dove'. In other words, if a player is confident that his opponent's strategy is 'If A, play "hawk"; if B, play "dove",' the best he can do is to adopt the same strategy himself. This equilibrium amounts to a rudimentary system of *de facto* property rights, in which rights to disputed resources are vested in A-players. To say that this equilibrium is stable is to say that these rules of property are self-enforcing.

The equilibrium (1,0) is a mirror image of the equilibrium I have just described, vesting *de facto* property rights in B-players. Since these are two stable equilibria, they are (by my definition) conventions.

The $(\frac{2}{3}, \frac{2}{3})$ equilibrium corresponds with the equilibrium for the symmetrical game (Section 4.2). In the symmetrical game the only equilibrium strategy was that of playing 'dove' in two-thirds of all games; and that strategy was stable. In the asymmetrical game, however, $(\frac{2}{3}, \frac{2}{3})$ is unstable. It can be invaded by any universal strategy (p, q) for which either $p > \frac{2}{3}$ and $q < \frac{2}{3}$ or $p < \frac{2}{3}$ and $q > \frac{2}{3}$. In other words, starting from a state of affairs in which everyone plays 'dove' with a probability of two-thirds, any tendency for A-players to play 'dove' more frequently and for B-players to do so less frequently will be self-reinforcing; and so will be the opposite tendency. Most obviously, the $(\frac{2}{3}, \frac{2}{3})$ equilibrium can be invaded by either (0,1) or (1,0). If only a few players start to follow one of these conventions, everyone has an incentive to do the same.

Following through the same reasoning as I used in the case of the crossroads game (Chapter 3), repeated playing of the hawk–dove game is likely to lead to the evolution of some convention of property. Even if initially the game is perceived as symmetrical, we should expect that sooner or later some players will recognize some asymmetry, and then a convention based on that asymmetry will start to establish itself.

So if the hawk–dove game is used as a model of the Hobbesian state of nature, Hobbes's conclusions seem unduly pessimistic: if individuals pursue their own interests in a society that is initially in a state of war of 'every man against every man', settled rules of property can evolve spontaneously. But what about the other two games?

4.6   Property conventions in the division game

The symmetrical form of the division game is described in Section 4.4. Recall that in this game each player makes a claim to a share (in the range from 0 to 1 inclusive) of a divisible resource; if these claims sum to 1 or less, each player gets what he claimed; if they sum to more than 1, there is a damaging fight. I shall now examine the asymmetrical form of this game, in which each game is played between one player labelled 'A' and another labelled 'B'.

Consider the class of strategies 'If A, claim c; if B, claim $1 - c$', where c takes some value in the range $0 \leq c \leq 1$. For any value of c in this range, this is a stable equilibrium strategy. It is easy to see why. Suppose you are confident that your opponent's strategy is: 'If A, claim c; if B, claim $1 - c$.' Then your best reply is to claim everything that your opponent will not claim, and this means claiming $1 - c$ if your opponent is A (i.e. if you are B) and claiming c if your opponent is B (i.e. if you are A). So 'If A, claim c; if B, claim $1 - c$' is the unique best reply to itself: it is a stable equilibrium strategy.

The game has no other stable equilibria. Why not? Recall the 'complementarity result' proved in Section 4.4 for the symmetrical division game. In the symmetrical game, if I and J are two strategies and if J is a best reply to I, then for every claim c contained in J there must be a complementary claim $1 - c$ contained in I. (To say that a strategy 'contains' a claim is to say that, under that strategy, there is a non-zero probability that that claim will be made.) Now consider the asymmetrical game. Any strategy in the asymmetrical game can be decomposed into an A-strategy ('If A, do ...') and a B-strategy ('If B, do ...'); an equilibrium consists of an A-strategy and a B-strategy, each of which is a best reply to the other. Using the complementarity result, an A-strategy cannot be a best reply to a B-strategy unless, for every claim c contained in the A-strategy, there is a complementary claim $1 - c$ contained in the B-strategy. And vice versa: a B-strategy cannot be a best reply to an A-strategy unless, for every claim $1 - c$ contained in the B-strategy, there is a complementary claim c contained in the A-strategy. Thus, if an A-strategy and a B-strategy are best replies to one another, the A-strategy must contain only some set of claims $c_1, c_2, \ldots$ and the B-strategy must contain only the complementary claims $1 - c_1, 1 - c_2, \ldots$.

Now let I be any equilibrium strategy in the asymmetrical game. Because of the argument of the previous paragraph, we know that I must take the form: 'If A, claim c_1 with probability p_1, c_2 with probability $p_2, \ldots$; if B, claim $1 - c_1$ with probability q_1, $1 - c_2$ with probability $q_2, \ldots$'. If I contains only one pair of complementary claims ('If A, claim c_1 with probability 1; if B, claim $1 - c_1$ with probability 1') it is a member of the class of stable equilibria I have already described. So suppose that it contains at least two pairs of complementary claims $(c_1, 1 - c_1)$ and $(c_2, 1 - c_2)$.

By assumption, I is an equilibrium strategy and therefore a best reply to itself. This implies that the two claims that A-players make, c_1 and c_2, are equally successful against B-players who are known to be following strategy I. Similarly, the two claims that B-players make, $1 - c_1$ and $1 - c_2$, are equally successful against A-players who are known to be following I. Thus the strategy J: 'If A, claim c_1 with probability 1; if B, claim $1 - c_1$ with probability 1' must be just as successful as I against an opponent who plays I. But J is the unique best reply to itself, and thus better than I as a reply to J. This establishes that I can be invaded by J – that I is an unstable equilibrium (cf. Section 2.6). This establishes what I set out to prove: that the only equilibria that can be stable are those based on a single pair of complementary claims.

So, provided that the players recognize *some* asymmetry, repeated playing of the division game can be expected to lead to the evolution of some convention assigning particular shares of the resource to each player. The convention that evolves might, like those of the hawk–dove game, assign the whole of the resource to one player; or it might prescribe an equal division; or it might prescribe a particular unequal division. Whatever the convention may be, it may be regarded as a *de facto* rule of property. This echoes the conclusions of Section 4.5.

4.7   Property conventions in the war of attrition

I have left the analysis of the asymmetrical war of attrition until last because it is particularly complicated, and because the conclusions I shall draw are not entirely in accord with received views. The symmetrical form of the war of attrition is described in Section 4.3. Recall that each player chooses a persistence time l; the players fight, at a cost in utility to each of them of c per unit of time, until the player with the shorter persistence time surrenders. The other player then takes the resource, whose utility value is v.

I shall now suppose that there is some asymmetry between the roles of the two players. Following the biological literature, I shall take the asymmetry to be between 'possessor' and 'challenger'. (Suppose that at the start of a dispute over some resource, one individual has possession of it, and the other is demanding that it be given to him.) I shall assume that each individual plays half his games as a possessor and half as a challenger.

Suppose that initially no one recognizes the asymmetry, so that the community settles down in a symmetrical equilibrium with a constant 'surrender rate' of c/v (cf. Section 4.3). This state of affairs will continue to be an equilibrium when individuals recognize the asymmetry between possessors and challengers, but like the symmetrical equilibrium of the hawk–dove game it will cease to be stable.

Since we are analysing an asymmetrical game, we must consider universal strategies of the form: 'If possessor, do ...; if challenger, do ...'. The pattern of behaviour in the symmetrical equilibrium can be described by the universal strategy I: 'If possessor, surrender at the constant rate c/v; if challenger, also surrender at the constant rate c/v.' Since all persistence times are equally successful against an opponent whose surrender rate is c/v (cf. Section 4.3), *all* universal strategies are best replies to I.

By analogy with the asymmetrical hawk–dove game, we might expect this equilibrium to be invaded by a universal strategy that prescribed which of the two player – possessor or challenger – should take the resource. Consider the convention that the possessor always keeps the resource. This might be represented by the universal strategy J: 'If possessor, never surrender; if challenger, surrender at time $t = 0$'. (Time t is measured from the start of the game.) A player following this strategy is always prepared to fight to keep the resource when he is the possessor and never prepared to fight when he is the challenger. Since all strategies are best replies to I, $\mathrm{E}(J, I) = \mathrm{E}(I, I)$ (i.e. the expected utility derived from playing J against I is equal to the expected utility of playing I against I). So J is a best reply to I. It is easy to calculate that $\mathrm{E}(I, J) = 0$ and $\mathrm{E}(J, J) = v/2$; so J is a better reply than I to J. This implies that I can be invaded by J : I is not a stable equilibrium.

As long as *some* individuals follow I, everyone else following J, J is the more successful strategy. It might seem, therefore, that if J began to invade I, the invasion would continue until everyone was following J, and that this state of affairs would be a stable equilibrium. However, this is not the case: J is not a stable equilibrium either.

The problem is that although J is *a* best reply to itself, it is not the *unique* best reply. Consider the strategy K: 'If possessor, surrender at $t = t^*$; if challenger, surrender at $t = 0$.' Here t^* may take any value greater than zero. Against individuals who play J, K is just as successful as J itself; since J-playing individuals always surrender immediately if they are challengers, any non-zero persistence time is as good as any other for their opponents. But, by exactly the same argument, K is just as successful as J against opponents who play K. Formally, then, J does not satisfy the condition for stability (cf. Section 2.6).

The implication of this is that there are no forces to prevent K from invading J. Admittedly, there are no forces to encourage such an invasion either; in a population in which some individuals followed J and the rest followed K, both sets of individuals would be equally successful. This sort of situation is called one of drift: the proportion of individuals playing each strategy is undetermined and is liable to drift in a random fashion. Notice, however, that if possessors, on average, choose persistence times of less than v/c, challengers have an incentive not to surrender. So the convention that challengers always surrender immediately is in danger of unravelling. If everyone follows this convention, there are no forces to prevent the persistence times of possessors from drifting downwards; but if persistence times drift downwards too far, the convention will collapse.

How real is this danger of unravelling? In cases like this it is often sensible to allow for the fact that players will not *always* choose the strategies that are most successful; they will only *tend* to choose such strategies. There are two main reasons why individuals will sometimes choose less successful strategies when more successful ones are open to them. First, individuals cannot find out which strategies are most successful unless they occasionally experiment with the others. Second, players can make mistakes. This seems particularly likely in cases where a convention is based on some asymmetry between the roles of players in a game. It often takes imagination and insight to interpret the convention that other individuals are following and, in particular, to decide how it applies to a specific case. For example, there are bound to be marginal cases in which it is not clear which of two individuals should be regarded as the possessor and which as the challenger; in such cases, a player who takes himself to be, say, the possessor may confront an opponent who believes the roles to be reversed.

This possibility has been explored by Hammerstein and Parker (1982).[10] Hammerstein and Parker assume that there is some difference between the utilities derived by players in the two roles. Let the value of the resource be v_A to those who take themselves to be possessors and v_B for those who take themselves to be challengers; and let the corresponding costs of fighting be c_A and c_B per unit of time. Suppose that $c_A/v_A < c_B/v_B$. Then, in Hammerstein and Parker's language, A is the 'favoured role'. (Either possessors value the resource more highly, or they incur less cost in fighting, or both.) The reason for this assumption will become clear in a moment.

Hammerstein and Parker then assume that individuals sometimes make mistakes in assessing their roles. Suppose that in every game one player is the 'real' possessor and the other is the 'real' challenger, but each player has a small probability of attributing the wrong role to himself. Then players who take themselves to be possessors will usually confront opponents who take themselves to be challengers, and vice versa; but occasionally self-styled possessors will meet self-styled possessors and self-styled challengers will meet self-styled challengers.

Now a universal strategy must specify how an individual will play when he *believes* he is the possessor and when he *believes* he is the challenger. Consider the strategy *J*: 'If (you believe yourself to be the) possessor, never surrender; if (you believe yourself to be the) challenger, surrender at $t = 0$.' In the original version of the asymmetrical game, in which mistakes were never made, this was an equilibrium strategy, although unstable. It is now no longer an equilibrium strategy, for two reasons. First, take the case of a player who believes he is the possessor, and whose opponent is following strategy *J*. If the opponent takes himself to be the challenger (as he probably will), he will surrender at $t = 0$. If, however, he does *not* surrender at $t = 0$, it will be because he takes himself to be the possessor; and if this is so, he will never surrender. So our player would do best to plan to surrender as soon as possible after $t = 0$: it is pointless to prolong a fight against an opponent who will not surrender. Second, take the case of a player who believes he is the challenger. There is some small chance that his opponent takes himself to be the challenger too; if this is so, the opponent will surrender at $t = 0$. It will thus be worthwhile for our player to plan to fight for a very short interval of time – just long enough to secure victory against an opponent who is playing as a challenger. The upshot of this is that the best reply to *J* – whichever role one attributes to oneself – is to surrender as soon after $t = 0$ as possible, but not at $t = 0$ itself. Clearly, then, *J* is not a best reply to itself.

However, as Hammerstein and Parker show, this game does have a stable equilibrium. In this equilibrium the game has two stages. Up to some time $t = t^*$, the only players to surrender are (self-styled)[11] challengers. Challengers surrender at a rate such that all persistence times from 0 to t^* are equally successful *for challengers*, but such that possessors do better to continue fighting. This is because possessors are more likely than challengers to confront challengers; so if the only players who surrender are challengers, possessors' opponents have a higher surrender rate than challengers' opponents. Beyond $t = t^*$, only possessors are left in the game, and so the game becomes effectively symmetrical. Possessors now surrender at the rate c_A/v_A. (Compare the equilibrium for the symmetrical game.) This surrender rate ensures that all persistence times greater than t^* are equally successful for possessors. Because $c_A/v_A < c_B/v_B$, this surrender rate is too slow to make it worthwhile for challengers to stay in the game beyond $t = t^*$.

This equilibrium can be regarded as a self-enforcing *de facto* rule of property: disputes between possessors and challengers are always settled in favour of possessors. But it is not a convention. It is not a convention because it is not one of *two or more* stable equilibria. In the asymmetrical hawk–dove and division games, *either* a rule favouring player A *or* a rule favouring player B might evolve; either rule, once established, would be self-enforcing. Thus, in those games, which player is favoured is a matter of convention. But on Hammerstein and Parker's analysis of the war of attrition, only one rule of property can be self-enforcing; which player is favoured is not a matter of convention, but is determined by the structure of the game.[12] This makes the logic of the war of attrition fundamentally different from that of the other two games.

I shall now suggest a slightly different way of allowing players to make mistakes in the war of attrition. This approach does not require there to be any favoured role; I shall therefore assume that possessors and challengers share common values of c and v.

In presenting Hammerstein and Parker's analysis, I described players as 'self-styled possessors' and 'self-styled challengers'. In some ways this use of words is misleading, since it suggests that each player thinks he *knows* his own role. If an individual plays the war of attrition repeatedly, and if he is prone to make mistakes in assessing his role, then he will learn by experience that he makes such mistakes. More precisely, he will learn that he sometimes fails to predict correctly which role his opponent will take on. (Notice that a player is not really concerned about his 'real' role: what matters to him is which role his opponent will assume.) It would therefore be more appropriate to talk in terms of probabilities. The 'self-styled possessor' is a player who thinks that he is probably the possessor, and hence that his opponent will probably play as a challenger. Similarly, the 'self-styled challenger' is a player who thinks that he is probably the challenger. For each player in any game there is some probability that he is the 'real' possessor; I shall call this probability the confidence level of the player in question.

Hammerstein and Parker, in effect, assume that only two confidence levels are possible: a player is either almost sure he is the possessor or almost sure he is the challenger. This may be a useful simplifying assumption, but – at least for contests among human beings – it is rather arbitrary. There seems no obvious reason to restrict the number of confidence levels to two. With sufficient experience of a game, an individual may come to distinguish many factors that influence conventional judgements about which player is the possessor; depending on the particular characteristics of the game he is playing, he may be more or less confident that he is the possessor. In some cases he will be almost sure that he is the possessor: he will have learned that in the vast majority of games of this kind that he has played, his opponent has taken on the role of challenger. In other cases he will be fairly sure that he is the possessor; and so on. I suggest that we should assume that many different confidence levels exist.

In the appendix I analyse the asymmetrical war of attrition on the assumption of many confidence levels, and consider the limiting case in which 'confidence' is a continuous variable. It turns out that in this limiting case the game has two stable equilibria. The essential characteristic of these equilibria is that players surrender in order of confidence.

There are two possibilities, depending on whether the convention that evolves favours possessors or challengers. Take the case in which possessors are favoured. Then, in equilibrium, there is a unique positive relationship between persistence time and confidence: the more sure a player is that he is the possessor, the longer he is prepared to fight. Thus contests are always won by the player who is more confident he is the possessor. This is a genuine convention. The more confident you are that you are the possessor, the less confident you will expect your opponent to be, and so the sooner you will expect him to surrender; thus the more confident you are, the less reason there is to surrender. Alternatively, the opposite convention may evolve. Then, in equilibrium, there is a unique *negative* relationship between a player's persistence time and his confidence that he is the possessor: contests are always won by the player who is more sure that he is the challenger.

If individuals are skilful in assessing their roles, the distribution of confidence levels will be such that in most games one player is fairly sure he is the possessor and the other is fairly sure he is the challenger. such contests will be settled quickly; there will be a brief fight, and then one player will back down. Which player backs down will be determined by convention: if the convention favours the possessor, the player who is less confident of being the possessor will be the one who surrenders. To an outside observer, it might look as though the player who surrenders is engaging in no more than a token fight, but in fact his brief period of fighting serves a purpose: it enables him to win the resource in the (unlikely) event that his opponent is even less confident than he is.

If this analysis is accepted, the logic of the war of attrition is, after all, very similar to that of the hawk–dove game and of the division game. In each of these games any asymmetry can form the basis for a convention specifying which of the two players should take the disputed resource, or how it should be divided between them. Such a convention is a *de facto* rule of property.

4.8   Extended games

So far I have assumed that games are played anonymously: players do not know who their opponents are, or how their opponents have played in previous games. In many cases in real life, however, we come into conflict with the same people over and over again; when one conflict occurs, we can remember how our previous conflicts with that opponent were resolved. We also observe conflicts in which we are not personally involved, and so we may know how our opponents have behaved in conflicts with other people. I shall now ask how far my conclusions are affected if the assumption of anonymity is dropped.

For the sake of brevity, I shall consider non-anonymous forms only of the simplest of the three games, the hawk–dove game. I shall suggest two alternative ways of modelling the idea that players know how their opponents have behaved in previous games; the first of these assumes that each player knows how his opponents have behaved in previous games *against him*, while the second assumes that each player knows how his opponents have behaved in previous games *against other people*. Here is the first. (The second is the subject of Section 4.9.)

Consider a community in which some game is played repeatedly between pairs of opponents drawn at random. These games are not anonymous: everyone remembers whom he has played before, and what happened in every previous encounter. However, no one knows anything about what happens in games in which he is not personally involved. Suppose also that people join and leave the community through some random process. Then any individual will constantly be coming across new opponents. Suppose Bill finds he is playing Charlie for the first time. This may turn out to be the only game they ever play (since either of them may leave the community before they have the chance to meet again). There is, however, some probability that they will play another game. Again, *this* may be their last game, but there is some probability that they will meet a third time; and so on. To make things simple, suppose that after any game, the probability that the two opponents will meet again is the same – irrespective of who they are, and of how many times they have met before. Let this probability be π.

We may now treat the sequence of games between any two particular opponents as a game in its own right. To avoid confusion, I shall call the individual games in the sequence rounds, and reserve the term game for the sequence itself; I shall call this type of game an extended game. (Such games are sometimes called 'supergames' or 'iterated games'.) Similarly, I shall call the strategies played in each round moves, and reserve the term strategy for a plan specifying how the whole game is to be played.

Notice that each individual plays the extended game repeatedly against different opponents, and that when he first meets a new opponent, he has no experience to guide him. Thus we may treat the extended game as one that is played anonymously, even though every round (apart from the first) is played against a known opponent. This allows us to use the usual concepts of equilibrium and stability at the level of the extended game.

The main problem in analysing extended games is the vast number of possible strategies – even when, as in the hawk–dove game, individual rounds are very simple. It is often relatively easy to show that certain strategies are stable equilibria, but extremely difficult to prove that a given list of stable equilibrium strategies is exhaustive. As far as the extended form of the hawk–dove game is concerned, I shall be content to describe two stable equilibrium strategies.

Suppose that there is some asymmetry between the players, so that *in each round* one is 'A' and the other is 'B'. In each round of a game, each player has some probability of being A and some probability of being B, the probabilities in each round being independent of those in every other. (For example: you and I repeatedly confront the problem of deciding which of us should have the pick of the driftwood on the shore. Sometimes you are on the shore before me; other times, I am there before you.) Now consider the following strategy for the extended game: 'In every round, play "hawk" if A and "dove" if B.'

It is easy to see that this is an equilibrium strategy, since in every round, 'dove' is the best reply to 'hawk' and vice versa. It can also be shown to be stable.[13] If this is true, then clearly the opposite strategy, 'In every round, play "dove" if A and "hawk" if B', is also a stable equilibrium. So conventions of property can evolve in the extended form of the hawk–dove game, just as they can in the simple game I presented in Section 4.5.

4.9 Games of commitment

Suppose that you and I are about to play the hawk–dove game. If you can convince me that you are irrevocably committed to playing 'hawk', and if I am still free to play 'dove', then you can guarantee victory. If I really believe that you are bound to play 'hawk', my best reply is clearly to play 'dove'. This feature of the hawk–dove game (or chicken game, as it is alternatively known) has been the subject of great interest ever since Schelling (1960) pointed out the paradox that it can be an advantage to have no freedom for manoeuvre. It seems clear that we should expect players in the hawk–dove game to *try* to convince their opponents of their unswerving commitments to play 'hawk'; but how are such statements of commitment to be made credible?

The problem, of course, is that words are cheap. Anyone can say 'I am absolutely committed to playing "hawk" ', without necessarily *being* committed. As long as games are anonymous, there can be no penalty for having one's bluff called; so everyone will try to bluff, and no one will be fooled. But suppose instead that games are played in public, so that everyone knows what threats everyone else has made, and whether these threats have been carried out. Then it is possible to earn a reputation as a person who means what he says – or, alternatively, as one who makes idle threats. I wish to suggest a simple way of modelling this concept of reputation in the framework of evolutionary game theory.[14]

If games are played repeatedly and in public, the way to make your threats credible is to carry them out. In the long run everyone has the power to bind himself in any way he chooses. All he has to do is to announce his intention invariably to act in a certain way, and then to do exactly what he said he would do. Here is the cost of commitment: to maintain your credibility you must carry out your threats even though from a short-term point of view you might be better off not doing so.

Notice that a player can bind himself before he meets his opponent. Someone who says 'I shall play "hawk" in every game, no matter who my opponent may be', and who then invariably does as he says, goes into every game with his commitment already on the record, so to speak. (Of course, he may be unfortunate enough to meet someone who has made exactly the same commitment, and then neither can back down without undermining his future credibility.) So when two players meet, the game is not simply won by whichever of them is first off the mark to declare his commitment to the 'hawk' strategy: they may both have committed themselves long before.

The making of commitments can be modelled by what I shall call a game of commitment. A game of commitment has two rounds. The second round consists of a conventional game, say the hawk–dove game, in which the players must simultaneously choose between alternative strategies. (I shall call these strategies 'moves'.) In the first round, each player has the option of making a commitment. A commitment is any unambiguous statement, conditional or unconditional, about the move that the player in question will make in the second round. For example, 'I shall play "hawk" ' is a commitment. So is: 'If I am assigned role A, I shall play "hawk" .' And so is: 'If my opponent has made no commitment, I shall play "hawk".' Commitments are made simultaneously. The crucial rule of a game of commitment is that the move a player makes in the second round must be consistent with any commitment he made in the first. This is a simple representation of what might be called the Matilda effect: in the long run there are no credible lies, only credible truths.

In a game of commitment a strategy has two components. There is a commitment (or a decision to make no commitment); and then there is a plan for the second round of the game, consistent with any commitment already made, in which the move to be made may be conditional on the opponent's commitment. The concepts of equilibrium and stability can now be defined in the usual way.

The game of commitment that incorporates the hawk–dove game is in important ways similar in structure to the hawk–dove game itself. The most aggressive strategy in the game of commitment is to make the unconditional commitment: 'I shall play "hawk".' The only strategies that are best replies to this are strategies that respond by playing 'dove'. These are relatively submissive strategies. But against any of *these* strategies, the most aggressive strategy is clearly a best reply. So the best replies to aggressive strategies are submissive, and vice versa. This is a characteristic feature of all the games I have described in this chapter.

It would not be surprising therefore to find that conventions of property could evolve from repeated play of the commitment form of the hawk–dove game. Proving this, however, is not easy. The difficulty is that there is no limit to the number of different statements of commitment that can be made. The best I have been able to do is to discover one form of commitment that is the unique best reply to itself.

Suppose, as usual, that in every game one player is 'A' and the other is 'B'. To represent the idea that commitments can be made in advance of particular games, I shall assume that the players do not know their roles until after they have declared their commitments. Now consider this commitment: 'If I am A, I shall play "hawk"; if I am B, I shall play "hawk" unless my opponent has made exactly the same commitment as this one.' Suppose you are confident that your opponent will make this commitment, which I shall call C. What commitment is best for you?

If you make any commitment other than C, or if you make no commitment at all, you will go into the second round of the game facing an opponent who is committed to playing 'hawk'. In these circumstances the best utility score you can achieve is 0. (If you have committed yourself to playing 'hawk', you will do worse than this.) If instead you make the commitment C, you will be able to achieve a score of 0 if you turn out to have role B. (In this event your opponent will be committed to 'hawk' and you will be free to play 'dove'.) And if you turn out to have role A, you will achieve a score of 2, provided that your opponent makes the only move that is sensible for him. (In this event, you are committed to 'hawk' while your opponent is free to play 'dove'.) So if you can count on your opponent not making a stupid move in the second round, C is the unique best commitment for you to make. In this sense C is the unique best reply to itself.

If everyone makes the commitment C, disputes are always resolved in favour of A-players. This may be interpreted as a convention of property, backed up by everyone's commitment to defend what, according to this convention, is his.

4.A   Appendix: the asymmetrical war of attrition with 'confidence levels'

Suppose that in every instance of the war of attrition, one player is the 'possessor' and the other is the 'challenger', but that players may be uncertain of their own roles. In particular, suppose that there are n different confidence levels, $L_1, \ldots, L_n$, that a player may experience. For a randomly selected player in a randomly selected game, there must be some probability r_i that this player has confidence level L_i; and clearly $\sum_i r_i = 1$. Let p_i be the probability that a player whose confidence level is L_i actually is the possessor. I shall number confidence levels so that $p_1 < \cdots < p_n$; in other words, higher numbers correspond with greater confidence in being the possessor.

Consider any one player in a particular game and let his confidence level for this game be L_i. Suppose it so happens that the more confident an opponent is (i.e. the higher *his* confidence level), the longer is his persistence time. My object is to show that this *will* be the case if everyone follows a particular equilibrium strategy; but for the moment I am simply assuming this. More precisely, suppose that there are times $t_0, t_1, \ldots, t_{n-1}$ where $0 = t_0 < t_1 < \cdots < t_{n-1}$ such that (1) for each $j = 1, \ldots, n-1$, opponents with confidence level L_j invariably choose persistence times in the range $t_{j-1} \leq l \leq t_j$, and (2) opponents with confidence level L_n invariably have persistence times greater than or equal to t_{n-1}.

Now suppose that our player is engaged in his game, that the time elapsed is t_{j-1}, and that his opponent has not surrendered. It is clear that his opponent must have one of the confidence levels $L_j, \ldots, L_n$. Consider the probability that the opponent's confidence level is L_j – in other words, that the opponent is one of the least confident players remaining in the game. Clearly, if $j = n$, this probability must be 1.0: when time t_{n-1} is reached, any opponent who remains in the game must have the confidence level L_n. But suppose that $j < n$. Then the following result can be proved: the higher is our player's confidence level, the greater is the probability that his opponent has the confidence level L_j. This makes intuitive sense: the more confident our player is that he is the possessor, the less likely it is that his opponent is the possessor, and so the less confident his opponent is likely to be.

Here is how the proof works. At time t_{j-1}, the probability that the opponent has confidence level L_j, conditional on his being the possessor is

$$r_j p_j \Big/ \sum_{k=j}^{n} r_k p_k \qquad (4A.1)$$

Similarly, the probability that the opponent has confidence level L_j, conditional on his being the challenger, is

$$r_j (1 - p_j) \Big/ \sum_{k=j}^{n} r_k (1 - p_k) \qquad (4A.2)$$

We know that $p_j < p_j + 1 < \cdots < p_n$. It follows from this that (4A.2) is greater than (4A.1) provided that $j < n$. Thus the opponent is more likely to have confidence level L_j if he is the challenger than if he is the possessor.

At time $t = 0$, the probability that the opponent is the possessor is $1 - p_i$; so the opponent is less likely to be the possessor, the higher is our player's confidence level. As the game proceeds, the probability that the opponent is the possessor increases. (The longer the game goes on without the opponent surrendering, the more evidence there is of the opponent's confidence.) Nevertheless, it follows from Bayes's theorem that at any given time, the opponent is less likely to be the possessor, the higher is our player's confidence level. Combining this result with the one stated in the previous paragraph, it is clear that at time t_{j-1} the opponent is more likely to have confidence level L_j, the higher is our player's confidence level.

Recall the definition of a surrender rate (Section 4.3). I shall define a player's victory rate as the surrender rate for his opponent. Consider our player's victory rate at any time between t_{j-1} and t_j. During this interval the only opponents who surrender are those whose confidence level is L_j. Thus our player's victory rate is the surrender rate for opponents with confidence level L_j, multiplied by the probability that the opponent has this confidence level. And this probability is greater, the higher is our player's confidence level. Hence the following result: at any time $t < t_{n-1}$, the higher is a player's confidence level, the greater is his victory rate.

It is now possible to describe an equilibrium strategy I as follows. In the first stage of the game, the only players who surrender are those whose confidence level is L_1; they surrender at such a rate that the victory rate for players whose confidence level is L_1 is c/v. A time will come when all such players have surrendered: this is t_1. In the second stage of the game, the only players who surrender are those whose confidence level is L_2; they surrender at such a rate that the victory rate for players whose confidence level is L_2 is c/v. And so on until t_{n-1}. In the final stage of the game the only players left are those with the confidence level L_n. They then surrender at the rate c/v, as in the symmetrical war of attrition; thus the victory rate for all players in the final stage of the game is c/v.

How can we be sure that I is an equilibrium strategy? Take a player whose confidence is L_i and whose opponents all follow I. Now consider what this player's victory rate would be if he chose never to surrender. Up to time t_{i-1}, the players who are surrendering are less confident than he is, so his victory rate is constantly greater than c/v. From t_{i-1} to t_i, the players who are surrendering are exactly as confident as he is, so his victory rate is exactly equal to c/v. And from t_i onwards, the players who are surrendering are more confident than he is; so his victory rate is never greater than c/v: it is less than c/v until t_{n-1}, and exactly equal to c/v thereafter.

Now recall a result that was proved in Section 4.3. Consider the relative success of the two strategies 'Surrender at time $t + \delta t$' and 'Surrender at time t' (where δt is a very short interval of time). The former is more successful than, just as successful as, or less successful than the latter according to whether at time t the victory rate for the player in question (or, equivalently, the surrender rate for his opponent) is greater than, equal to, or less than c/v. Applying this result to the present case, it must pay a player whose confidence level is L_i to delay his surrender at least until time t_{i-1}. From t_{i-1} to t_i, our player's victory rate is exactly c/v, so all persistence times in this range are equally successful: it does not matter when he surrenders. If our player's confidence level L_i is less than L_{n-1}, there will be an interval of time after t_i when his victory rate is less than c/v; and it will never again exceed c/v. (If he stays in the game to the bitter end, his victory rate will eventually get back to c/v.) Thus it must pay our player not to stay in the game beyond t_i. If the player's confidence level is L_{n-1}, it does not matter whether he stays in the game beyond t_{n-1} or not, since his victory rate will never fall below c/v; but he has nothing to gain by staying in the game.

This argument establishes that I is a best reply to itself. (Recall that I requires players whose confidence level is L_i to choose persistence times in the range from t_{i-1} to t_i; for players with this confidence level, this is a best reply to an opponent following strategy I.) However, if the number of confidence levels is finite, I is not a stable equilibrium. The problem concerns those players whose confidence level is L_{n-1}. For these players – in contrast to those at lower confidence levels – the victory rate never falls below c/v. Thus they have nothing to lose (although nothing to gain) by delaying their surrender beyond t_{n-1}. If they do so, the equilibrium may unravel.

This is the problem that confronted Hammerstein and Parker (1982). Their model is essentially equivalent to the one I have presented, but with just two confidence levels. The lower confidence level – L_1 in my notation – is that of the player who takes himself to be the challenger, but may have made a mistake. The higher confidence level, L_2, is that of the player who takes himself to be the possessor, but also may have made a mistake. If all players share common values of c and v, there can be an equilibrium in which players at one confidence level surrender before players at the other.

However, for the reasons I have outlined, this equilibrium is not stable. Hammerstein and Parker respond by assuming that the value of c/v differs according to a player's confidence level. This allows a stable equilibrium in which players who believe themselves to be in the 'unfavoured role' (the role with the higher value of c/v) surrender first.

An alternative approach is to drop the assumption of a finite number of confidence levels. Instead we may assume that 'confidence' (the probability, say p, that one is the possessor) is a random variable whose distribution can be described by a continuous probability density function. On this assumption, the special problem posed by players at confidence level L_{n-1} evaporates.

I have described an equilibrium strategy I for the case in which the number of confidence levels is finite. Its continuous analogue is as follows. For every value of p (that is, for every degree of confidence) there is a unique persistence time $l(p)$; higher values of p are associated with longer persistence times. For a player whose degree of confidence is p, the victory rate is greater than c/v up to $l(p)$, exactly equal to c/v at $l(p)$, and less than c/v thereafter. Thus $l(p)$ is the unique best persistence time for a player whose degree of confidence is p. It follows that this equilibrium strategy is the *only* best reply to itself: it is stable. This strategy can be interpreted as a convention of property that favours possessors.

Needless to say (since in my model 'possessor' and 'challenger' are no more than labels) there is another stable equilibrium strategy, identical apart from labelling, in which the order in which players surrender is reversed. This amounts to a convention of property that favours challengers.

5
Possession

5.1 Nine points of the law

When oil and gas reserves were discovered under the North Sea the problem arose of who had the right to exploit them. The potential claimants were nation states.[1] Given the power of most nation states to inflict harm on most others, it was important to find some way of dividing up the reserves that would be generally acceptable. In effect, nations were involved in a variant of the division game, but with many players instead of just two.

The solution reached was to allocate each portion of the sea bed to the country whose coastline happened to be nearest. In terms of any abstract theory of justice, this seems completely arbitrary. The main beneficiaries from this arrangement were the United Kingdom and Norway. West Germany, despite its large population and its considerable length of North Sea coastline, came out badly. Why did West Germany acquiesce in such an unfair partition? Why, for that matter, should the share-out have been restricted to countries with a North Sea coastline? The poor countries of Africa and Asia might have used arguments of distributive justice to support claims to North Sea oil. If it is replied that these countries lack the military power to support such claims, how much military power does Norway have? And the United States and the Soviet Union are overwhelmingly more powerful than any of the North Sea countries; yet they too got nothing.

One answer might be that this peculiar division of the sea bed was prescribed by international law. In 1958 an international conference in Geneva had drafted a convention which was to come into force when it had been ratified by 22 states; the 22nd state signed in 1964. According to this convention, each state has a right to exploit the continental shelf adjacent to its coastline. International boundaries on the continental shelf are to be fixed by agreement between the states concerned, but in case of dispute, median lines (i.e. lines equidistant from the coasts of two countries) are to be used. In fact, however, the agreement among the North Sea countries departed from this convention quite significantly. There is a deep trench between the Norwegian coast and the North Sea oilfields; according to the Geneva Convention these oilfields were all on the British continental shelf, even though in some cases the closest coastline was Norway's. In the event the North Sea countries opted for the simpler rule of ignoring the depth of the sea bed and allocating every portion of continental shelf to the country with the closest coastline. So the partition of the North Sea was not arrived at simply by applying existing international law. And in any case, we should need to explain why the Geneva Convention was agreed in the first place. The participants in the Geneva Conference were also playing a kind of division game: why did the median line solution appeal to them?

Suppose, suggests Milton Friedman, that:

> you and three friends are walking along the street and you happen to spy and retrieve a $20 bill on the pavement. It would be generous of you, of course, if you were to divide it equally with them, or at least blow them to a drink. But suppose you do not. Would the other three be justified in joining forces and compelling you to share the $20 equally with them? I suspect most readers will be tempted to say no. (Friedman, 1962, p. 165)

This is another example of the division game, this time with four players. Friedman suggests that if his readers played the game they would recognize the rule of 'finders keepers'. Although we may tell our children that the right thing to do is to take the money to a police station, I feel sure Friedman is right: most people *would* recognize that the person who finds the $20 bill keeps it. At any rate, the finder's claim is far stronger than that of the friends who happen to be with him when he finds it.

Suppose you are driving your car and approaching a long bridge over a river. The bridge is only wide enough for one car. Another car is approaching the bridge from the other side. It reaches the bridge before you do and begins to cross. Do you stop and allow the other car to cross, or continue on in the expectation that the other driver will see you coming and reverse? My observation is that most drivers recognize a convention that the first car on the bridge has the right of way.

In each case, I suggest, a conflict is resolved by appeal to a convention. In each case the convention works by assigning each disputed object to the claimant with whom the object is already most closely associated – 'associated' in some sense that is itself conventional. The first driver on the bridge has a special association with it – the relation of being the first claimant, or of being the person in possession. The person who first picks up the $20 bill has a similar relation to it. In the case of the North Sea, each portion of the sea bed is assigned to the nation whose land is closest to it.

In the rest of this chapter I shall argue that many of the property conventions that are used to resolve human conflicts work in this way: they exploit existing associations between claimants and objects. Such conventions inevitably tend to favour possessors, since to be in possession of something is to have a very obvious association with it. The maxim that possession is nine points of the law is more than a description of a feature of a particular legal system; it describes a pervasive tendency in human affairs. I shall suggest some reasons why this kind of convention tends to evolve from repeated play of games of property – that is, games of the general family to which the hawk–dove game, the division game and the war of attrition all belong.

5.2 Asymmetries in the structure of a game

In Section 3.2 I suggested that the relationship between alternative conventions was like that between seedlings in a crowded plot of ground. Each seedling, if allowed space to grow to maturity, is capable of becoming a viable plant; but the one whose first growth is most vigorous will choke out the others. Similarly, there may be many conceivable conventions, each of which would be a stable equilibrium for a particular game, were it able to establish itself; but in order to establish itself a convention has to develop before its rivals. A convention begins to develop when individuals begin to realize that it is in their interests to follow it. So we should ask what properties a convention must have in order for individuals to come to this conclusion quickly. It is both convenient and graphic to speak of conventions as being rivals, as in competition with one another; but of course it must be remembered that no element of purpose or intention is involved. There is only a process of natural selection in which some conventions are more successful than others; the most successful convention becomes established.

As I argued in Section 3.2, a convention has a head-start over its rivals if it exploits an asymmetry that is already embedded in the structure of the relevant game in the following way: if initially no one recognizes the asymmetry, the first person to do so will have an immediate incentive to behave in the way the convention would prescribe. This argument applies to the games of property I described in Chapter 4 just as much as it does to the games of coordination I described in Chapter 3.

Consider the hawk–dove game, and suppose that at the start of every contest one individual is in possession of the disputed resource while the other is not. I shall call the first player the possessor and the second the challenger. This is an asymmetry of labelling. However, we might expect that in reality the asymmetry would go a little deeper than this, for two main reasons. First, we might expect an individual, on average, to value disputed resources more highly when he is the possessor than when he is the challenger, because at any time the things a person has in his possession are likely to be things he particularly values. (That is why he is carrying them around with him, keeping close watch on them, or whatever. And people develop habits of life around, and acquire skills to use, the things they have long possessed.) Second, we might expect that in the case of a fight, possession confers some advantage; thus an individual may be slightly more likely to win fights when he is the possessor than when he is the challenger.

I shall consider the second of these possibilities here. (The analysis of the first leads to essentially the same conclusions.) Figure 5.1 shows a variant of the hawk–dove game in which A (the possessor) comes out of the average fight slightly less badly than B (the challenger). The difference between the expected utilities of A and B in the event of a hawk–hawk encounter (-1.9 and -2.1) reflects the assumption that A is slightly more likely to emerge as the winner. Notice that this difference is *not* an interpersonal utility comparison. It is a proposition about the preferences of each individual player; the comparison is between each player's experience as a possessor and his experience as a challenger.

The asymmetry in this game is rather slight, and might for some time pass unnoticed. Although on average, possessors win more often than

		B's strategy	
		Dove	Hawk
A's strategy	Dove	1, 1	0, 2
	Hawk	2, 0	−1.9, −2.1

Figure 5.1   A variant of the asymmetrical hawk–dove game

challengers, challengers often win. A player might have to engage in many fights before he realized that possession made a difference to his chance of success. For a player who does not notice the asymmetry, and who therefore pools his experiences as possessor and challenger, the game will appear to have the structure of the original hawk–dove game (Figure 4.1). If initially no one recognizes the asymmetry, the community will settle down in an equilibrium in which either player in a randomly selected game has a probability of $\frac{2}{3}$ of playing 'dove' (cf. Section 4.2). In this situation, anyone who comes to recognize the asymmetry will find that 'hawk' is slightly more successful than 'dove' in the games he plays as possessor, and that 'dove' is slightly more successful in the games he plays as challenger. Thus there will be a tendency for people to adopt the convention that possessors demand all the resource and that challengers back down; and this tendency will be self-reinforcing.

So in games of the hawk–dove kind, the conventions that evolve are likely to favour classes of players who on average attach relatively high value to the disputed resource; or who attach relatively low cost to the act of fighting; or who are particularly likely to win fights if they occur. Similar conclusions apply to the war of attrition and to the division game. (In the war of attrition players cannot differ in their fighting ability, since fights are lost only when one player chooses to surrender; in this game the conventions that evolve are likely to favour those players for whom the value of the resource, relative to the cost of fighting per unit of time, is greatest – i.e. those with a low value of c/v.) Notice, however, that if it could become established, a convention could be self-perpetuating without favouring these particular classes of player; it could even discriminate against them.[2] The point is that such a convention would be unlikely to establish itself in the first place.

This line of argument supplies one reason why conventions favouring possessors might tend to be relatively successful in a world of natural selection. However, many other conventions have similar advantages. Take, for example, the convention that a disputed resource goes to the best fighter, or the convention that it goes to the person who needs it most. Either of these seems more directly connected with a relevant asymmetry than the convention favouring possessors. Wouldn't these conventions be more likely to establish themselves?

5.3   Prominence and possession

If a convention is to develop it must first be recognized by people: each person must come to see that there is some pattern in the behaviour of his fellows, and that it is in his interest to follow this pattern himself. In the early stages of the development of a convention, when only a small proportion of the population are following it, these patterns are likely to be hard to spot. People are more likely to find those patterns that – consciously or unconsciously – they are looking for. Thus a convention is more likely to develop if people have some prior expectation that it will.

This is not as circular as it sounds. Such prior expectations correspond with Schelling's concept of prominence, discussed in Section 3.3. Despite the elusiveness of this concept, and the way it seems to lie beyond the reach of rational analysis, there can be no doubt that some solutions *are* more prominent than others.

Hume seems to have had in mind something like Schelling's notion of prominence when writing his *Treatise on Human Nature* – particularly the two penetrating passages entitled 'Of the origin of justice and property' and 'Of the rules, which determine property' (Hume, 1740, Book 3, Part 2, Sections 2–3). As I have pointed out before, Hume argued that rules of property are conventions that have evolved spontaneously – that have arisen, as he put it, gradually and acquired force by slow progression and by our repeated experience of the inconveniences of transgressing them. He tried to answer the question I am confronting: Why does one particular convention of property evolve rather than another? To answer this question, he wrote, we must look to 'the imagination' rather than to 'reason and public interest' (1740, Book 3, Part 2, Section 3).

Hume presents the following example of a division game:

> I first consider men in their savage and solitary condition; and suppose, that being sensible of the misery of that state, and foreseeing the advantages that wou'd result from society, they seek each other's company, and make an offer of mutual protection and assistance. I also suppose, that they are endow'd with such sagacity as immediately to perceive, that the chief impediment to this project of society and partnership lies in the avidity and selfishness of their natural temper; to remedy which, they enter into a convention for the stability of possession, and for mutual restraint and forbearance. I am sensible, that this method of proceeding is not altogether natural; but besides that I here only suppose those reflexions to be form'd at once, which in fact arise insensibly and by degrees; besides this, I say, 'tis very possible, that several persons, being by different accidents separated from the societies, to which they formerly belong'd, may be oblig'd to form a new society among themselves; in which case they are entirely in the situation above-mention'd.

'Tis evident, then, that their first difficulty, in this situation, after the general convention for the establishment of society, and for the constancy of possession, is, how to separate their possessions, and assign to each his particular portion, which he must for the future inalterably enjoy. This difficulty will not detain them long; but it must immediately occur, as the most natural expedient, that every one continues to enjoy what he is at present master of, and that property or constant possession be conjoin'd to the immediate possession. (1740, Book 3, Part 2, Section 3)

Notice that this is a one-off game, even though it is being used as a simple model of a process of evolution ('reflexions . . . which in fact arise insensibly and by degrees'). Hume is claiming that the rule favouring possessors has a natural prominence; this leads people to converge on it as a solution in a game in which any agreement is better than none.

Why is this solution particularly prominent? Hume appeals to what he claims is a natural tendency of the human mind to seek out relations between objects:

'Tis a quality, which I have already observ'd in human nature, that when two objects appear in a close relation to each other, the mind is apt to ascribe to them any additional relation, in order to compleat the union ... Thus for instance, we never fail, in our arrangement of bodies, to place those which are *resembling* in *contiguity* to each other, or at least in *correspondent* points of view; because we feel a satisfaction in joining the relation of contiguity to that of resemblance, or the resemblance of situation to that of qualities ... As property forms a relation betwixt a person and an object, 'tis natural to found it on some preceding relation; and as property is nothing but a constant possession, secur'd by the laws of society, 'tis natural to add it to the present possession, which is a relation that resembles it. (1740, Book 3, Part 2, Section 3)

I think there is an important truth here. If we are playing a game in which we have to agree on a way of assigning objects to persons, there *is* a natural prominence to solutions that base the assignment on some pre-existing relation between persons and objects. And the closer the resemblance between the pre-existing relation and the one to be determined in the game, the more prominent is the solution based on that relation.

If this sounds like a conservative rationalization of the law of property, consider the following pure coordination game, of the kind discussed

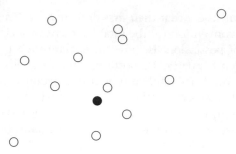

Join the black circle to one of the white circles. If you choose the same circle as your partner, you win £10; otherwise, you win nothing.

Figure 5.2   A pure coordination game

by Schelling (cf. Section 3.3). You and a partner are separated and not allowed to communicate. Then you are each shown the pattern of circles drawn in Figure 5.2. You are told to draw a line joining the black circle to any one white circle. If you both hit on the same white circle, you will each be given £10; otherwise, you get nothing. Which circle would you choose? My hunch is that most people would choose the white circle closest to the black one. The reason, I think, is the one given by Hume. You are asked to establish a relation between the black circle and a white one (the relation of being linked by a line). It is natural to look for some other relation, already there in the diagram, by which one and only one white circle can be linked to the black one; the most prominent such relation, surely, is that of being closest. (I cannot *prove* that this is the most prominent relation. Why not the relation of lying directly below the black circle, or of being farthest away from it? I can only say that closeness seems the most prominent relation to me, and hope the reader has the same reaction.)

Prominence, as I argued in Section 3.3, is often dependent on analogy. When people face new problems of the kind that are resolved by convention, they tend to look for prominent solutions by drawing analogies with other situations in which conventions are well established. Thus conventions can spread from one context to another. The conventions that are best able to spread are those that are most general (i.e. that can be applied in the greatest range of cases) and most fertile (i.e. most susceptible to extension by analogy). The idea that disputes are resolved in favour of possessors seems to be peculiarly fertile and general.

Conventions favouring possessors can be found everywhere. Perhaps the purest case is the principle, embodied in English law, that a right to a parcel of land or to a right of way can be established by a long period of undisputed occupation or use. However arbitrary this principle may be from any moral point of view, it seems to be generally recognized as a working convention, even in cases in which litigation is out of the question. Consider minor disputes between neighbours, between workmates, or between employers and employees. Think how much importance is attached to precedents, to 'custom and practice'. If your neighbour or workmate or employer starts doing something that annoys you, the time to complain is *straight away* – before a precedent is established. Why do precedents matter so much, if not because there is some convention that established practices are allowed to continue? And notice how very general this convention is – how many different kinds of disputes it can be used to resolve.

Closely analogous with conventions favouring possessors are conventions favouring first claimants – those people who first register, in a way that is itself defined by convention, their claims on disputed resources. Take the convention of the queue, or of 'first come, first served'. The principle here is that, of all the people who might dispute over something – perhaps the opportunity to use a public telephone, or to be served in a shop, or to get on a bus – the person who was there first has established the strongest claim. Or take the principle of 'last in, first out' for determining who must go when someone in a factory or office has to be made redundant. Or take the convention, well established on planes and trains, that once a person has occupied a seat it is his for the rest of his journey, even if he leaves it temporarily.

The author Leo Walmsley has described a convention that was recognized on the Yorkshire coast up to the 1930s. After a storm, valuable driftwood could be washed up. The first person to go on to any stretch of the shore after high tide was allowed the pick of the driftwood; anything he collected into piles and marked with two stones was regarded as his, to carry away when he chose (Walmsley, 1932, pp. 70–1). This is an interesting mixture of two principles – the principle of first claims and the principle that property can be acquired by labour. When driftwood is washed up on the shore it belongs to no one, but by gathering it into piles a person makes it his.

This latter principle is formulated most famously by Locke, who gives it the status of natural law – a moral law that is evident to the natural reason of man:

> Though the Water running in the Fountain be every ones, yet who can doubt, but that in the Pitcher is his only who drew it out? His *labour* hath taken it out of the hands of Nature, where it was common, and

belong'd equally to all her Children, and *hath* thereby *appropriated* it to himself.

Thus this Law of reason makes the Deer, that *Indian's* who hath killed it ... And amongst those who are counted the Civiliz'd part of Mankind, who have made and multiplied positive Laws to determine Property, this original Law of Nature for the *beginning of Property*, in what was before common, still takes place; and by vertue thereof, what Fish any one catches in the Ocean, that great and still remaining Common of Mankind ... is *by* the *Labour* that removes it out of that common state Nature left it in, *made* his *Property* who takes that pains about it. (1690, Second Treatise, Ch. 5)

Like Hume, I am not convinced that this principle of property can be discovered out of nothing, by reason alone. But Locke is surely right in saying that, in the absence of 'positive laws', this principle *is* widely recognized as a way of resolving disputes. It is, I suggest, a convention that has evolved.

The convention that a person has a special claim to those things on which he has expended labour may be interpreted as a member of the general family of conventions that favour possessors. Hume argues this persuasively. The concept of possession, he says, cannot be defined in any exact way; the definitions we use are grounded in the imagination and not in reason or public interest. Nevertheless, our definitions of possession will be in agreement in straightforward cases:

A person, who has hunted a hare to the last degree of weariness, wou'd look upon it as an injustice for another to rush in before him, and seize his prey. But the same person, advancing to pluck an apple, that hangs within his reach, has no reason to complain, if another, more alert, passes him, and takes possession. (Hume, 1740, Book 3, Part 2, Section 3)

Hume interprets these examples as illustrating the principle that by expending his labour on something a person can establish a claim to possession. Comparing the cases of the hare and the apple, he asks:

What is the reason of this difference, but that immobility, not being natural to the hare, but the effect of industry, forms in that case a strong relation with the hunter, which is wanting in the other? (1740, Book 3, Part 2, Section 3)

The expenditure of labour establishes a relation between an object and a person, and relations of this kind have a natural prominence as solutions to problems that require an assignment of objects to persons. In addition, there is, I think, a natural association of ideas between the relation created by labour and that created by simple possession. We associate first claims with possession, and what counts as a first claim is a matter of convention; expending labour on an object may be thought of as a way of registering a claim on it. It is also a matter of common experience that the expenditure of labour is often the first step towards physical possession, as in the case of the piles of driftwood or Hume's example of the hare.

Hume suggests another form of prominence that is related to possession:

> We acquire the property of objects by *accession*, when they are already connected in an intimate manner with objects that are already our property, and at the same time inferior to them. Thus the fruits of our garden, the offspring of our cattle, and the work of our slaves, are all of them esteem'd our property, even before possession. (1740, Book 3, Part 2, Section 3)

In other words, conventions may exploit two-step relations between persons and objects: if I am in possession of object X, and if there is some especially prominent relation between object X and some 'inferior' object Y, then this may be enough to establish a prominent relation between me and Y. This idea may help to explain the attraction of the median-line solution to the problem of partitioning the North Sea. Among geographical features, the relation of closeness seems to have an inescapable prominence, and in this sense it is natural to associate each portion of the sea bed with the closest land mass, and thus with the nation that is in possession of that land.

An alternative explanation of the median-line solution is that it derived its prominence from the existence of long-standing conventions about fishing rights. It has long been recognized that each nation has the right to control fishing off its own coasts, although how far this right extends has often been a matter of dispute – as in the 'cod wars' between Britain and Iceland. The median-line rule is a natural extension of this principle, and so this may be an example of the spread of conventions by analogy. But then why did the convention of coastal fishing rights become established? Hume's idea of accession may help to explain why this convention seems a natural solution to fishing disputes.

5.4   Equality

I have argued, following Hume, that conventions that favour possessors have a natural prominence. Or, more generally, that conventions that exploit relations between individual players and disputed objects have a natural prominence in games of property. I suspect that many readers will be inclined to object that there is another kind of prominent solution, at least for the division game: the solution of equal division. Perhaps, it might be added, this solution did not occur to Hume in the way that it does to us because we live in a more egalitarian age than he did. No doubt there would be some truth in saying that. Nevertheless, the equal-division solution is not as easily defined – and hence not so uniquely prominent – as it seems at first sight.

Consider the case of the North Sea. Why didn't the disputants agree to divide the sea bed equally between them? As soon as one begins to take this possibility seriously, all sorts of difficulties start to emerge. The first is to decide who are the disputants, each of whom is to receive an equal share. Suppose we accept that only nation states can count as claimants – a presupposition which also underlies the median-line rule. Then *which* nations are to be allowed to claim? Unless we answer, 'All the nations in the world', where is the line to be drawn? Nations with a North Sea coastline? European nations? Nations with *any* coastline? Similar problems arise with the case of the $20 bill. If equal division is to be the rule, how close do you have to be to the finder of the bill in order to make a claim? In *this* case it is obviously absurd to treat everyone in the world as a claimant. Notice that the problem is not that of a neutral arbitrator looking for a fair solution. Each of us, if put in the arbitrator's position, might be able to find a solution that he or she could defend as fair. The problem, rather, is this: is there any single definition of 'claimant' that is so prominent as to be recognized *by the disputants themselves* as uniquely obvious or natural? To the question, 'How close must a disputant be to the object in order to have a share?', one answer is inescapably prominent, in the same way that the number 1 stands out in the set of positive integers. This is: 'Nearer than everyone else'.

A second problem in the North Sea case (although not in the case of the $20 bill) is that the resource in dispute is far from homogeneous. The disputants knew that some areas of the North Sea were more likely to yield oil and gas than others; so an equal division of the *area* of the North Sea would not have been appropriate. But an equal division of the *value* of the sea bed would have required a unit of value – prior to the detailed exploration that would not be carried out until the division had been agreed. There does not seem to be any uniquely obvious way of defining an equal share. Contrast these difficulties with the simplicity of the rule that each piece of sea bed goes to the nearest country. This latter rule may be arbitrary, in a way that a rule of equal division is not; but the arbitrariness of the median-line solution is, in a sense, part of its prominence. By this I mean that the arbitrariness of the solution provides few footholds for special pleading by aggrieved parties; there is much less scope for sophisticated argument around the question 'Where are the median lines?'[3] than around 'What is an equal share?'.

This is an instance of a general point made by Schelling, that uniqueness is an important element of prominence. If two people are separately shown the same map and each is asked to pick a point at which to meet the other, they will look for a rule that prescribes a single point. If the map shows one house and several crossroads, they will go to the house; if it shows several houses and one crossroads, they will go to the crossroads (Schelling, 1960, p. 58). This tends to work against conventions that are ambiguous or open to rival interpretations: people have a prior expectation that ambiguous conventions will not become established.

5.5 Ambiguity

Ambiguous rules are also handicapped in another way. Imagine a community of individuals playing the hawk–dove game, and suppose that initially two conventions start to evolve side by side, exploiting two different asymmetries in the game. Some players follow the strategy, 'If A, play "hawk"; if B, play "dove"'. Others follow the strategy, 'If X, play "hawk"; if Y, play "dove"'. Given the number of players following either of these strategies, they will all be more successful, the less ambiguous the convention is. To say that a convention is ambiguous is to say that players are sometimes unsure which role they are playing; thus there will be some games in which both players are trying to follow the same convention, but both play 'hawk'. The more ambiguous the convention, the greater is this danger. When two conventions are evolving side by side, players are attracted to whichever is currently yielding the better results (cf. Section 3.1); so in the race to become established, ambiguous conventions are at a disadvantage.

In games of the hawk–dove kind there is a conflict of interest between the players. It is in each individual's interest to follow an established convention, whatever it may be, but players are not indifferent as to what the convention is. This opens up the possibility that players may try to turn ambiguities to their own advantage – in a word, may try to cheat. If in the hawk–dove game there is a convention that A-players play 'hawk', it is in each player's interest that he should be regarded as an A-player by his opponent. Thus if it is possible to fake the characteristics that make up A-ness, people will find that faking pays. But if everyone fakes, the convention collapses. Thus we should expect the conventions that eventually establish themselves to exploit asymmetries that are not only relatively unambiguous but also relatively cheat-proof.

These considerations count against conventions – however much we might approve of them from a moral point of view – that are subtle or subjective, or that require fine judgements. Take, for example, the rule that resources should be allocated according to need. In terms of games of property, this might be translated as the rule that a disputed resource should go to the player for whom it has the greater utility. To apply this rule it is necessary to make an interpersonal comparison of need or utility. Such comparisons are notoriously hard to make. Some writers – particularly in economics – have maintained that interpersonal utility comparisons are meaningless. This, I think, is going too far; there are many cases in which almost everyone could agree on the answer to a question of the form, 'Who needs X more?' (Who needs a bowl of rice more, you or a starving peasant in Ethiopia?) If interpersonal comparisons of need really were meaningless, it would be hard to explain how we all manage to agree on any case, however 'obvious': there are no obvious answers to meaningless questions. But in run-of-the-mill cases, people are likely to give different answers to 'Who needs X more?' questions. Even the most committed utilitarian would surely concede this. In addition, many of the kinds of evidence that could serve as the basis for judgements of relative need are far from cheat-proof. (Suppose a healthy-looking man asks you to give him your seat in a crowded train. He says he has a heart condition. Do you believe him?) Conventions based on possession may seem morally arbitrary, but they tend to be fairly unambiguous and to rely on definitions of possession that are not easy to fake.

Even after a convention has become established, there will be a tendency for it to evolve in the direction of greater precision: conventions will become less ambiguous over time. To take a far-fetched example, imagine a community of players of the hawk–dove game in which the convention, 'If the better-looking player, play "hawk"; if the less good-looking player, play "dove"' succeeds (against the odds) in becoming the established convention. Now everyone is confident that everyone else expects the better-looking of two players to take the resource. Each player's problem is that he is not sure how to interpret the convention in particular cases. But notice that each person wants to interpret it in the same way as other people. Suppose I am playing the hawk–dove game against Paul Newman, and I know there is a convention that the better-looking player takes the resource. Suppose I prefer my looks to his. Should I therefore play 'hawk'? Not if I am convinced that he will interpret the convention as favouring him. If my experience of the game has shown me that people who look like Paul Newman almost always play 'hawk', then the best I can do is play 'dove'. What matters to me is not how I think the convention *ought* to be interpreted, but how it is *conventionally* interpreted.

So in my example people will find themselves playing a game with something of the same structure as the one famously described by Keynes – the newspaper competition of the 1930s:

> in which the competitors have to pick out the six prettiest faces from a hundred photographs, the prize being awarded to the competitor whose choice most nearly corresponds to the average preferences of the competitors as a whole; so that each competitor has to pick, not those faces which he himself finds prettiest, but those which he thinks likeliest to catch the fancy of the other competitors, all of whom are looking at the problem from the same point of view. (1936, p. 156)

If this sort of game is played repeatedly, we should expect conventions of beauty to become established. More generally, if an ambiguous convention has become established in a game, repeated play of the game will lead to the evolution of further conventions, determining how the original convention is to be interpreted.

What forces determine *which* interpretation of an ambiguous convention becomes established? Clearly, the same sort of forces as determine which of a set of rival conventions becomes established. So we should expect a process of social natural selection that favours prominent, unambiguous and cheat-proof interpretations. Thus a subtle and subjective concept like beauty is unlikely to persist as the basis of a convention; it will tend to be supplanted by cruder and more objective proxies like tallness or hair colour. Once it is generally known that (say) the taller player always takes the resource, no one will care that tallness was once a proxy for beauty; the more objective convention will take on a life of its own. Similarly, a convention based on relative need would be unlikely to last indefinitely, even if it managed to establish itself. It would tend to be replaced by less ambiguous proxies – like possession.

So, I suggest, it is no accident that many of the conventions that we use to settle disputes about property seem morally arbitrary. (They may have moral force for us because they are established conventions; but we find it hard to provide any independent moral justification for them.) The forces of social evolution favour conventions that are crude and robust, and that leave no room for fine judgements.

5.6   The evidence of biological evolution

I have said several times that I am not writing a book about biological evolution or sociobiology. Nevertheless, biological evidence is not entirely irrelevant. It is a striking fact that in many different animal species, contests over resources are settled by what amount to conventions in favour of possessors. Male speckled wood butterflies use patches of sunlight as places in which to attract females; they defend these against intruding males. When two males come into conflict they engage in a few seconds of spiral flight – a kind of ritual fight – until one of them flies away and the other returns to the patch of sun. The successful male is almost invariably the one who previously occupied the patch. Male swallow-tails use hilltops as territories; again, contests almost always end in a victory for the previous possessor. Male lions contest for oestrous females; the first male to start to guard a particular female – often some days before her oestrous period begins – establishes possession until the end of that period, and other males respect this (Maynard Smith, 1982, pp. 97–100). And so on. 'Conventions' favouring possessors have evolved independently in species after species.

These 'conventions' are, of course, genetically determined. Male butterflies do not learn by experience that it is in their interest to hold out when they are in possession of a patch of sunlight and to back down when they intrude on another male's patch. Rather, they have an in-built drive or impulse or desire to behave in this way. The human conventions I have been describing are not of this kind. We have in-built desires for food and warmth and sex, but we have no in-built aversion to taking a seat on a train on which some other passenger has left a briefcase or coat.

Why, then, is the biological evidence of any interest? For two reasons. First, because of the many structural similarities between the processes of social evolution and biological evolution. The theory of social conventions is not an instance of the biological theory of animal behaviour; but the two theories are remarkably isomorphic. If apparent conventions favouring possessors show a consistent tendency to evolve in animal behaviour, we should not be surprised to find true conventions of the same kind establishing themselves in human societies. A critic of the arguments of this chapter might easily – but not, I hope, convincingly – claim that it was all an *ex post* rationalization of the law of property as it exists in liberal democracies. (Or perhaps: of the law of property as it used to exist in nineteenth-century liberal states.) It might be said that it is only because we have been brought up under such a law of property that the conventions I have described seem natural. It is only because we look at the problem through bourgeois eyes that possession assumes such prominence for us; perhaps the conventions that would evolve in a socialist society would be quite different. The biological evidence does not prove that this criticisim is invalid. It does not prove that conventions based on property have an inherent tendency to evolve in human society. But it is at least suggestive.

There is a second reason for taking the biological evidence seriously. Since so many animals do have an innate sense of possession and territory, it would not be surprising if this was true for our species. The notion that things can be owned by particular individuals, that possession establishes ownership and that ownership should be defended, may not be entirely a matter of human invention: we may be born with some innate capacity to think in this way. This would certainly not mean that we would be *forced* to follow conventions based on possession. If other kinds of conventions became established, we would have sufficient reason to recognize that our interests lay in following them. But the concept of possession would have a natural prominence – natural in the most literal sense of being part of the nature of our species.

6
Reciprocity

6.1 The prisoner's dilemma

Suppose you are an American academic. I am an English one. We are on exchange visits to each other's universities, and have exchanged houses. Having met a crowd of boisterous Americans, I should like to throw a party in your house on the night before I return to England. I know what this will lead to – cigarette burns on the chairs, beer stains on the carpets – but this doesn't greatly concern me: I won't have to live with the mess afterwards. Meanwhile you have met a crowd of unrestrained Brits, and you would like to throw a party for them on the night before you leave ...

Suppose that, whatever damage is caused by either party, recourse to the law is out of the question. (You can't be extradited for damaging carpets.) Suppose that neither we nor our institutions will have any dealings with one another once our exchange visits are over. Then we are playing a simple one-off game: the exchange-visit game.

Each of us has a choice between two strategies: to throw a party, or to refrain. I shall treat the state of affairs in which we both throw parties as the datum, and assign a utility of zero to this outcome, seen from my point of view. Then 'refraining from having a party' is an action that imposes costs on the person who refrains, but confers benefits on the other. Let c be the utility I lose if I refrain, and let b be the utility I gain if you refrain. Then the worst outcome for me is the one in which I refrain and you don't; the utility of this outcome for me is $-c$. The best outcome for me is the one in which you refrain and I don't; the utility of this outcome for me is b. If we both show restraint, the utility I derive is $b-c$.[1] Needless to say, b and c are both positive. I shall also assume that $b > c$: i prefer the outcome in which we both show restraint to the outcome in which neither of us does. Now suppose that the game looks just the same from your point of view as it does from mine. Then (ignoring any labelling asymmetries for the moment) we have the symmetrical game set out in Figure 6.1.

This game, of course, is a version of the famous prisoner's dilemma game. In the prisoner's dilemma game, each player has a choice of two strategies, 'co-operate' and 'defect'.[2] For each player, the worst outcome occurs if he co-operates and his opponent defects. Next worst is the outcome in which they both defect. Better than this is the outcome in which they both co-operate. But the best outcome of all for each player is the one in which he defects while his opponent co-operates. In the exchange-visit game throwing a party is the strategy of defection while showing restraint is the strategy of co-operation. The utility scores I have assigned to the outcomes of the exchange-visit game ensure that my game has the same structure as the prisoner's dilemma game.[3]

Now imagine a world community of academics in which individuals play the exchange-visit game against one another repeatedly *but anonymously*. Thus each individual accumulates experience of the game in general, but not of the behaviour of particular opponents. Then the analysis of the game is extremely simple. There is only one equilibrium strategy: the pure strategy 'defect' (throw a party). And this equilibrium is stable.

Notice that 'defect' is the unique best reply, not only to itself, but to *all* strategies, pure or mixed. In common-sense terms: nothing that I do can affect whether or not you have a party in my house, since you will not know what I have done until you get home. If you are having a party, the best I can do is to have one too. And if you are showing restraint, I still do best to exploit your good nature and have a party anyway. Because 'defect' is a dominant strategy, it makes no difference whether players perceive the game as symmetrical or asymmetrical. Whatever my role, and whatever I expect you to do, it is always best for me to defect.

| | | Opponent's strategy | |
		Co-operate (refrain)	Defect (throw party)
Player's strategy	Co-operate (refrain)	$b-c$	$-c$
	Defect (throw party)	b	0

Figure 6.1 The exchange-visit game

Note: $b > c > 0$ and $\pi > c/b$

One way of describing this result is to say that there is an opportunity for mutually-beneficial trade – we would both like to be able to make a no-party agreement – but this opportunity cannot be exploited because, although we can make agreements, we cannot enforce them. (We might each *promise* to take care of the other's home, but then each of us has an incentive to break that promise.)

Here is another example of the same kind of problem. I shall call it the trading game. Suppose you inherit a rare postage stamp from a distant relative's collection. You are not interested in stamps and unsentimentally decide to sell it. You advertise in a magazine and eventually receive a phone call from a stamp collector who offers you £50. You accept. Now you have to decide how to arrange the exchange of the stamp and the money. The collector lives 300 miles away, so a meeting is impractical. You suggest that he sends you £50 in cash through the post; you will post the stamp to him as soon as you receive the money. This way you are safe from the danger that he will cheat you out of the stamp. He responds with a counter-proposal: that you send him the stamp and that he will send the money as soon as the stamp arrives. That way *he* is safe. It is clear that your position and his are symmetrical with one another; you cannot both be safe. So eventually you agree to a symmetrical solution. You promise to put the stamp in the post straight away and he promises to do the same with the money. Will he keep his promise? Will you?

This game has the same structure as the exchange-visit game: keeping the promise is the strategy of co-operation and breaking it is the strategy of defection. Again (assuming repeated and anonymous play) the only stable equilibrium is one in which everyone always defects: although everyone would benefit from trade, no one trades.

Here is a final example, presented by Hume:

> Your corn is ripe to-day; mine will be so to-morrow. 'Tis profitable for us both, that I shou'd labour with you to-day, and that you shou'd aid me to-morrow. I have no kindness for you, and know you have as little for me. I will not, therefore, take any pains upon your account; and should I labour with you upon my own account, in expectation of a return, I know I shou'd be disappointed, and that I shou'd in vain depend upon your gratitude. Here then I leave you to labour alone: You treat me in the same manner. The seasons change; and both of us lose our harvests for want of mutual confidence and security. (1740, Book 3, Part 2, Section 5)

There is a slight difference between this game and the two previous ones, in that Hume's players choose *in turn* (rather than simultaneously) whether to co-operate or defect. But this difference is not significant; a full analysis of Hume's game would show the only stable equilibrium (given repeated anonymous play) to be one in which no one ever helps anyone else. That, in effect, is Hume's own conclusion, less elegantly expressed.

6.2 Reciprocity in the extended prisoner's dilemma game

The games I considered in Section 6.1 were all played anonymously. In situations of anonymity, promise keeping is unlikely to pay dividends. If you break a promise in one game, there is no way in which the person you have cheated can take reprisals, since by assumption he will not meet you again – or will not recognize you if he does. And since, again by assumption, your opponents never know how you have behaved in previous games, there is no way to build up a reputation for keeping your word. I shall now consider what would happen in games of the exchange-visit or prisoner's dilemma type if there was some chance that the players would meet again.

I shall do this by analysing the extended form of the prisoner's dilemma game. The idea of an extended game (sometimes called an iterated game, or a supergame) was presented in Section 4.8. An extended game consists of a sequence of rounds played by the same two individuals; each round is a simple game in its own right, in which the two individuals each choose between alternative strategies or moves. I shall analyse the extended game in which each round takes the form set out in Figure 6.1 – that is, the game that consists of repeated plays of the exchange-visit game. (The exchange-visit game, of course, is an instance of the prisoner's dilemma game.) After each round of the extended game there is a probability $1 - \pi$ that the game comes to an end; otherwise, another round is played. Thus games do not last for ever, but there is never a stage at which the players know they are meeting for the last time. This, I suggest, is the way much human interaction works.

We may now analyse the extended game using the usual concepts of equilibrium and stability.[4] The main difficulty with such an analysis is the vast number of possible strategies. A strategy is a plan for playing the whole extended game. Because a strategy may make a player's move in one round conditional on his opponent's moves in previous rounds, the number of possible strategies increases explosively with the number of rounds that may be played. If only one round of the prisoner's dilemma game is played, each player has only two possible strategies. If there are two rounds, there are eight possible strategies; if there are three rounds, there are 128 strategies; if there are four rounds, there are 2^{15} or 32,768 strategies; if there are five rounds, there are 2^{31} or approximately 2,150 million! In the extended game that I am analysing, of course, there is no limit to the number of rounds that might be played.

One way of starting out on an analysis of this very complicated game is to consider a few particularly simple strategies. Before doing this, however, I shall make an important assumption about the value of π.

Throughout this chapter I shall assume that $\pi > c/b$. To see what this means, imagine an agreement between two players by which they both co-operate in every round. If this agreement is kept, both players derive an expected utility of $(b - c)(1 + \pi + \pi^2 + \cdots)$, or $(b - c)/(1 - \pi)$. Now suppose that each player knows that if he breaks the agreement once, his opponent will never co-operate again. (Notice that this is the *worst* his opponent can do by way of retaliation.) Then if one player breaks the agreement in the first round while his opponent keeps to it, the first player will derive a utility of b. Thereafter he will derive a utility of zero from every round, since neither player will co-operate. Whether it pays to keep the agreement, then, depends on whether $(b - c)/(1 - \pi)$ is greater than or less than b or, equivalently, on whether π is greater than or less than c/b. To assume that $\pi > c/b$ is to open up the *possibility* of agreements of mutual co-operation.

The extended prisoner's dilemma game has a quite different structure in the case in which $\pi < c/b$. We know that if the prisoner's dilemma game ends after one round, the only stable equilibrium strategy is to defect. To say that the game is certain to end after one round is to take the case $\pi = 0$. We might expect, therefore, that strategies of reciprocal co-operation would not be stable equilibria if π was *close to zero* – if the game was *very likely* to end after one round. It turns out that the critical value of π is c/b: so long as π is greater than this, reciprocal co-operation can be a stable equilibrium. Notice that the assumption that $\pi > c/b$ need not imply that typical games are long: for example, if $b = 2$ and $c = 1$, the assumption is satisfied if $\pi > \frac{1}{2}$ – that is, if the average number of rounds played per game is greater than 2.0.

Now I shall examine some simple strategies for the extended prisoner's dilemma game. My main concern will be with strategies that make a player's co-operation conditional on his opponent's co-operation – strategies of reciprocity. But first I shall consider the two simplest strategies of all. These are unconditional co-operation – playing 'co-operate' in every round, irrespective of your opponent's behaviour – and unconditional defection – playing 'defect' in every round. I shall denote these strategies *S* (for sucker) and *N* (for nasty).

It is immediately clear that *S* cannot be an equilibrium strategy. If you know that your opponent is going to co-operate whatever you do, there is never any point in your co-operating. So the only strategies that are best replies to *S* are those (like *N*) that reply to *S* by defecting in every round; *S* is not a best reply to itself.

It is equally obvious that *N* *is* an equilibrium strategy. If you know that your opponent is going to defect whatever you do, there is again no point in your ever co-operating. So the only strategies that are best replies to *N* are those that reply to *N* by defecting in every round. Since *N* is such a strategy, it is a best reply to itself. In other words: in a world of nasties, you cannot do better than to be nasty yourself.

Is *N* a stable equilibrium strategy? The only best replies to *N* are those strategies that, when playing against *N*, defect in every round. But *N* is not the only strategy with this property. I shall say that a player is following a cautious strategy if he never co-operates unless his opponent has previously co-operated at least once. *N* is a cautious strategy, but it is not the only one. It is easy to see that *all* cautious strategies (and no other strategies) are best replies no *N*. Notice also that if two players following cautious strategies meet one another, they never co-operate. Thus as long as everyone follows cautious strategies of one kind or another, *all* cautious strategies produce the same result: no one ever co-operates. The upshot of this is that there are no forces to prevent a world of *N*-players being invaded by some other cautious strategy, but neither are there any forces to foster such an invasion. The situation is one of drift (cf. Section 4.7).

If we are to say more about the stability or instability of *N*, we must allow for the possibility that players occasionally make mistakes. I shall model mistakes by assuming that in each round there is some small probability that a player who intends to defect will actually co-operate, and vice versa. I shall assume that a player who makes a mistake is immediately aware of what he has done; his opponent knows which move has actually been made but he does not know whether it was made deliberately or accidentally. Given these assumptions, suppose your opponent is playing strategy *N* – that is, he *intends* to defect in every round. If he ever co-operates, this is a mistake and not a sign that he has any intention of co-operating in future. So your best reply – your only best reply – is never to co-operate deliberately, irrespective of what your opponent does. In other words, *N* is the unique best reply to itself: it is a stable equilibrium strategy.

This is not to say, however, that N is the *only* stable equilibrium strategy. I shall now consider a simple strategy of reciprocity – of co-operating with those who co-operate with you. This strategy is tit-for-tat (T for short). A player following strategy T co-operates in the first round. In every subsequent round he makes exactly the same move ('co-operate' or 'defect') as his opponent made in the previous round. Notice that if two T-players meet, they co-operate in every round. If, however, a T-player meets an N-player, the T-player will co-operate only in the first round; thereafter he will defect. T-players, then, are willing to co-operate with people like themselves; but they are not prepared to be suckers.

Is T an equilibrium strategy? The following argument is based on one presented by Axelrod (1981). Suppose you know your opponent is playing strategy T, and suppose you are about to play the *i*th round of the game. There are two possibilities, depending on whether this is the first round and, if it is not, on how you played in the previous round: *either* your opponent will co-operate in round *i* or he will defect in round *i*. You know which of these is the case. Given this knowledge, it must, in principle, be possible for you to work out a best reply to your opponent's moves for the rest of the game (since his moves in rounds $i+1, i+2, \ldots$ will be entirely determined by moves that you have yet to make). In addition, it is not hard to see that the value of *i* is irrelevant to your calculations; the best way for you to play in rounds $i+1, i+2, \ldots$ is independent of *i*. Thus each of the following two questions must have a determinate answer, independent of *i*:

1 If your opponent will co-operate in round *i*, can it be part of a best reply for you to co-operate in round *i* too?
2 If your opponent will defect in round *i*, can it be part of a best reply for you to co-operate in that round?

Suppose that the answer to question 1 is 'Yes'. Then let $i = 1$. You know your opponent will co-operate in the first round, so it is a best reply for you to co-operate too. But if you co-operate in round 1, your opponent will co-operate in round 2. It will then be a best reply for you to co-operate too. And so on. Thus if the answer to question 1 is 'Yes', co-operating in every round must be a best reply to T.

Now suppose instead that the answer to question 1 is 'No'. Then any best reply to T must defect in round 1. This ensures that your opponent defects in round 2. There are now two possibilities, depending on the answer to question 2. If the answer to that question is 'No', any best reply to T must defect in round 2 also. And so on: defecting in every round is a best reply to T. If instead the answer to question 2 is 'Yes', then it will be a best reply for you to co-operate in round 2. This will ensure that your opponent co-operates in round 3. This repeats the position of round 1, so you must defect again. And so on: defecting in odd-numbered rounds and co-operating in even-numbered ones is a best reply to T.

Now consider three possible replies to T: T itself, N (i.e. defecting in every round) and a new strategy, A. A (for alternation) is the strategy of defecting in odd-numbered rounds and co-operating in even-numbered ones. We know from the argument of the preceding paragraphs that one of these three strategies must be a best reply to T. We may now evaluate the expected utility derived from playing each of these strategies against T. Using the utility indices of Figure 6.1:

$$E(T, T) = (b - c)(1 + \pi + \pi^2 + \ldots)$$

$$= \frac{b - c}{1 - \pi} \tag{6.1}$$

$$E(N, T) = b \tag{6.2}$$

$$E(A, T) = b - \pi c + \pi^2 b - \pi^3 c + \pi^4 b \ldots$$

$$= \frac{b - \pi c}{1 - \pi^2} \tag{6.3}$$

It is not difficult to work out that if (as I have already assumed) $\pi > c/b$, then $E(T, T) > E(N, T)$ and $E(T, T) > E(A, T)$. In other words, T is better than N or A as a reply to T. But one of these strategies is a *best* reply to T. So T must be a best reply to itself: tit-for-tat is an equilibrium strategy.

6.3 Punishment and reparation

Is tit-for-tat a convention? I have shown that tit-for-tat is an equilibrium strategy in the extended prisoner's dilemma game. I have also shown that it is not the *only* equilibrium. The nasty strategy N ('never co-operate') is also an equilibrium; and the equilibrium in which everyone is nasty is stable. On my definition a convention is one of two or more stable equilibrium strategies in a game; so to show that tit-for-tat is a convention I must show that it is a *stable* equilibrium strategy.

In Section 6.2 I showed that the only best replies to the tit-for-tat strategy, T, are those strategies that, when playing against T, co-operate in every round. T has this property – that is why T is an equilibrium strategy – but so do many other strategies. The most obvious example is S, the sucker's strategy of unconditional co-operation. And against S, S is just as successful as T. As long as everyone follows one or other of these two strategies, there are never any defections. This means that there are no forces to prevent a world of T-players being invaded by S-players; but neither are there any forces to foster such an invasion. Again we have a situation of drift.

I shall therefore assume, as before, that players occasionally make mistakes. Because of this assumption I shall need to make a minor change in the definition of the tit-for-tat strategy. Suppose you are pretty sure that your opponent is playing tit-for-tat. You therefore co-operate in every round, and your opponent co-operates too. Then in one round, say round i, you make a mistake: you intended to co-operate, but you end up defecting. What should you do now? You can expect your opponent to defect in round $i + 1$ in response to your accidental defection. If you followed the strict principles of tit-for-tat, you would respond by defecting in round $i + 2$, then your opponent would defect in round $i + 3$, and so on. It may be better to cut short this endless chain of retaliation and counter-retaliation by co-operating in round $i + 2$. This is the intuition behind the following variant of tit-for-tat, which I shall call T_1.

T_1 starts from a concept of being in good standing. The essential idea is that a player who is in good standing is entitled to the co-operation of his opponent. At the start of the game both players are treated as being in good standing. A player remains in good standing provided that he always co-operates when T_1 prescribes that he should. If in any round a player defects when T_1 prescribes that he should co-operate, he loses his good standing; he regains his good standing after he has co-operated in *one* subsequent round. (This is why I call this strategy T_1; if it took two rounds of co-operation to regain good standing, the strategy would be T_2 and so on.) Given all this, T_1 can be formulated as follows: 'Co-operate if your opponent is in good standing, or if you are not. Otherwise, defect.'

For a player who never makes mistakes, T and T_1 are equivalent to one another. (If you follow T_1 without ever making a mistake, you will always be in good standing, so T_1 will prescribe that your opponent should co-operate in every round. Thus whether your opponent is in good standing in any round depends entirely on whether or not he co-operated in the previous round. If he co-operated in round $i - 1$, T_1 requires you to co-operate in round i; if he defected in round $i - 1$, T_1 requires you to defect in round i.) The only difference between T_1 and T concerns the moves that a player makes after he has defected by mistake. Suppose you are following T_1 and are about to play round i; you and your opponent are both in good standing. You should therefore co-operate in round *i*. Suppose, however, that you defect by mistake while your opponent co-operates. Then you lose your good standing. Now, according to T_1, you should co-operate in round $i + 1$. Since you have lost your good standing, your opponent may defect in round $i + 1$ without losing his; so whatever he does in round $i + 1$, T_1 will require you to co-operate in round $i + 2$ also.

Provided that the probability of mistakes is sufficiently small, T_1 is a stable equilibrium strategy. Why? Suppose you know your opponent is following T_1, and you are about to play round *i*. Assume that, whatever may have happened in the past, neither you nor your opponent will make any further mistakes. I shall show that, on this assumption, the only best reply is 'Co-operate if your opponent is in good standing, or if you are not; otherwise, defect'. But if this is the *only* best reply when there is no possibility of further mistakes – that is, if this reply is *strictly* better than any other – it must remain the only best reply when there is *some* possibility of further mistakes, provided the probability of mistakes is sufficiently small. So what I shall be proving is that 'Co-operate if your opponent is in good standing, or if you are not; otherwise, defect' is the only best reply to T_1 if there is some, sufficiently small, probability of mistakes. But this reply is T_1. So I shall be proving that T_1 is a stable equilibrium strategy.

Now for the proof itself. When you go into round *i*, there are only three possibilities:

1 *Either* you and your opponent are both in good standing, *or* neither of you is in good standing. Then your opponent will co-operate in round *i* and thereafter play tit-for-tat (i.e. repeat your last move).
2 Your opponent is in good standing but you are not. Then he will defect in round *i* and thereafter play tit-for-tat.
3 You are in good standing but your opponent is not. Then he will co-operate in round *i*, co-operate again in round $i + 1$, and thereafter play tit-for-tat.

Notice that in the first round of the game, case 1 must apply. This, then, is the case analysed in Section 6.2, in which I proved that if no mistakes were made, the best reply to strategy *T* was to co-operate in every round (the proof was in fact Axelrod's). So we know that in case 1 your only best move in round *i* is to co-operate.

Now consider case 2. Notice that if you co-operate in round *i*, then round $i + 1$ will be an instance of case 1: your opponent will co-operate in that round and then play tit-for-tat. We know that in case 1 your only best reply is 'co-operate, co-operate ...'; so if it is a best move to co-operate in round i, it must be a best move to co-operate in round $i + 1$, and so on. If instead you defect in round i, then round $i + 1$ will be another instance of case 2; so if it is a best move to defect in round i, it must be a best move to defect in round $i + 1$, and so on. Thus one of two sequences of moves for rounds $i, i + 1, \ldots$ must be a best reply – *either* 'co-operate, co-operate, ...' *or* 'defect, defect, ...'. Given the assumption that $\pi > c/b$, the former sequence generates the greater expected utility. So in case 2, as in case 1, your only best move in round i is to co-operate.

Finally consider case 3. In this case you are free to defect in round i without losing your good standing; whatever you do in round i, round $i + 1$ will be an instance of case 1. So your best move must be to defect in round i. This completes the proof: your best move in round i is to co-operate if your opponent is in good standing or if you are not (cases 1 and 2), but to defect otherwise (case 3).

Strategy T_1, then, is a stable equilibrium – but not the only stable equilibrium. (Recall that unconditional defection is also a stable equilibrium.) In other words, T_1 is a convention. Consider what this convention amounts to in everyday terms.

To begin with, it is clearly a convention of reciprocity: a person following T_1 is willing to co-operate provided his opponent is willing to do the same. But it is also a convention of punishment. Suppose that in some round i your opponent mistakenly defects while you co-operate. Then he has breached the convention and for this round you have been made a sucker. The convention now prescribes that in the next round your positions should be reversed: he should co-operate while you defect. Then in round $i + 2$ you both co-operate again. What happens in round $i + 1$ may be interpreted as a punishment for your opponent's previous breach of the convention: he suffers the worst possible outcome for that round (a utility loss of c). Notice that this is worse for him than the outcome that would have resulted had he, like you, defected in round $i + 1$. In this sense, your opponent chooses to accept punishment (knowing that if he did otherwise, the long-term consequences for him would be worse still).

To say that your opponent has been punished is, however, to tell only half the story. In round $i + 1$ you receive the best possible outcome – a utility gain of b. This is better for you than the outcome of a round of mutual co-operation, let alone the outcome of a round of mutual defection. So the events of round $i + 1$ not only inflict harm on your opponent; they also benefit you. In other words, what is going on is not only punishment but also reparation. The convention, we might say, prescribes that your opponent performs an act of reparation. Your defection in round $i + 1$ and his co-operation are both parts of this act.

Strategy T_1 prescribes one round of reparation following any unjustified defection (that is, any defection not prescribed by T_1). After this one round, the two players co-operate again. Why only one round of reparation? After all, this reparation is insufficient to compensate the injured party fully for the losses he has suffered from the other player's breach of the convention. (The original breach – say in round i – imposes a cost of b on the injured party: this is the benefit he should have received from his opponent's act of co-operation, but which in fact he never received. The act of reparation in round $i+1$ allows the injured party to save c, since he receives the benefits of his opponent's act of co-operation without having to incur the costs of co-operating himself. But we know that $b > c$. In addition, the cost saving c must be discounted to allow for the possibility that round $i + 1$ will never be played.) The answer is that the extent of reparation is itself a convention. The injured party demands just as much reparation as he expects his opponent to concede, and his opponent offers just as much as he expects the first player to insist on.

We might imagine a strategy T_2 prescribing two rounds of reparation for each unjustified defection, or a strategy T_3 prescribing three rounds of reparation – and so on. It can be proved (but I shall not give the proof here) that any such strategy T_r is a stable equilibrium provided that $\pi^r > c/b$. Thus any strategy T_r is a stable equilibrium if π is sufficiently close to 1, but the higher is the value of r, the closer to 1 the value of π must be in order to ensure stability.

Why is this? The higher the value of r, the greater are the reparations that a player must make to regain his good standing after a mistake; we might say, following Axelrod (1981, p. 310) that strategies with lower values of r are more forgiving. There is an obvious limit to how forgiving a strategy may be if it is to be an equilibrium: reparations must be sufficiently burdensome to deter deliberate defections. But this is true even for T_1, the most forgiving of the strategies. Beyond this point there is a danger in being unforgiving. Once having made a mistake, a player is not *compelled* to make reparation; he may instead resign himself to the loss of his good standing and continue to defect. The less forgiving his opponent is, the more attractive this second option will be. It will also be more attractive at lower values of π, since the sooner the game is likely to end, the less there is to gain from being in good standing.

6.4   Does evolution favour reciprocity?

The tit-for-tat strategies I have been considering are members of a much larger class, which I shall call strategies of brave reciprocity. These strategies have two defining characteristics. First, against an opponent who defects in every round, these strategies defect in every round except the first (provided no mistakes are made). Second, if two players following strategies of brave reciprocity meet, they both co-operate in every round (again, provided no mistakes are made). Notice that the two players need not be following the *same* strategy.

A strategy can only satisfy the second condition if it always co-operates in the first round (since until the first round has been played, neither player can know anything about his opponent's strategy). This is why I call these strategies brave. By being prepared to co-operate in advance of any evidence that your opponent will reciprocate, you are leaving yourself open to exploitation by an opponent who always defects. If you are following a strategy of brave reciprocity, this exploitation will be limited to one round, but it is exploitation none the less. This is a price that has to be paid if you follow *any* strategy that 'co-operates with itself' – that is, any strategy such that if both players in a game are following it, they will both co-operate. (If neither player will co-operate until the other has already done so, they will never co-operate at all; so if a strategy is to co-operate with itself, it must be willing to co-operate before there is any evidence of the same willingness on the part of the opponent.)

Now suppose that when people play the extended prisoner's dilemma game, they consider only two kinds of strategy – strategies of brave reciprocity, and the nasty strategy of unconditional defection, N. This is, of course, an heroic simplification when the number of strategies actually available is infinitely large. (Remember that even the five-round prisoner's dilemma game has more than two billion strategies!) But we have to start somewhere.

There are now three possibilities. First, two N-players may meet. They will defect in every round; each will derive a utility of zero from the game. Second, an N-player may meet someone following a strategy of brave reciprocity (I shall call him a B-player). They will both defect in all rounds except the first; but in the first round the N-player defects and the B-player co-operates. Thus over the whole game the N-player derives a utility of b and the B-player derives a utility of $-c$. The third possibility is that two B-players meet. They both co-operate in every round, gaining a utility of $b - c$ in each round; the expected value of this utility stream is $(b - c)/(1 - \pi)$. Notice that it does not matter whether all B-players follow the same strategy or not; all that matters is that each B-player follows *some* strategy of brave reciprocity.

This situation can be represented by the simple symmetrical game shown in Figure 6.2. This game can now be analysed in the usual way.

	Opponent's strategy	
	B (Brave reciprocity)	N (Unconditional defection)
Player's strategy — B (Brave reciprocity)	$\dfrac{b-c}{1-\pi}$	$-c$
Player's strategy — N (Unconditional defection)	b	0

Figure 6.2   A simple version of the extended prisoner's dilemma game

Note: $b > c > 0$ and $\pi > c/b$

Notice that N is the best reply to N and that, provided $\pi > c/b$, B is the best reply to B. So which is the better strategy for a player to choose depends on the probability that his opponent will choose one strategy rather than the other. Let p be the probability that a random opponent will choose strategy B. Then there will be some critical value of p, say p^*, such that B is more successful than, just as successful as, or less successful than N according to whether p is greater than, equal to, or less than p^*. It is easy to calculate that this critical value is

$$p^* = \frac{c(1 - \pi)}{\pi(b - c)} \tag{6.4}$$

If the probability of meeting an opponent again is fairly high, this critical value of p can be quite close to zero. Suppose, for example, that $b = 2$ and $c = 1$ (which would seem to be as neutral an assumption as any). Then if $\pi = 0.9$, implying that the average length of a game is 10 rounds, the critical value of p is 0.11. If $\pi = 0.98$, so that the average game has 50 rounds, the critical value is 0.02. This reflects the fact that playing B is a kind of risky investment. By incurring the risk of being exploited by an N-player in the *first* round, you are able to co-operate with a B-player in *every* round. The longer the game is likely to last, the more time there is to recoup on a successful investment.

This result seems to suggest that, in games which on average have many rounds, a convention of brave reciprocity has a good chance of evolving. Even if initially the great majority of players are nasties, the nasties may do less well than the small minority who are following strategies of brave reciprocity; and then there will be a self-reinforcing tendency for the minority group to grow.[5] Notice that this argument works even if the members of the minority group are not all following the same strategy. In other words, a *general* convention of brave reciprocity may establish itself in advance of any *specific* convention about reparation.

Now here is another argument for expecting evolution to favour strategies of brave reciprocity. This argument does not require any critical mass of brave reciprocators: provided there are *any at all*, a convention of brave reciprocity can evolve. However, it is necessary to assume that all the brave reciprocators follow the same convention about reparation.

Notice that there can be strategies of reciprocity that are cautious rather than brave. (A cautious strategy is one that is never the first to co-operate, see Section 6.2.) An individual following a strategy of cautious reciprocity waits for his opponent to make the first co-operative move; then, but only then, he co-operates too. The great advantage of this type of strategy is that it leads to co-operation with brave reciprocators without incurring the risk of being exploited by nasties. Its main disadvantage, of course, is that it cannot co-operate with itself: cautious players cannot distinguish between opponents who are nasty and opponents who are merely cautious (cf. Section 6.2).

If cautious strategies are to be successful, they need to be tailored to the conventions of reparation that prevail among their brave opponents. Suppose, for example, that all brave players follow T_1 – the tit-for-tat strategy that prescribes just one round of reparation for each unjustified defection (cf. Section 6.3). Thus a cautious player who defects in the first round and then finds that his opponent has co-operated is virtually certain that the opponent is playing T_1 (not *absolutely* certain, because the opponent may have intended to defect, but made a mistake). The cautious player is now in the same position as a T_1-player who, almost certain he is facing an opponent like himself, accidentally defects in the first round. So the cautious player's best plan is to do exactly what the T_1-player would do: co-operate for the next two rounds and then play tit-for-tat.

Here is a simple formulation of this type of strategy: 'Defect in round 1. If your opponent defects in round 1, defect in all subsequent rounds. If your opponent co-operates in round 1, play all subsequent rounds as though your strategy was T_1, treating your defection in round 1 as though it had been a mistake.' I shall call this strategy C_1. (It is easy to see that cautious strategies $C_2, C_3, \ldots$ can be designed to dovetail with the brave strategies $T_2, T_3, \ldots$.)

Now consider the game that results if we assume that the only strategies available are N, T_1 and C_1. This game is set out in Figure 6.3.[6] To illustrate the argument, I shall use the numerical values $b = 2, c = 1$ and $\pi = 0.9$, which gives the game set out in Figure 6.4. Nothing depends on these numbers, however; all that matters for the argument to go through is that (as I have been assuming throughout this chapter) $\pi > c/b$.

Opponent's strategy

		T_1	C_1	N
Player's strategy	T_1	$\dfrac{b-c}{1-\pi}$	$\dfrac{b-c}{1-\pi}-b+\pi c$	$-c$
	C_1	$\dfrac{b-c}{1-\pi}+c-\pi b$	0	0
	N	b	0	0

Figure 6.3   Another version of the extended prisoner's dilemma game

Note: $b > c > 0$ and $\pi > c/b$

Opponent's strategy

		T_1	C_1	N
Player's strategy	T_1	10	8.9	−1
	C_1	9.2	0	0
	N	2	0	0

Figure 6.4   Illustrative utility indices for the game in Figure 6.3

Note: These indices have been derived by setting $b = 2$, $c = 1$ and $\pi = 0.9$.

Now imagine a community in which initially some people play T_1, some C_1 and some N. Let the probabilities associated with these strategies be pq, $p(1 - q)$ and $1 - p$ respectively. In other words, p is the probability that a random opponent will play a strategy of reciprocity (T_1 or C_1). Given that an opponent is playing a strategy of reciprocity, q is the probability that he is playing the brave strategy T_1.

Provided that $pq > 0$, the best strategy must be either T_1 or C_1. (N is dominated by C_1: it does worse than C_1 against an opponent who plays T_1 and no better than C_1 against any strategy.) Thus so long as *some* people play T_1, the value of p must rise steadily as people learn by experience not to play N. But notice that T_1 is the best reply to both T_1 and C_1. Thus if the value of p is sufficiently high, T_1 must be the most successful strategy. So even if T_1 was not initially the most successful strategy, it will eventually become so; and it will remain the most successful, however many people switch to it.

Translating into more common-sense terms, imagine a community in which initially almost everyone is nasty. In this community it does not pay to be a brave reciprocator, since co-operative initiatives will almost always be repulsed. But there is nothing to lose[7] by being a cautious reciprocator: this allows you to co-operate with any brave reciprocators you happen to meet, while protecting you from exploitation by nasties. So people will gradually learn that cautious reciprocation pays dividends. But cautious reciprocators are too cautious to co-operate with one another; they can co-operate only with brave reciprocators. As the number of cautious reciprocators grows, and as the number of nasties falls, there will come a time when bravery pays. In this model the role of cautious reciprocation is rather like that of some kinds of plant that grow on disturbed ground – plants that colonize habitats that others find inhospitable, but whose presence helps to bring about the conditions that favour other species that eventually invade and take over.

I have now presented two arguments that suggest that the processes of social evolution might favour strategies of brave reciprocation. But I must confess that neither argument is altogether compelling. The trouble is, it is hard to see how any argument purporting to show that evolution will favour particular kinds of strategies can be more than suggestive. In the extended prisoner's dilemma game there are countless billions of strategies; it seems that we can analyse the game only by restricting ourselves to a few basic types of strategy, which means that any analysis must be incomplete.

This problem, I think, can never be completely solved; but Axelrod (1981) has proposed a fascinating way of making some progress. Axelrod's approach – which he calls the tournament approach – is to specify a particular form of the extended prisoner's dilemma game and then to invite all comers to submit strategies for playing the game. These strategies are then set loose against one another in some kind of tournament in which all play against all, to see which emerges as the winner. The beauty of this approach is that, although the number of strategies that are analysed is limited – that, of course, is inevitable – no arbitrary limits are imposed. No one can complain that the analyst has fixed his results by excluding particular strategies that might have done well, or that he has overlooked particular strategies because he has been too dull to perceive their merits. If you have a pet strategy that you are convinced would do well, all you have to do is enter it in the tournament. The only limits are set by human ingenuity – and that, of course, imposes limits in real-life games too.

Axelrod organized a tournament of this kind. His version of the extended prisoner's dilemma game was slightly different from the one I have been analysing. In my version of the game, the four possible outcomes for a player (defect when opponent defects, co-operate when opponent co-operates, defect when opponent co-operates and co-operate when opponent defects) have utility indices of 0, $b-c$, b and $-c$, with $b > c > 0$. Axelrod's game had the utility indices 1, 3, 5 and 0. These two formulations are not strictly compatible, but the essential structure of the game is the same.[8] The value of π was set at 0.99654, so that the median length of games was 200 rounds; the expected length was 289 rounds. The tournament was organized on the round-robin principle, strategies being submitted as computer programs.

Axelrod's tournament had 62 entries. The entrants, he reports, included 'game theorists in economics, psychology, sociology, political science and mathematics' and 'professors of evolutionary biology, physics, and computer science' (Axelrod, 1981, pp. 309–10). The winner was the simple tit-for-tat strategy T, submitted by the game theorist Anatol Rapoport.

In interpreting this result, a few qualifications must be borne in mind. First, the value of π was rather high, which would tend to favour strategies of brave reciprocity relative to cautious or nasty ones. Second, a round-robin tournament is not quite the same thing as an evolutionary process. In a round-robin tournament it is possible to amass a high score by doing well against poor opponents, whereas the processes of evolution will tend to weed out the least successful strategies at an early stage.[9] Third, in the evolution of conventions, prominence plays a very important part; and prominence can sometimes be a matter of imaginative leaps and associations of ideas that are not easily reduced to mathematics. By setting up his experiment in an abstractly mathematical form, and by requiring strategies to be written as computer programs, Axelrod may unwittingly have built in a bias towards mathematical concepts of prominence.

All this said, however, the success of tit-for-tat in Axelrod's tournament remains remarkable. It provides further grounds for believing that, if games of the extended prisoner's dilemma type are played repeatedly in a community, conventions of brave reciprocity will tend to evolve.

7
Free Riders

7.1 Free riding and the prisoner's dilemma game

In the one-off prisoner's dilemma game, the two players face only one problem: that of enforcing an agreement that they would both like to make. If some external mechanism for enforcing agreements is made available to the players, the game becomes trivial. There is no way in which either player can sensibly try to hold out for anything better than an agreement of mutual co-operation. The only threat a player has is to refuse to co-operate; but if one player refuses to co-operate it will be in the other player's interest to defect, and then the outcome will be worse for both players than if they had agreed to co-operate. To put this another way, neither player can have any expectation of a free ride: there is no possibility that a player will be able to defect while his opponent co-operates.

In the extended game, and in the absence of any mechanism for enforcing agreements, a player may be able to take a free ride in *occasional* rounds, by exploiting his opponent's uncertainty about his intentions; but no one can realistically expect to free ride *consistently*. As soon as your opponent realizes that you have no intention of co-operating with him, it will it will not be in his interest to co-operate with you.

I shall argue that it is because free riding is not a real option in the prisoner's dilemma game that strategies of reciprocal co-operation can evolve so easily. (That such strategies do tend to evolve was, of course, the central argument of Chapter 6.) I shall present this argument by investigating some games with a family resemblance to the prisoner's dilemma game; in some of these games free riding is not a real option for the players, but in others it is.

7.2 The mutual-aid game

Before the introduction of state insurance schemes, the sickness of a wage-earner could easily lead to financial ruin for working-class families. The problems caused by sickness were mitigated by various institutions for mutual aid. In nineteenth-century and early twentieth-century England, there were an enormous number of 'friendly societies' and 'sick clubs' run by working men; members paid weekly subscriptions and received benefits during periods when they were too ill to work. In addition to these formal schemes, there were informal practices with essentially the same effect; indeed it seems possible that friendly societies may have evolved as codifications of pre-existing traditions of informal mutual aid. Lady Florence Bell has described the practices of mutual aid that she observed amongst ironworkers in Middlesbrough around the turn of the century:

> Then there is a form of expenditure frequently met with which, if it may not be wise, is generous and beautiful – the amount expended on charity by the very poor, who, with self-sacrificing kindness, seem constantly ready to help one another. It often happens that if one of their number is struck down by accident or sudden illness, a 'gathering' is made at the works, the hat is passed round, and each one contributes what he can to tide over the time of illness, or, in the case of death, to contribute to funeral expenses. (1907, p. 76)

These 'gatherings' raised significant sums of money from workmen who had very little to spare; Lady Bell gives an example of a collection that raised £5 for a sick workman, and this was at a time when most ironworkers earned between £1 and £2 per week (Bell, 1907, pp. 26 and 175).

I shall now present a game which provides a simple model of the kind of problem faced by the ironworkers. I shall call it the mutual-aid game.

This is a game for any number of players, from two upwards. Let the number of players be n. Like the extended prisoner's dilemma game, the mutual-aid game consists of a series of rounds; after each round there is a probability of $1 - \pi$ that the game comes to an end. Each round is played as follows. One player is chosen at random to be the recipient; each player has the same probability $1/n$ of being chosen. The other players are the donors. Then each donor has a choice between two moves, 'co-operate' and 'defect'. If he co-operates, he scores $-c$; if he defects, he scores zero. The recipient scores Nb where N is the number of donors who have co-operated, and where $b > c$. The idea, then, is that each person has a chance of being in a situation (say sickness) in which he needs the help of the others, and that the benefits he then derives from each other person's act of assistance is greater than the cost to him of assisting another person, when that person is in need.

One special case of this game is the case in which $n = 2$. Then the game is very similar to the exchange-visit and prisoner's dilemma games (Section 6.1). It is not identical, however, because in each round of those games there are *two* possible acts of assistance, each with a cost of c to one player and a benefit of b to the other; the two players decide simultaneously whether each will assist the other. In a round of the two-person mutual-aid game, in contrast, there is only one possible act of assistance, and so only one player has a decision to make. The two-person mutual-aid game is more like Hume's game of the two farmers (Section 6.1).

In the two-person mutual-aid game, as in the prisoner's dilemma game, both players stand to gain from an arrangement of mutual co-operation. In each round, before it is revealed which player is to be the recipient and which the donor, each of them would derive an expected utility of $(b - c)/2$ from an arrangement that whichever player became the donor would co-operate; since $b > c$, this expected utility is positive. In contrast, if donors always defect, each player derives a utility of zero from each round. Also as in the prisoner's dilemma game, neither player can realistically expect to enjoy an indefinite free ride at the expense of the other. Acts of co-operation are costly; one player will, therefore, assist the other only if there is some prospect of return.

These features of the two-person game carry over into the more general n-person game. Any group of players stands to benefit – that is, every member of any group of players stands to benefit – from an arrangement that each member will co-operate if any other member is the recipient. The larger the group, the more each member stands to gain from this sort of arrangement. But since acts of co-operation are costly, and since in each round the identify of the recipient is clear to all, a player who consistently refuses to co-operate can have no realistic expectation of benefiting from the co-operation of his fellows. The mutual-aid game, then, is very close to being an n-person generalization of the prisoner's dilemma game. It is a generalization that preserves one of the most important features of that game: no one can realistically expect a free ride.

Now consider the n-person mutual-aid game. If only one round is played – that is, if $\pi = 0$ – each of the players has a choice of just two pure strategies: 'If donor, co-operate' and 'If donor, defect'. For each player the latter strategy is clearly the more successful, irrespective of the strategies chosen by his opponents. So the one-round game has a unique and stable equilibrium, in which no one co-operates.

What if $\pi > 0$, so that the game may run to many rounds? As in the prisoner's dilemma game, the sucker's strategy 'Co-operate in every round in which you are a donor' (S for short) cannot be an equilibrium. In a world of suckers, it never pays to co-operate. It is equally clear that the nasty strategy 'Defect in every round in which you are a donor' (N for short) *is* an equilibrium. In a world of nasties, just an in a world of suckers, co-operation never pays. If we allow for the possibility of mistakes, it turns out that N is a stable equilibrium strategy. (Compare the discussion of the stability of the nasty strategy in the prisoner's dilemma game, Section 6.2.)

By analogy with the prisoner's dilemma game, we might expect to find that some kind of tit-for-tat strategy would be a stable equilibrium provided that the value of π was sufficiently high. This is indeed the case.

Consider the following strategy, which I shall call tit-for-tat or T_1 (since it is closely analogous with the corresponding strategy in the prisoner's dilemma game). This strategy is based on a partition of the set of players into two groups, those who are in good standing and those who are not. At the start of the game everyone is treated as being in good standing. Now consider any round i, and let j be the player who is the recipient. Strategy T_1 prescribes that all donors should contribute if j is in good standing, but defect if he is not. If j was in good standing at the start of round i, then at the start of round $i + 1$ the players who are in good standing are j and all those donors who co-operated in round i. If j was not in good standing at the start of round i, then at the start of round $i + 1$ the players who are in good standing are simply those who were in good standing at the start of round i.

T_1 is a strategy of brave reciprocity, punishment and reparation (cf. Sections 6.3–6.4). It is strategy of reciprocity because it requires a player to co-operate with those who show a willingness to co-operate with him. To be more precise, the essential maxim behind this strategy is: 'Co-operate with those people who co-operate with people like you'; I shall call this the maxim of multilateral reciprocity. (Compare the maxim of bilateral reciprocity that lies behind tit-for-tat strategies in two-person games: 'Co-operate with those people who co-operate with you'.) T_1 is a brave strategy because it is prepared to make the first co-operative move in advance of any evidence that the beneficiary of this co-operation will reciprocate: in short, it gives opponents the benefits of the doubt.

(This is the implication of the proposition that everyone is treated as being in good standing at the start of the game.) As long as a player keeps to T_1 he is entitled to the co-operation of his fellow players if he becomes the recipient. If some player A fails to co-operate in any round in which the recipient is entitled to this co-operation, A loses his own entitlement to the co-operation of others. This is A's punishment. A may regain his entitlement by co-operating in one round in which the recipient is entitled to the co-operation of the others; this may be regarded as an act of reparation. (Why is *one* round of reparation sufficient? This is purely a matter of convention. It is easy to construct strategies $T_2, T_3, \ldots$ which differ from T_1 by requiring two, three, $\ldots$ rounds of co-operation before a player who has lost his good standing may regain it. Among the set of strategies $T_1, T_2, T_3, \ldots, T_1$ is the most forgiving, cf. Section 6.3.)

Now suppose you are playing the mutual-aid game, and that you know that all your fellow players are following strategy T_1. Assume, for the moment, that mistakes are never made. This means that your fellows will always be in good standing. Consider any round i. If you are the recipient, you have no decision to make. So suppose you are a donor. The decision you make now will determine whether or not you are in good standing until the next round in which you are a donor; but then you make a new decision. That decision will determine your standing until the next round in which you are a donor, and so on. So in evaluating your two possible moves in round i you need consider their effects only over rounds $i, i+1, \ldots, i+r$, where r is the number of subsequent rounds in which you are the recipient before the next round in which you are a donor. Of course r is a random variable: you cannot know in advance how many rounds – if any – will be played before you are a donor again.

If you defect, your expected utility over these rounds is zero: if you become the recipient, no one will co-operate. If instead you co-operate, you are certain to lose c, the cost of co-operating in round i. However, there is a probability π/n that round $i + 1$ will be played, and that in that round you will be the recipient. In this event you gain $(n - 1)b$ from the co-operation of your fellows. Given that this event does occur, there is a further probability π/n that round $i + 2$ will be played, and that you will be the recipient again. And so on. Thus if you co-operate your expected utility over rounds $i, i + 1, \ldots, i + r$ will be positive if

$$-c + (n - 1)b\left[\frac{\pi}{n} + \left(\frac{\pi}{n}\right)^2 + \cdots\right] > 0 \tag{7.1}$$

This expression reduces to

$$\pi > \frac{nc}{(n-1)b+c} \tag{7.2}$$

So if (7.2) holds, it is better to co-operate than to defect.

This inequality is rather similar to the inequality $\pi > c/b$ in the prisoner's dilemma game – indeed, as $n \to \infty$ the right-hand side of (7.2) tends to c/b – and plays the same role in the analysis. It sets a limit on the value of π below which a tit-for-tat strategy cannot be an equilibrium. From now on I shall assume that (7.2) holds.

Then it is immediately clear that T_1 is an equilibrium strategy. If all your fellow players are following T_1, your best reply is to co-operate in every round in which you are a donor. And this reply is exactly what is prescribed by T_1; T_1, then, is a best reply to itself.

To test the stability of T_1, we must allow there to be some very small probability that players make mistakes – defecting when they intended to co-operate, and co-operating when they intended to defect. Given this assumption, it is easy to see that T_1 is the unique best reply to itself. Suppose your fellow players are all trying to follow T_1, but very occasionally make mistakes. Provided this probability is sufficiently small, it is always best for you to co-operate whenever you are the donor and the recipient is in good standing. (This follows from the argument that shows T_1 to be a best reply to itself.) So if you ever defect by mistake, the best you can do is to regain your good standing as soon as you get the opportunity. On very rare occasions you will be a donor when the recipient is not in good standing (having made a mistake in an earlier round, and not having had the opportunity to rectify it). In this event you can defect without suffering any penalty; since co-operation is costly in itself, your best move must be to defect. These responses are exactly the ones prescribed by T_1.

So in the mutual-aid game, T_1 is a stable equilibrium strategy (provided that the value of π is sufficiently high, and that occasional mistakes are made). It is not, however, the only stable equilibrium strategy. Whatever the value of π, the nasty strategy 'Never co-operate' is clearly a stable equilibrium too. So T_1 is a convention – a convention of brave, multilateral reciprocity and of punishment and reparation.

I am inclined to think that in games of the mutual-aid kind, the processes of social evolution will tend to favour strategies of this kind. The argument in support of this claim is rather similar to the one I presented in Section 6.4 for the prisoner's dilemma game, so I shall not spell it out. Like the argument in Section 6.4 it is, unfortunately, far from decisive.

What does seem clear is that practices of mutual aid can be self-enforcing: they can be conventions. Lady Bell thought that the ironworkers' expenditure on helping their sick workmates was generous but not wise. It seems at least possible that her interpretation was mistaken, and that the ironworkers were being prudent rather than generous; the practice she observed may have been an informal system of mutual insurance and not, as she thought, a form of charity.

7.3   The snowdrift game

Suppose you are driving your car on a lonely road in winter, and you get stuck in a snowdrift, along with one other car. You and the other driver have both sensibly brought shovels. It is clear, then, that you should both start digging. Or is it? The other driver cannot dig his own way out of the drift without digging your way out too. If you think he is capable of doing the work on his own, why bother to help him?

This snowdrift game is set out in Figure 7.1 which describes a simple symmetrical game for two players. Each has a choice of two strategies, 'co-operate' (dig) and 'defect' (not dig). Then there are four possible outcomes for a player: that he and the other player both defect; that he and the other player both co-operate; that he co-operates while the other defects; and that he defects while the other co-operates. Let the utility scores for these outcomes be 0, $v - c_2, v - c_1$ and v. Here v represents the benefit that each player gains by escaping from the snowdrift. Provided that at least one player co-operates, both gain the benefit. The utility cost of the labour of digging is c_1 for a player who has to do it alone and c_2 for a player who does only a half-share of the work. Clearly $v > 0$ and $c_1 > c_2 > 0$. I shall assume in addition that $v > c_2$ and $c_1 > 2c_2$. The first of these inequalities means that if both players co-operate the outcome is better for both of them than if they both defect. (It is better to do half the digging and get out of the snowdrift than to remain stuck.) The second inequality means that

		Opponent's strategy	
		Co-operate	Defect
Player's strategy	Co-operate	$v - c_2$	$v - c_1$
	Defect	v	0

Figure 7.1   The snowdrift game

Note: $v > c_1 > 2c_2 > 0$.

the job of digging can be done more efficiently by two people than by one.

If we assume $v < c_1$ we have a game with the familiar prisoner's dilemma structure:[1] mutual co-operation is preferred to mutual defection, but whatever your opponent does, your best strategy is to defect. In terms of the example, the work involved in digging alone is so hard that each driver would prefer to stay in his car in the snowdrift and wait to be rescued. In this case neither player can have any sensible expectation of a free ride (of being dug out by the other driver).

I shall assume instead, however, that $v > c_1$: it is so important to get out of the snowdrift that each player would rather do all the digging himself than remain stuck. The snowdrift game, then, is defined by the utility indices shown in Figure 7.1 along with the condition $v > c_1 > 2c_2 > 0$. Now if you are sure that your opponent will defect, it is in your interest to co-operate. Because of this, it may make sense for a player to try to hold out for a free ride.

The snowdrift game has the same basic structure as the hawk–dove game (or chicken game) analysed in Chapter 4. In the hawk–dove game, two players are in dispute over the division of some resource that they both want. To play 'hawk' is to hold out for the whole of the resource; to play 'dove' is to claim only a half-share and to be ready to back down if an opponent demands more. The cost of playing 'hawk' is that when two hawks meet there is a fight, and this is the worst outcome of all. In the snowdrift game, the two players are in dispute over the division of something they both want *to avoid*, namely the labour of digging. To play 'defect' is to hold out for taking none of this bad thing; to play 'co-operate' is to offer to take a half-share but to be ready to back down and take it all if an opponent refuses to take any. The cost of playing 'defect' is that if both players do this they remain stuck in the snowdrift, and this is the worst outcome of all.

Because the two games share a common basic structure, much of the analysis of the hawk–dove game can be carried over to the snowdrift game. Consider the simple case in which the snowdrift game is played for only one round, rather than in some extended form; and suppose that the members of some community play this game repeatedly but anonymously against one another.

If the game is perceived as symmetrical, there is a unique and stable equilibrium. This is the mixed strategy in which 'co-operate' is played with the probability $(v - c_1)/(v - c_1 + c_2)$. Against an opponent following this strategy, 'co-operate' and 'defect' are equally successful. This equilibrium is stable, because if there is any increase in the probability that an opponent will co-operate, defection becomes the best strategy; and vice versa (cf. Section 4.2).

In practice it seems unlikely that a game of this kind would be played continually without the players coming to recognize some asymmetry, if only of labelling. If the game is perceived as asymmetrical, the mixed strategy described in the last paragraph ceases to be a stable equilibrium. Instead, there are two stable equilibria or conventions. Suppose the asymmetry is between two roles A and B (perhaps A is the driver of the first car to get stuck). Then one stable equilibrium strategy is: 'If A, co-operate; if B, defect.' The other is: 'If A, defect; if B, co-operate' (cf. Section 4.5).

Now consider an extended version of the snowdrift game. As usual, I shall assume that a game consists of a series of rounds; after each round, there is some probability π that a further round will be played. Suppose that the players all recognize some asymmetry between the roles A and B. (I shall assume that players' roles are fixed for the duration of a game.) It is immediately obvious that 'If A, always defect; if B, always co-operate' and 'If A, always co-operate; if B, always defect' are both equilibrium strategies for this extended game. If we allow there to be some very small probability that players make mistakes, these strategies are both stable (cf. Section 4.8).

However, there may be *other* stable equilibria in the extended game. In the snowdrift game, as in the prisoner's dilemma game, both players prefer mutual co-operation to mutual defection. Because of this it can make sense for one player to say to the other: 'If you will co-operate, so will I; but if you don't, neither will I.' In the prisoner's dilemma game the statement 'If you don't, neither will I' is not so much a threat as a report of the speaker's interests: he has nothing to gain from co-operating if his opponent is going to defect. In the snowdrift game, the statement is a pure threat: the speaker is holding out for an agreement of mutual co-operation by threatening an action that will hurt both himself and his opponent. Nevertheless, such threats make sense. A tit-for-tat strategy in the extended snowdrift game may be interpreted as an offer of mutual co-operation, backed up by just such a threat. Can a tit-for-tat strategy be a stable equilibrium?

Consider the tit-for-tat strategy T_1 that I presented for the extended prisoner's dilemma game (Section 6.3). For the purposes of this strategy, a player is in good standing at the start of the game and remains in good standing provided that he always co-operates when T_1 prescribes that he should. If he defects in any round when T_1 prescribes that he should co-operate, he loses his good standing; he regains his good standing after he has co-operated in one subsequent round. Then T_1 is: 'Co-operate if your opponent is in good standing, or if you are not. Otherwise, defect.'

If turns out that T_1 is a stable equilibrium strategy for the extended snowdrift game, provided that there is a very small probability that players will make mistakes, and provided that the value of π is sufficiently close to 1. (More precisely, it is necessary that $\pi > \max [c_2/v, c_2/(c_1 - c_2)]$.) The proof of this is very similar to the corresponding proof for the prisoner's dilemma game (Section 6.3) and is given in an appendix, as part of the proof of a more general result.[2]

So there are at least two distinct kinds of convention that might evolve in the extended snowdrift game. One kind of convention exploits some asymmetry in the game, and prescribes that one player co-operates while the other defects. These might be called conventions of licensed free riding: they prescribe who may take a free ride at whose expense. The other possibility is a convention of reciprocity.

These two kinds of convention are not equally desirable from the viewpoint of a typical individual. Suppose that each person plays half his games in the role of A and half in the role of B. Then under a convention of licensed free riding a player derives an expected utility of $v - c_1/2$ per round of a randomly selected game.[3] (He derives the benefit v whether he is A or B; there is a 0.5 probability that he will be playing the role in which he is required to incur the cost c_1.) Under a convention of reciprocity a player derives a utility of $v - c_2$ from every round. (He always derives the benefit v and he always incurs the cost c_2.) Since, by assumption, $c_1 > 2c_2$, it is clear that everyone is better off under a convention of reciprocity than under a convention of licensed free riding. Nevertheless, either convention, if once established, is self-perpetuating. Suppose I live in a community in which a convension of licensed free riding is firmly established. I should certainly *wish* that everyone would simultaneously switch to a convention of reciprocity; but I cannot change the way everyone else behaves. As long as everyone else is following a convention of licensed free riding, the best I can do is to follow it too.

Both kinds of convention seem to be found in everyday life. The allocation of minor tasks among workmates and neighbours and between the members of families and clubs often seems to be determined by conventions of licensed free riding. A certain kind of job has to be done; we all want it to be done, but no one wants to do the work. We all expect Joe to volunteer – perhaps because this is the kind of job Joe always does, or because it is Joe's turn to volunteer for something, or because there is some special relationship between Joe and the job in question that makes 'Leave it to Joe' a uniquely prominent solution. Because we all expect this, we feel safe in sitting tight. Joe expects us to sit tight, so he volunteers. For a more concrete example, suppose that you and your next-door neighbour have lawned front gardens with no fence in between. You hate seeing either plot of ground untidy – so much so that you would prefer to mow your neighbour's lawn yourself rather than see it never cut. Naturally you would also prefer to mow your own lawn than see it never cut; and you would welcome any offer by your neighbour to cut your lawn for you. Suppose your neighbour's preferences are symmetrical with yours. Then this is a game with the same basic structure as the snowdrift game. In most neighbourhoods this sort of problem is solved by a simple and very general convention: each household is responsible for the jobs that have to be done on its own plot.

In other cases, however, conventions of reciprocity seem to have become established. Take the case of the snowdrift. I guess that most people, if put in this situation, would expect the work to be shared between the two drivers – at least if they were of the same sex and if neither was old or infirm. It might be objected that my analysis cannot apply to real-life versions of the snowdrift game, since I assumed that the same two people were likely to play the game against one another many times. The objection would have a lot of force if we interpreted each occasion on which two drivers are stuck in a snowdrift as a round in the extended game. It might be quite realistic, however, to model each such occasion as an entire extended game, in which each round represents an interval of time during which a player can be either co-operating or defecting (digging or resting). Then a tit-for-tat strategy makes a lot of sense. Stuck in the snowdrift, I get out my shovel and start to dig, expecting you to join me. If you don't, I stop digging, to show that you can't expect a free ride. If you do join me, we dig together; but if you then try to sidle off, I stop work too. This sort of convention may have been what Hume had in mind when he wrote: 'Two men, who pull the oars of a boat, do it by an agreement or convention, tho' they have never given promises to each other' (1740, Book 3, Part 2, Section 2).[4] At any rate, the situation of two people in a rowing-boat might well be modelled as an extended snowdrift game, and their co-operation might by explained by their both adopting strategies of reciprocity.

7.4   The public good game

In the snowdrift game, the clearing of the snow is a public good for the two drivers: it is a good that both drivers want and that, if provided for one, must be provided for both (cf. Samuelson, 1954). This good will be provided only if one or both of the drivers chooses to incur some cost. The snowdrift game, then, is about the supply of public goods through voluntary contributions.[5]

In the snowdrift game there are only two players, but public goods often benefit many people. The favourite example of economists is the lighthouse. Since the whole point of a lighthouse is that it should be as visible as possible, a lighthouse provides benefits to any sailor who wishes to navigate by it: if it is there for the benefit of one sailor, it is there for the benefit of all. The defence of a community against attack from outside is another well-known example.

The conservation of natural resources is often beset by public-good problems. Take the case of a community of fishermen harvesting a common fishing ground. Every fisherman might be made better off by an agreement that limited everyone's catch so as to prevent over-fishing; but each would prefer still more that everyone else observed limits, he alone having a free hand. Here the fishing ground is a public good whose quality is maintained by the restraint of individual fishermen; and restraint is costly to the individual. This is one instance of a general problem of conservation, often called the 'tragedy of the commons' (Hardin, 1968).

Hume presents a famous example of this problem – although in Hume's case it is the improvement rather than the degradation of common land that is at stake:

Two neighbours may agree to drain a meadow, which they possess in common; because 'tis easy for them to know each others mind; and each must perceive, that the immediate consequence of his failing in his part, is, the abandoning the whole project. But 'tis very difficult, and indeed impossible, that a thousand persons shou'd agree in any such action; it being difficult for them to concert so complicated a design, and still more difficult for them to execute it; while each seeks a pretext to free himself of the trouble and expence, and wou'd lay the whole burden on others. (1740, Book 3, Part 2, Section 7)

The case of the two neighbours seems to be a game of the prisoner's dilemma or snowdrift type. In games of these kinds, Hume suggests, conventions of reciprocity can become established; but if the number of players if increased, co-operation is much less likely. Everyone will try to 'lay the whole burden on others' – to take a free ride. Hume mentions a further problem, that of coordinating the labour of many individuals, but I am not sure that this is as intractable a problem as Hume suggests. If we abstract from the free-rider problem, and suppose that each person has already committed his labour to the project, then we are left with a coordination game in which everyone has a common interest in their all working to *some* concerted plan; any remotely sensible plan is better than none. It is not difficult to imagine conventions that would solve coordination problems of this kind – the most obvious being a convention of leadership, by which a particular individual takes responsibility for directing everyone's labour. The real problem, I suggest, is getting people to commit their labour to the project in the first place.

Here is a simple game that models the problem of supplying public goods through voluntary contributions. I shall call it the public-good game. There are n players, where n may take any value from two upwards. In the one-round or non-extended version of the game, each player has a choice of two strategies, 'co-operate' or 'defect'. Let r be the number of players who co-operate. Then if $r = 0$, everyone scores zero. If $r > 0$, everyone who defects scores v and everyone who co-operates scores $v - c_r$. Here v stands for the benefit each player derives from some public good that will be produced only if at least one person volunteers to incur some cost; c_r is the cost borne by each volunteer in the case in which there are r volunteers. I shall assume that $v > c_n$, so that the outcome in which everyone co-operates is preferred by everyone to the outcome in which everyone defects; and that $c_1 > 2c_2 > \cdots > nc_n > 0$, so that the greater the number of volunteers, the more efficiently the public good is produced.

First consider the case in which $n = 2$ – the two-person public-good game. This game has two forms, depending on the value of v. If $v > c_1$, the two-person public-good game is identical to the snowdrift game; if $v < c_1$, it becomes a game of the prisoner's dilemma type. In the extended form of each of these games it is possible for a convention of reciprocity to evolve: each player co-operates conditional on the co-operation of the other. In the extended snowdrift game, but not in the extended prisoner's dilemma game, conventions of licensed free riding may evolve instead: one player co-operates while the other takes a free ride. In the extended prisoner's dilemma game, but not in the extended snowdrift game, conventions of nastiness may evolve instead of ones of reciprocity: no one co-operates.

These results can be generalized for the n-person game. Here I shall only outline the most important conclusions that can be drawn from an analysis of the extended n-person public good game; more details are given in an appendix.

In any given case of the public-good game it is possible to define a number m which represents the size of the smallest group of players who can benefit from an arrangement of mutual co-operation in the face of the defection of all the other players. If $v > c_1, m = 1$; otherwise m is defined[6] so that $c_{m-1} > v > c_m$. Thus in the two-person game $m = 1$ corresponds with the snowdrift game and $m = 2$ with the game with the prisoner's dilemma structure. To say that $m = n$ is to say that no one can realistically expect a free ride, since in such a case, if it is known that even one player is sure to defect, it cannot be in the interests of the others to co-operate. If, however, $m < n$ it may be possible for a player to take a free ride: he may defect and hope that the others will come to some arrangement among themselves whereby they all co-operate even though he does not.

One conclusion is fairly obvious: provided that $m > 1$, the nasty strategy 'Defect in every round' is a stable equilibrium. (When I use the concept of stability I shall always assume that players make very occasional mistakes.) If you are sure that, whatever you do, everyone else is going to defect, your decision turns on the relative size of v (the benefit you derive from the public good) and c_1 (the cost of supplying it alone). If $c_1 > v$ – as must be the case if $m > 1$ – the best you can do is to defect along with the others. The nasty strategy of the extended prisoner's dilemma game is one instance of this general class of stable equilibrium strategies.

Provided that π, the probability of playing a further round after any given one, is sufficiently close to 1, there is another class of stable equilibrium strategies. These correspond with conventions of the following two-part kind. The first part of each convention defines some set of players A who are made responsible for providing the public good. Here it is essential that A contains at least m players, so that it can be in these players' interests to co-operate with one another in the face of the free riding of the others. The second part of the convention prescribes reciprocal co-operation among those players who are responsible for providing the public good. Essentially, each of these players adopts a kind of tit-for-tat strategy whereby he co-operates if and only if all the others do so too.

One special case of this kind of convention is the one in which all n players are held responsible for providing the public good. The tit-for-tat strategies of the snowdrift game and prisoner's dilemma game are instances of such conventions. Another special case is the one in which only one player is responsible for providing the public good; then this one player simply co-operates in every round. The 'licensed free riding' conventions of the snowdrift game are examples. If there are more than two players there can be conventions intermediate between these two extremes, prescribing that more than one player, but less than all, provide the public good through an arrangement of reciprocal co-operation.

Why are such conventions stable equilibria? This question is answered in more detail in the appendix, but here is a quick answer. Suppose you are playing the public-good game and you know that all your $n - 1$ fellow players are following some particular convention of the kind I have described. Then if this convention allows you to take a free ride, there is no point in co-operating: the public good will be provided for you anyway. If instead you are one of the people responsible for providing the public good, you know that in the long run the other people who are responsible will not co-operate unless you do. Since you would rather co-operate along with them than see everyone defect, it is in your interest to co-operate.

In principle, then, it is quite possible for public goods to be supplied through the voluntary contributions of many self-interested individuals, each pursuing a tit-for-tat strategy of reciprocal co-operation.[7] In practice, however, conventions of reciprocal co-operation are likely to be increasingly fragile as the number of co-operators increases.

One problem is that if a convention is to work it must be reasonably unambiguous, and not so complicated that people have difficulty interpreting it. One of the beauties of the original tit-for-tat strategy (Section 6.2) was its extreme simplicity. Even the dullest player of an extended prisoner's dilemma game would surely grasp the logic of this strategy eventually, if his opponent followed it consistently. (The success of this strategy in Axelrod's tournament (Section 6.4) suggests that its logic can be grasped even by the dullest computer program.) The principle of tit-for-tat can be generalized for the case of many individuals in a theoretically satisfactory way; but some of its original simplicity is lost.

Perhaps the most serious source of ambiguity arises when a convention defines a set of players as being responsible for supplying a public good, allowing the rest to take a free ride. Co-operation may break down completely if players do not all interpret the convention in the same way. Suppose that all the players in a game except one believe there to be a convention prescribing that some particular set of players A is responsible for providing some public good: each member of A should co-operate provided the others do. Let the maverick be player i and suppose that *he* believes that some different set of players A' is responsible for the public good. If i is not a member of A there is no problem since, whatever i does, the A-players can establish a practice of reciprocal co-operation among themselves. But suppose i *is* a member of A. Then reciprocal co-operation cannot be established if i is not a member of A' – if i believes that the convention allows him to take a free ride. Acting on this belief, he will persistently defect; the other A-players will defect in retaliation for what, to them, is an unjustified defection. Reciprocal co-operation will also fail to become established if A' is not a subset of A – if there is any player whom *i* believes to be responsible for the public good, but whom no one else does. In this case *i* will defect in retaliation for what he sees as an unjustified defection by another player; the other A-players will then defect in retaliation for *i*'s defection, which *they* see as unjustified.

How serious is this danger? This seems to depend on two main factors – on the number of players in A, and on the ambiguity or otherwise of the convention that defines A.

As far as numbers are concerned, it is clear that a convention is more vulnerable, the larger is the set of players A that is responsible for the public good. Suppose that in any game there is a 'true' interpretation of the convention, but that each player has a small chance, say 0.05, of misinterpreting it. An arrangement of reciprocal co-operation will be established if *all* members of A interpret the convention correctly. (It is possible that reciprocal co-operation might be established in other circumstances, but only by a fortunate accident.) If the number of players in A is q, the probability that all A-players will interpret the convention correctly is 0.95^q. If $q = 1$, this probability is 0.95; if $q = 10$ it is 0.60; if $q = 50$ it is only 0.08. (In Hume's case, with $q = 1000$, the probability is less than one in a thousand million million million!) This seems to suggest that if tit-for-tat conventions evolve in the public-good game, the number of players made responsible for the public good is likely to be relatively small.

To this it might be objected that lack of ambiguity is related to prominence, and that the most prominent and least ambiguous definition of A is that it contains *all* players. Surely, it might be said, a convention prescribing that everyone co-operates, conditional on everyone else's co-operation, is so simple and obvious that the problem of misinterpretation could hardly arise. For the game in its mathematically pure form, this is, I think, true. But in real life public-good problems do not come with a set of *n* potential co-operators neatly defined. Suppose a patch of public open space in a housing estate becomes littered with rubbish, and can be cleared only by volunteer labour. This is an *n*-person public-good game, but who are the *n* players? It seems natural to define the game so that the players are those people who live relatively close to the open space, or who make most use of it; but the questions 'How close?' and 'How much use?' may have no obvious answers. By defining the game as involving a particular set of players and then saying that the convention 'Everyone co-operates, conditional on everyone else's co-operation' is uniquely prominent, we are supposing that the problem of defining the set of individuals responsible for the public good has already been solved. In real life, this problem can only be solved by convention, and a successful convention must be based on some general rule that can be adapted to many different contexts. It is remarkably difficult to think of any general, simple and cheat-proof rule to prescribe which individuals should be responsible for which public goods.

This problem is in many ways analogous with that of dividing up the North Sea (Section 5.1). That problem was a division game for *n* players; the set of players was clearly *some* subset of the nations of the world, but it was not clear *which*. The problem was solved by an unambiguous convention that assigned each portion of the sea bed to a single country – the nearest. The prominence of this solution stems in part from what seems to me to be an inescapable fact: the unique prominence of the number 1 in the set of positive integers. The analogue in the public-good game is a convention prescribing that each public good should be supplied by the efforts of just one person, that person being identified by appeal to some relation of closeness or special association between the person and the good. As I pointed out in my discussion of the snowdrift game (Section 7.3), such conventions are quite common in everyday life. But they can work only if it is in the interests of one person to supply the good unaided, and for many public goods this is not the case.

These problems are compounded by a further one. A convention of reciprocal co-operation works because it is not in the interests of any individual co-operator to opt out: he knows that if he defects, everyone else will, and given this knowledge, he prefers not to defect. In the pure mathematical form of the game it is easy to think of conventions that are stable in this sense. But what about real life?

Any practical convention prescribing who should be responsible for a public good is bound to be rough and ready – indeed, crudeness is often an important factor in making a convention prominent and unambiguous (cf. Section 5.5). Thus cases may arise in which a convention prescribes that a particular person should join a co-operative arrangement to produce a public good, when the value of this good to him is less than the cost he would have to incur if he co-operated. Then the tit-for-tat threat of his fellows is in fact no threat at all: knowing that his defection will wreck the whole scheme, he *prefers* to defect. It might seem that the solution to this problem is a convention that defines the group of contributors in terms of their preferences; but of course such a convention would be wide open to cheating. As an example of exactly this problem, consider the convention that each person looks after his own garden. Suppose one person really doesn't care what his garden looks like, and so chooses to leave it full of rubbish and weeds. Perhaps some of his neighbours would actually prefer a co-operative arrangement among themselves, whereby they looked after the offending garden – if only to protect the value of their own property. But they don't do this because they know that if they did, all their other neighbours would start to profess a love of untidiness.

7.5   Are conventions fragile?

Of course, problems of these kinds can arise with *all* conventions. In most cases, however, conventions are such that a community-wide scheme of co-operation cannot be wrecked by the actions of just one or a few individuals who misinterpret the conventions or who have unusual preferences. Take the case of a coordination problem, like the use of money, or the problem of determining who gives way to whom at cross-roads. If a few eccentrics refuse to trade in anything except French francs when everyone else is using US dollars they will cause occasional irritation to the rest of the community. If a few drivers give priority to vehicles approaching from the left when everyone else gives priority to vehicles approaching from the right, there will occasionally be serious consequences. But in neither case is the convention itself seriously threatened: it is still in everyone else's interest to use US dollars and to give priority to vehicles approaching from the right, and so most people can continue to co-operate with one another despite the existence of mavericks. The same is true of the public-good game when individual games involve only a few players. Take my example of gardens. If a few people are happy to leave their gardens in a mess, they impose costs on their immediate neighbours; but so long as most people want their own gardens to be tidy, the convention 'Everyone looks after his own garden' allows most people to co-operate tolerably well with most others. Whenever social interactions can be factored down into a large number of separate games, each involving only a few players, mavericks do not pose particularly serious problems.

Even in games which involve many players, co-operative arrangements are not necessarily vulnerable to the actions of mavericks. Take the mutual-aid game (Section 7.2), which may be played by many individuals. In this game the benefits of co-operation accrue not to all players, but only to those who actually co-operate. Suppose that one person in a large community refuses to join an arrangement of mutual aid, always refusing to go to the help of anyone in need. Then everyone else can continue to help one another, only slightly the worse off for the one person's defection; the defector's punishment is that no one helps *him*.

Many of the situations in which individuals are able to benefit by co-operation have the structure of the mutual-aid game rather than that of the public-good game. In the mutual-aid game those who choose to co-operate can exclude other people from enjoying the benefits of their co-operative arrangements; these arrangements are essentially *clubs* (cf. Buchanan, 1965). A great deal of voluntary co-operation takes place within clubs. Think of the importance of clubs in organizing sports, recreations and entertainments; or of the growing tendency for welfare services to be supplied by reciprocal self-help organizations such as Alcoholics Anonymous or Gingerbread (for one-parent families) or the Multiple Sclerosis Society (cf. Kramer, 1981, p. 211; Johnson, 1981, pp. 76–7). Although law and order is often regarded as a classic case of a public good, it is possible even for certain basic policing services to be provided by clubs. Think of communities in which official police forces have lost control, and that are preyed on by petty criminals. A common response is the setting up of vigilante groups. Since vigilantes can *choose* whom they protect – can choose whether or not to go to a person's aid if he is attacked, or, failing this, whether or not to try to hunt down his attackers and extract reparation – the situation has the structure of the mutual-aid game. In international affairs military alliances serve purposes similar to those of vigilante groups. So in a state of nature there may be co-operative arrangements to enforce conventions of property.[8]

The peculiarity of the many-person public-good game is that the benefits of any player's co-operation are reaped by all players – co-operators and defectors alike. It is this that makes co-operation so difficult to organize. Each potential defector can be deterred only by the threat that if he defects, the whole co-operative scheme will be brought down: no one will co-operate with anyone. This means that the scheme *must* be fragile: it cannot work at all unless it is capable of being wrecked by any maverick who refuses to co-operate when the rules of the scheme prescribe that he should.

The implication seems to be this: if each person pursues his own interests it is most unlikely that genuine public goods will be produced by co-operative arrangements involving many individuals. (Most unlikely, but not impossible: there may be no maverick around to wreck the arrangement.) But this leaves us with a puzzle. As I pointed out in Section 1.2, some public goods *are* paid for by the voluntary sacrifices of many individuals. Take the case of the British lifeboat service,[9] which is financed by the gifts of many thousands of donors. Since most donors do not know even the identities of other donors, this cannot be a case of a tit-for-tat convention. On any sensible definition of interests, I suggest, the person who contributes towards the costs of the lifeboat service is acting against his own interests: any benefit that *he* derives from *his contribution* is surely insignificant. Why then does anyone contribute?

If we are to answer this question we must, I believe, recognize that individuals sometimes choose to act contrary to their own interests, out of some sense of moral obligation, or as Sen (1977) puts it, some sense of 'commitment'. In the final two chapters I shall argue that there is more to spontaneous order than a set of conventions that it is in everyone's interest to follow: these conventions are likely to be supported by a system of morality. Spontaneous order, I shall argue, has a moral dimension.

7.A   Appendix: tit-for tat strategies in the prisoner's dilemma, snowdrift and public-good games

The extended public-good game is defined as follows. There are n players, where $n \geqslant 2$, playing a series of rounds; after each round there is a probability π that a further round will be played. In each round each player has a choice of two moves – 'co-operate' or 'defect'. If at least one player co-operates, everyone who co-operates scores $v - c_r$ where r is the number of players who co-operate; everyone who defects scores v. If no one co-operates, everyone scores zero. It is assumed that $v > c_n$ and that $c_1 > 2c_2 > \cdots nc_n > 0$. The number m is defined so that $m = 1$ if $v > c_1$, otherwise m is such that $c_{m-1} > v > c_m$. (To simplify the analysis I leave aside the possibility that v might be exactly equal to one of $c_1, \ldots, c_n$.) The extended snowdrift game is the special case in which $n = 2$ and $m = 1$. The extended prisoner's dilemma game is the special case in which $n = 2$ and $m = 2$.

I shall assume that the extended public-good game is played repeatedly but anonymously in some community; in each game the n players are drawn at random from the community. I shall also assume that there is some asymmetry in the roles of the players, such that in every game it is possible to identify some group of players as being of 'Type A', the rest being of 'Type B'. And I shall assume that in every game the number of A-players is always the same, this number being q, where $n \geqslant q \geqslant m$. Notice that this formulation includes as a limiting case the case in which *all* players are A-players.

First consider the nasty strategy N: 'Defect in every round, whether you are an A or a B.' This is clearly a stable equilibrium strategy provided that $c_1 > v$. (Throughout this appendix I shall define stability by assuming that in each round each player has a very small probability of making a mistake.)

Now consider the following strategy of reciprocity, which I shall call R_1. The essential idea is that B-players defect while each A-player co-operates provided that all other A-players do the same. The strategy rests on a concept of 'being in good standing' that applies only to A-players. At the start of a game, all A-players are treated as being in good standing. As long as an A-player co-operates in every round in which this is prescribed by R_1, he remains in good standing. If he defects when R_1 prescribes co-operation, he loses his good standing; but he regains his good standing as soon as he has co-operated in *one* subsequent round (hence the subscript 1 in 'R_1'). Then R_1 is as follows: 'If you are a B-player, defect in every round. If you are an A-player, then co-operate provided that all other A-players are in good standing. Also co-operate if you yourself are not in good standing. Otherwise, defect.'

In the special case of the snowdrift game, R_1 reduces to the strategy of licensed free riding if we set $q = 1$; it reduces to the tit-for-tat strategy T_1 if we set $q = 2$. In the prisoner's dilemma case $m = n = 2$, which entails that $q = 2$. Then R_1 reduces again to the tit-for-tat strategy T_1.

For the public-good game in general: any strategy R_1 is a stable equilibrium provided that π is sufficiently close to 1. Here is a sketch of the proof.

Suppose you are playing the extended public-good game, and you know that your $n - 1$ fellow players are all following R_1. You are about to play round i. Assume that, whatever may have happened so far, the probability that any mistakes will be made in the rest of the game is so small that it can be safely ignored.

First suppose that you are a B-player. Then you know that at least one A-player will co-operate in round i. (If all A-players are in good standing, they will all co-operate; if one or more are not in good standing, the players who are not in good standing will co-operate.) So your best move must be to defect: the public good will be provided whether you co-operate or not, so why co-operate?

Now suppose you are an A-player. One possibility is that $q = 1$: you are the *only* A-player. Then whatever you do, everyone else will defect. Since by assumption $q \geqslant m$, it is clear that $m = 1$ or, equivalently, $v > c_1$. This entails that your best move for round i is to co-operate.

Suppose instead that $q > 1$: you are not the only A-player. Then there are four possible cases:

1 You and all the other A-players are in good standing.
2 You are not in good standing but all the other A-players are.
3 You are not in good standing, and at least one other A-player is not in good standing either.
4 You are in good standing but at least one A-player is not.

In case 1 you know that all the other A-players will co-operate in round i; in every subsequent round they will all repeat your last move in a tit-for-tat fashion. Using Axelrod's argument (Section 6.2), one of the following sequences of moves must be a best reply: *either* co-operate, co-operate, . . .; *or* defect, defect . . .; *or* defect, co-operate, defect, co-operate, ... It turns out that 'co-operate, co-operate, . . .' is the best reply, provided that

$$\pi > \max \left[\frac{c_q}{v}, \frac{c_q}{c_1 - c_q} \right] \tag{7A.1}$$

This must be the case if π is sufficiently close to 1. From now on I shall assume that (7A.1) holds.

In case 2 you know that all the other A-players will defect in round i; in every subsequent round they will all repeat your last move in a tit-for-tat fashion. Your best reply must be *either* 'co-operate, co-operate, . . .' *or* 'defect, defect, . . .' *or* 'co-operate, defect, co-operate, defect, . . .'. Provided that (7A.1) holds, it turns out that 'co-operate, co-operate, . . .' is your best reply if

$$\pi > \frac{c_1 - v}{c_1 - c_q} \tag{7A.2}$$

This must be the case if π is sufficiently close to 1. From now on I shall assume that (7A.2) holds.

In case 3 you know that in round i all the A-players who are in good standing will defect, while all those (apart from you) who are not in good standing will co-operate. Thus if you co-operate now, round $i + 1$ will be an instance of case 1; if you defect now, round $i + 1$ will be an instance of case 2. In either case your best moves for rounds $i + 1, i + 2, \ldots$ will be 'co-operate, co-operate, . . .'. Given that you will co-operate from round $i + 1$, your best move in round i is 'co-operate' provided that $\pi > c_s/(c_1 - c_q)$ where s is the number of A-players, including yourself, who are not in good standing at the start of round i. The value of

$c_s/(c_1 - c_q)$ is at a maximum when $s = 2$ (i.e. the lowest possible value of s), so 'co-operate' must be the best move if

$$\pi > \frac{c_2}{c_1 - c_q} \tag{7A.3}$$

This must be the case if π is sufficiently close to 1. From now on I shall assume that (7A.3) holds.

Finally, consider case 4. In this case you know that the player(s) who is(are) not in good standing will co-operate in round i, so you will receive the benefit v whether you co-operate or not. Since R_1 does not require you to co-operate, you will retain your good standing even if you defect in round i; thus your best move is to defect.

So to sum up, in cases 1, 2, and 3 your best move in round i is 'co-operate'; in case 4, your best move is 'defect'. This is exactly what is prescribed by R_1. Therefore R_1 is the unique best reply to itself: it is a stable equilibrium strategy. This, of course, is conditional on the value of π being sufficiently high, as defined by (7A.1)–(7A.3). Since $c_2 \geqslant c_q$, these conditions may be compressed into the single condition

$$\pi > \max\left[\frac{c_q}{v}, \frac{c_2}{c_1 - c_q}, \frac{c_1 - v}{c_1 - c_q}\right] \tag{7A.4}$$

It is a special case of this proof that the strategy of licensed free riding is a stable equilibrium for the (extended) snowdrift game. It is also a special case of this proof that the tit-for-tat strategy T_1 is a stable equilibrium for the (extended) snowdrift game and for the (extended) prisoner's dilemma game. For the snowdrift game, $q = 2$ and $v > c_1$, so the restriction on π that makes T_1 a stable equilibrium strategy is

$$\pi > \max\left[\frac{c_2}{v}, \frac{c_2}{c_1 - c_2}\right]$$

This is the result I stated in Section 7.3. For the prisoner's dilemma game, $q = 2$ and $c_1 > v$, so the restriction is

$$\pi > \max\left[\frac{c_2}{v}, \frac{c_2}{c_1 - c_2}, \frac{c_1 - v}{c_1 - c_2}\right]$$

We may reproduce the exchange-visit version of the prisoner's dilemma game – the version set out in Figure 6.1 and discussed in Chapter 6 – by substituting $v = b, c_1 = b + c$ and $c_2 = c$. Then the restriction on π reduces to $\pi > c/b$, the result proved in Sections 6.2–6.3.

8
Natural Law

8.1 Conventions as natural law

In the preceding chapters I have shown how social life can be regulated by rules that evolve spontaneously and that, once established, are self-enforcing. These rules are conventions.

The conventions I have analysed fall into three broad categories. The first of these is made up of conventions of coordination – the kinds of convention I examined in Chapter 3. These conventions evolve out of repeated play of games of pure coordination, like Schelling's rendezvous game, or out of games of the crossroads or 'leader' kind, in which the degree of conflict of interest between the players is relatively minor. Typical examples of these conventions in social life are: 'keep left' (or 'keep right') and 'give way' rules on the roads; the use of money; weights and measures; market-places and market days; and languages.

The second class of conventions is made up of what I shall call conventions of property – the kinds I examined in Chapters 4 and 5. These conventions evolve out of the repeated play of games of the hawk–dove or chicken kind, or related games such as the war of attrition and the division game. In all of these games there is a real conflict of interest between the players: they are in dispute over something that they all want, but all cannot have. This something may be a physical object, like the $20 bill of Friedman's example (Section 5.1), or an opportunity such as the use of a public telephone or a seat on a train, or the privilege of taking a free ride on other people's contributions towards the supply of a public good. Typical examples of these conventions in social life are: the 'finders keepers' rule; the principle of 'prescriptive rights' (i.e. the principle that a right can be established by long occupation or usage); the importance of 'custom and practice' in labour disputes; queues; and the principle that everyone is responsible for the tidiness of his own front garden.

The final class of conventions is made up of conventions of reciprocity – the kinds I examined in Chapters 6 and 7. These conventions evolve out of the repeated play of games of the exchange-visit or prisoner's dilemma kind, or related games like the mutual-aid, snow-drift and public-good games. In these games individuals choose between strategies of 'co-operation' and 'defection'; it is contrary to the immediate interest of an individual to choose 'co-operate' but by doing so he confers benefits on others. Conventions of reciprocity prescribe that individuals should co-operate with those people who co-operate with them – but not with others. Conventions of this kind can be found in practices of mutual restraint (I respect your interests if you respect mine), mutual aid (I help you when you need my help if you help me when I need yours), trade and exchange (I keep my promises if you keep yours), and contributions towards the supply of public goods (I contribute towards goods that benefit both of us if you contribute too).

These conventions regulate interactions between individuals in situations in which their interests are in conflict. (The conflict of interest is most obvious in the case of conventions of property and of reciprocity, but there is some conflict of interest in many of the games from which conventions of coordination evolve. Only in the special case of a pure coordination game do individuals have completely common interests.) Situations of conflict of interest are ones in which we typically invoke ideas of *justice*; in cases of serious conflict we may be able to appeal to the courts. Thus conventions fulfil some of the same functions as positive laws (that is, laws promulgated by some authority, such as Parliament or Congress or the King); but whereas positive laws are the product of conscious human design, these conventions have evolved spontaneously, out of the repeated interactions of individuals with conflicting interests. In this sense, conventions of coordination, property and reciprocity are natural laws.

In saying this I am – as in so much else – following Hume. The account I have given of the evolution of conventions is, I believe, essentially the same as Hume's account of the origin of justice – fleshed out with more details and formulated in game-theoretic terms. Hume argues that justice is a virtue 'that produce(s) pleasure and approbation by means of an artifice or contrivance, which arises from the circumstances and necessities of mankind' (1740, Book 3, Part 2, Section 1), by which he seems to mean that principles of justice are social conventions: our sense of justice is not innate in the way that our 'natural affections' (such as our feelings towards our own children) are. Hume's way of putting this is to say that justice is an 'artificial' rather than 'natural' virtue. But:

> when I deny justice to be a natural virtue, I make use of the word, *natural*, only as oppos'd to *artificial*. In another sense of the word; as no principle of the human mind is more natural than a sense of virtue; so no virtue is more natural than justice. Mankind is an inventive species; and where an invention is obvious and absolutely necessary, it may as properly be said to be natural as any thing that proceeds immediately from original principles, without the intervention of thought or reflexion. Tho' the rules of justice be *artificial*, they are not *arbitrary*. Nor is the expression improper to call them *Laws of Nature* ... (1740, Book 3, Part 2, Section 1)

Notice that for Hume justice is a *virtue*. Our sense of justice has evolved out of repeated interactions between individuals pursuing their own interests; but it is a *moral* sense: we believe we *ought* to keep to the 'Laws of Nature'. In Hume's words, we 'annex the idea of virtue to justice' (1740, Book 3, Part 2, Section 2).

In this respect Hume's conception of natural law should be distinguished from another conception that has been much discussed by political theorists – that of Thomas Hobbes's *Leviathan* (1651). Hobbes starts unashamedly from each individual's pursuit of his own interests. Natural law, for Hobbes, is a system of rules that it is in each individual's interest to follow – and nothing more. So far, I must concede, my approach has been essentially Hobbesian. Conventions, I have argued, are stable because once they have become established, it is in everyone's interest to keep to them. I have been more optimistic than Hobbes about the possibilities for co-operation in a state of nature, but my starting point has been the same as his. (The similarities between Hobbes's theory and those presented in this book are explored in an appendix.) However, I now wish to follow Hume in suggesting that natural laws can come to have moral force for us. Let me make it clear that I am not presenting a moral argument: I am not going to argue that we ought to behave according to natural law. What I am going to argue is that we tend to believe that we ought to.

8.2 Breaches of conventions

On a strict application of my definition of 'convention' (Section 2.8), it can never be in a person's interest to behave contrary to a convention, provided he can be sure that other people will abide by it. Nevertheless, people sometimes *do* behave contrary to the sort of practical rules that I have claimed are conventions.

One reason for this is that people can make mistakes. Conventions have to be *learned*, and a person may fail to grasp the principles of a convention, or interpret it incorrectly (i.e. unconventionally) in a particular case. For example, there may be a convention that disputes over resources are resolved in favour of the possessor; but it is not always clear which disputant is the possessor. (Compare the discussion of mistakes in Section 4.7.) This problem may be compounded by wishful thinking.[1] If, according to established convention, I am the challenger, it is not in my interest to act as though I were the possessor; but I still wish the convention made me the possessor. It is a human weakness to allow our judgements about what really *is* the case to be confused by our thoughts about what we should *like* to be the case. We may also be absent-minded and behave in ways that we would not have done, had we thought carefully first. (We all occasionally break the conventions of the roads through absent-mindedness.)

A second reason is that people can suffer from weakness of will, and yield to temptations to act in ways they know to be contrary to their long-term interests. For example, in the extended prisoner's dilemma game it is in each player's short-term interest to defect: this gives the best outcome in the round in which a player first defects. If a tit-for-tat convention is established, the defector will be punished in the next round, provided the game does not come to an end first; taking a long-term view, defection does not pay. Nevertheless, there is a temptation to go for the immediate benefit that comes from defection.

A third reason is that it sometimes *is* in a person's interest to break the kind of rules that I have described as conventions. Take, for example, a 'give way' convention at a crossroads. If I am driving a large car and you are riding a bicycle, and if it is clear that you have seen me and have time to stop, it may be in my interests to pull out in front of you, even if there is an established rule that you have the right of way. Or take the case of a convention of mutual restraint between neighbours. Normally it pays me not to annoy my neighbours too much because if I do, they may retaliate; but if I am about to move house, it may no longer be in my interest to show restraint.

That such cases can arise reflects the fact that the games I have been analysing are no more than models of real life; equally, the theoretical definition of a convention as a certain kind of equilibrium strategy in a game is only a model of the practical rules that in ordinary speech would be called conventions. For the purposes of theory, it is convenient to use a single matrix of utilities to describe a whole class of interactions, such as all cases in which two vehicles meet at a crossroads, or all cases of disputes between neighbours. Nevertheless, such a matrix can represent only some kind of average of many matrices, each slightly different from every other. A convention, then, is a rule that, in the typical case, is a stable equilibrium – that it is in each player's interest to follow, provided that his opponents follow it too. But there can be atypical cases in which it is in a player's interest to break the convention, even if his opponents do not.

If we take a Hobbesian approach we shall say that the first two kinds of breaches of conventions – those arising out of mistakes and weakness of will – generate their own punishment. Thus although natural law will sometimes be broken, there will be a strong *tendency* for it to be kept. But the Hobbesian response to the third kind of breach must, I think, be that in these atypical cases conventions *will* be broken. Or, more accurately, it must be that maxims like 'Give way to the vehicle on the right' and 'Show restraint towards neighbours who show restraint towards you' are only rules of thumb. If natural law is no more than a system of rules for promoting an individual's own interest, then a fuller specification of the appropriate rules would be something more like 'Give way to the vehicle on the right – unless you are sure you can get away with not doing so' and 'Show restraint to neighbours who show restraint towards you – unless you are sure they cannot retaliate if you annoy them.'

I wish to suggest, however, that this is *not* how we typically think of the conventions that regulate social life. When we meet people who break conventions through carelessness or stupidity or weakness of will, we are not content to let them go to the devil in their own way; if their behaviour harms us we feel resentment and anger; we believe that we have been wronged. (Suppose you are driving along a British road and narrowly avoid a collision with a car that is being driven on the right-hand side of the road. Perhaps the driver is drunk, or perhaps he is an absent-minded French tourist. How would *you* react?)

Further, we recognize that conventions are rules that apply to the atypical as well as the typical cases. It is usually in our interest to follow these rules; but even if it is not, we still believe that we ought to follow them. And if we meet with opponents who break these rules we believe we have been wronged – even if we know that those opponents were acting in their own interests. (Suppose you are travelling on a crowded train, and you leave your seat to go to the lavatory. Following the usual practice, you leave a coat on the seat to mark it as yours. When you return you find the coat has been moved on to the luggage rack and a hefty young man has taken your seat. Don't you feel some sense of resentment against the man who has taken your seat, some sense that he has not merely *harmed* you but *wronged* you?)

The point of these examples is that conventions of the kind I have analysed in this book are maintained by something more than the interest that each individual has in keeping to them – most of the time. We expect that our dealings with other people will be regulated by convention, but this expectation is more than a judgement of fact: we feel *entitled* to expect others to follow conventions when they deal with us, and we recognize that they are entitled to expect the same of us. In other words, conventions are often also norms, or, to use Hume's expression, principles of natural law.

8.3   Why other people's expectations matter to us

Suppose you want me to perform some action X. You also have a confident expectation, based on your experience of other people's behaviour in similar circumstances, that I will do X. In the event I do something else, leaving you worse off than you had expected to be. Then you will probably feel some resentment against me.

In order to explain this sense of resentment, I suggest, it is not necessary to call on any sophisticated moral theory. You had expected me to do X; other people, in my situation, would have done X; my not doing X has hurt you. In these circumstances resentment is a primitive human response.

It is another natural human response to feel uneasy about being the focus of another person's resentment. Because of this, our actions – and our evaluations of our actions – are influenced by other people's expectations of us. We can probably all remember foolish actions – actions that we knew to be foolish at the time – that we did merely because other people wanted us to do them and expected us to do them. Curiously, we can be motivated by what we take to be other people's expectations about us even when those other people are total strangers, and when there seems to be no solid reason for us to care about their opinions of us.

Suppose you are driving a car and waiting to pull out into a main road. It is difficult to find a gap in the traffic and you have waited some time. A queue of vehicles has built up behind you. Doesn't the mere presence of these other vehicles, with drivers who are waiting for you to pull out, put psychological pressure on you? I can only record my own response to this sort of situation. I know that the drivers behind will never remember me, even if we do happen to meet again, so there is no way they can reward me for acting in their interests or punish me for not doing so. (Thus the relationship between them and me is not like those of the games that generate conventions of mutual assistance.) But at the time it does seem to matter what the driver behind thinks of me. I know he wants me to pull out as quickly as possible; I know he has expectations about normal driving behaviour; and because of this I feel under some kind of pressure not to behave in a way that he might judge over-cautious.

Here is another example. Suppose you take a taxi ride. You know it is normal to give the driver a tip, but you have reached your destination safely and you can be as good as sure that you will have no more dealings with this particular driver. (Perhaps you are a tourist in a city to which you do not expect to return.) In any case, the driver is unlikely to remember your face. So, in the ordinary sense of the words, it is not in your interest to give a tip. Nevertheless, many people do tip in circumstances like these; others (and here, I regret to confess, I speak also from personal experience) keep their hands in their pockets – but with sensations of unease and guilt. It is one thing to adopt a policy of not tipping, and another thing to carry it off with panache. Why isn't it *easy* for us not to tip? A large part of the answer, I suggest, is that it matters to us what the taxi-driver thinks of us. We know he wants a tip. We know he expects a tip. We know that he knows that we know he expects one. If we don't tip we shall be the focus of his ill-will, if only for a few minutes. Admittedly, there is very little he can do to us; the worst we can expect is a sarcastic remark. But isn't the mere knowledge of his ill-will towards us a source of unease?

In each of these examples it is important that the other person not only *wants* us to do something but also *expects* us to do it; and his expectation is based on his experience of what other people normally do. If we were motivated simply by a desire that other people's wants should be satisfied – that is, by altruism – their expectations would not matter to us. But in these kinds of cases expectations do matter. We feel under pressure not to slow down other road users by driving in unusual ways, but we do not feel under the same kind of pressure to speed them along by showing them unexpected degrees of courtesy. We don't feel under pressure to give the taxi-driver a bigger tip than we think he expects. No doubt bus-drivers are as much in need of extra income as taxi-drivers, but we don't feel under pressure to tip them.

In the examples I have given, the people whose opinions of us matter to us are, in the game-theoretic sense, our opponents: they are people whose interests are directly affected by our actions. But theirs are not the only opinions that matter to us. When we play a game we also care about the opinions of third parties – people with no direct interest in the game, but who happen to observe it, or who are told about it afterwards. This is evident from the impulse we seem to feel, when engaged in any quarrel, to appeal to others to take our part. When we have been – as we see it – wronged, we want our interpretation of events to be confirmed by others. Even though other people may be unable to give us material help, we want them to share our resentments.

One consequence of this was noted by Adam Smith with his usual realism:

> we are not half so anxious that our friends should adopt our friend-ships, as that they should enter into our resentments. We can forgive them though they seem to be little affected with the favours which we may have received, but lose all patience if they seem to be indif-ferent about the injuries which may have been done to us: nor are we half so angry with them for not entering into our gratitude, as for not sympathizing with our resentment. (1759, Part 1, Section 1, Ch. 2)

We can take more satisfaction in our resentments when other people share them. (This is one instance of what Smith called the 'pleasure of mutual sympathy'.) Because of this, we are more prone to express – and indeed to cultivate – feelings of resentment, the more confident we are that other people regard us as in the right. Conversely, our unease at being the focus of one person's ill-will is compounded if that person has the sympathy of others. (Suppose you go back to a shop to complain about the quality of some goods you have bought. The manager is called and he refuses your demand for a refund. Aren't you emboldened if you sense that other customers in the shop are taking your side? And don't you feel under more pressure to back down if instead they seem to be on the manager's side?)

So other people's expectations of us do matter. They matter because we care what other people think of us. Our desire to keep the good will of others – not merely of our friends, but even of strangers – is more than a means to some other end. It seems to be a basic human desire. That we have such a desire is presumably the product of biological evol-ution. We are social animals, biologically fitted to live in communities. Some in-built tendency to accommodate oneself to others – some nat-ural inclination to what Hobbes called 'complaisance'[2] – must surely be an aid to survival for a social animal.

It might be objected that all this has nothing to do with morality. That the taxi-driver expects me to tip him, that he wants me to tip him, that he would resent my not tipping him, that other people's sympathies would be on his side if I didn't tip him, that I should be uneasy at being the focus of this resentment and ill-will – these propositions may all be true, but can they entail that I *ought* to give a tip? If this is a question about the logic of moral propositions, then the answer must be 'No'. 'Ought' statements cannot be derived from 'is' statements by any logically valid chain of reasoning: this is Hume's Law,[3] which I have no intention of questioning. There would be nothing self-contradictory in saying: 'I know the taxi-driver expects to be tipped, I know he wants to be tipped, etc., but I have no moral obligation to tip him.'

But my argument is not about the logic of moral propositions; it is about the psychology of morals. It is a matter of common experience, I suggest, that we are strongly inclined to believe that we ought to do what other people want and expect us to do; when we go against other people's wants and expectations, we are inclined to feel guilt. Any plausible theory of moral learning – of how we judge some things right and others wrong – would surely have to assign a good deal of importance to praise and blame. We learn to think wrong those actions that other people censure. That other people censure them does not *make* them wrong; but it is a powerful force influencing us to *judge* them wrong.

Some readers, I suspect, will still object that I am misusing the terms 'right' and 'wrong', 'praise' and 'blame'. The psychological urge we feel to meet other people's wants and expectations, the objection would run, may be real enough; but it is an improper use of words to describe this urge as a sense of moral obligation. Equally, it might be said, it is improper to describe the resentment we feel when other people frustrate our expectations as moral censure, or to describe our pain at being the subject of such resentment as a sense of guilt. If I am to answer this objection I must make clear what I mean when I use words like 'right' and 'wrong'.

My position is a Humean one. The famous passage in which Hume presents what has come to be called his 'law' is part of a section headed 'Moral Distinctions not deriv'd from Reason'. He presents the following argument in support of his 'law':

> But can there be any difficulty in proving, that vice and virtue are not matters of fact, whose existence we can infer by reason? Take any action allow'd to be vicious: Wilful murder, for instance. Examine it in all lights, and see if you can find that matter of fact, or real existence,

which you call *vice*. In which-ever way you take it, you find only certain passions, motives, volitions and thoughts. There is no other matter of fact in the case. The vice entirely escapes you, as long as you consider the object. You never can find it, till you turn your reflexion into your own breast, and find a sentiment of disapprobation, which arises in you, towards this action. Here is a matter of fact; but 'tis the object of feeling, not of reason. It lies in yourself, not in the object. So that when you pronounce any action or character to be vicious, you mean nothing, but that from the constitution of your nature you have a feeling or sentiment of blame from the contemplation of it. (1740, Book 3, Part 1, Section 1)

One implication of this position – which is fairly conventional among economists, if not among philosophers – is that moral propositions can be derived only from other moral propositions. A person's moral beliefs must therefore include some beliefs that cannot be justified by any appeal to reason or evidence. Following Sen (1970, pp. 59–64), economists often call these non-justifiable beliefs 'basic value judgements'. If we want to explain why a person subscribes to one basic value judgement rather than another, we cannot use *moral* reasoning. (We cannot say that the reason why we tend to believe that killing people is wrong is because killing people *is* wrong.) The explanation must be a psychological one: as Hume put it, we must look to the constitution of human nature.

Does this mean that a moral judgement is no more than a personal preference? No, because a moral judgement is a statement of *approval* or *disapproval*, and this is not the same thing as a like or dislike. And moral judgements are more than bald reports of sensations of approval or disapproval. Hume put it like this:

The approbation of moral qualities most certainly is not deriv'd from reason, or any comparison of ideas; but proceeds entirely from a moral taste, and from certain sentiments of pleasure or disgust, which arise upon the contemplation and view of particular qualities or characters. Now 'tis evident, that those sentiments, whence-ever they are deriv'd, must vary according to the distance or contiguity of the objects; nor can I feel the same lively pleasure from the virtues of a person, who liv'd in *Greece* two thousand years ago, that I feel from the virtues of a familiar friend and acquaintance. Yet I do not say, that I esteem the one more than the other.... Our situation, with regard both to persons and things, is in continual fluctuation... and 'tis impossible we cou'd ever converse together on any reasonable terms, were each of us to consider characters and persons, only as they appear from his peculiar point of view. In order, therefore, to prevent those continual *contradictions*, and arrive at a more *stable* judgement of things, we fix on some *steady* and *general* points of view; and always, in our thoughts, place ourselves in them, whatever may be our present situation. (1740, Book 3, Part 3, Section 1)

In other words, it is a *convention of language* that moral judgements are invariant with respect to changes in viewpoint. I stress 'convention of language' because this is not a hypothesis about human psychology. We are naturally inclined to disapprove more strongly of actions, the more their ill-effects impinge on us; but we use moral language to express our general disapproval of *classes* of actions. Moral judgements are in this sense universalizable.[4]

My position is that any universalizable statement of approval or disapproval is a moral judgement. Suppose there is some established convention that anyone in a particular situation should behave in a particular way, for example the convention that queues should be respected. Suppose that I should feel a strong sense of disapproval if you pushed past me in a queue. Suppose also that if I, as a bystander, saw you push past someone else in a queue, I should still disapprove, even if my resentment against you would be less lively than in the first case. Finally suppose that if *I* pushed past *you* in a queue, I should feel some degree of guilt, that is, I should not altogether approve of my own action. Then my disapproval of queue-jumping is universalizable: it is, on my account, a moral judgement.

8.4 Conventions, interests and expectations

It is in the nature of an established convention that everyone *expects* everyone else to keep it. Is it also in everyone's *interest* that everyone else keeps to it? If it is, then we should expect breaches of conventions to provoke general resentment and censure; and this will predispose people to the moral judgement that conventions ought to be kept.

I shall now examine the extent to which it is in one individual's interest for other individuals to follow conventions. I shall consider these conventions in their pure forms, that is, as equilibrium strategies in 'typical case' games. Strictly speaking, then, my arguments will apply only to those breaches of conventions that arise out of mistakes and weakness of will. I am inclined to think that my conclusions will carry over to most of the atypical cases in which it is in an individual's interest to behave contrary to convention, but I cannot prove this. (A proof would require a catalogue of all the atypical forms that the various games could take, and an analysis of each; this would be a huge task.) I shall argue that conventions are normally maintained by *both* interest *and* morality: it pays us to keep to conventions and we believe we ought to keep to them. If this belt-and-braces conclusion is correct, then it is at least plausible to suppose that morality may sometimes motivate us to behave according to natural law even when interest does not.

The question, 'Is it in one person's interest that other people follow a convention?' can be posed in various ways; but if we are concerned with the possibility that breaches of conventions will provoke resentment, the most obvious question to ask seems to be this: 'If one individual follows a convention, is it in his interests that his opponents follow it?'.

The connection between this question and the possibility that people will resent breaches of convention *by their opponents* is obvious enough. If a convention is established, each individual will expect his opponents to follow it. Because he has this expectation, it is in his interests to follow it himself. Then if the answer to my question is 'Yes', each individual will not only *expect* his opponents to follow the convention; he will also *want* them to. Resentment in the face of breaches of the convention would be a natural response.

What about the responses of bystanders? In what sense can anyone have an interest in whether or not other people keep to a convention in a game in which he is not involved? The most obvious answer seems to be this. If the bystander is a member of the community within which the game is played, then the individuals whom he observes may be his opponents in future games. Thus the bystander's interest in the behaviour of other people is the interest of a potential opponent. Take an example. Suppose you are driving along a British road, and see two drivers, A and B, narrowly miss an accident. The cause of the problem was that A was driving on the left while B was driving on the right. It will surely occur to you that B and drivers like him are a threat, not just to A, but *to you*. So you have some cause for resentment against B, which will predispose you to take A's side. This brings us back to the question, 'If one individual follows a convention, is it in his interests that his opponents follow it?' If, for a given convention, the answer is 'Yes', then breaches of the convention are likely to provoke *general* resentment – from bystanders as well as from opponents.

However, *is* the answer to this question 'Yes'? There is nothing in my definition of 'convention' that entails that everyone wants his opponent to follow an established convention (although this *is* entailed by David

Lewis's definition: cf. Section 2.8). I shall therefore consider in turn the three kinds of convention I have investigated in this book.

Conventions of coordination

The crossroads game (or leader game) is typical of the games from which conventions of coordination evolve. As a typical convention, consider the rule 'Give way to vehicles approaching from the right' in the crossroads game. It is easy to see that an individual who follows this convention has an interest in his opponents doing the same. This is true even if the convention favours the opponent. If you are approaching from my right, then the convention of 'priority to the right' favours you; in this instance, at least, I should prefer the convention to be 'priority to the left'. Nevertheless, it is in my interest to slow down, because I expect you to follow the established convention; and because I shall slow down, it is in my interest that you maintain speed. In other words, I want you to follow the convention that has actually become established, even though I may wish we all followed some other convention.

This example may seem slightly artificial, because it is in the nature of a convention that it applies to a wide class of cases, and *in the long run* the rule of 'priority to the right' does not seem to favour anyone relative to anyone else. But consider the convention 'Cars give way to buses'. (Clearly this rule would resolve only some instances of the crossroads game, but for games involving a car and a bus it is a perfectly workable convention. Compare the old nautical rule 'Steam gives way to sail'.) If I am a car driver who never travels by bus, this convention favours my opponent in every game to which it applies; taking a long-run view, then, I should certainly prefer the opposite convention to be established. But even so, if 'Cars give way to buses' is the established convention, I do not want *individual* bus drivers to try to give way to cars.

There is, however, one significant difference between 'Priority to the right' and 'Cars give way to buses.' Notice that they are both asymmetrical conventions – that is, they both exploit some asymmetry between the roles of the two players in a game. (In contrast, 'Keep left' as a convention for dealing with cases where two vehicles approach one another head-on is a symmetrical convention.) But 'Priority to the right' exploits what I shall call a cross-cutting asymmetry. By this I mean that in the community of players of the crossroads game, each individual will sometimes find himself on one side of the asymmetry and sometimes on the other. (If, as is surely true in the case of 'Priority to the right', each individual has *the same* probability of being assigned each role as every other individual has, I shall say that the asymmetry is perfectly cross-cutting.)

In contrast, the asymmetry exploited by 'Cars give way to buses' is *not* cross-cutting: there are many car drivers who never drive or ride in buses and perhaps a few bus drivers who never have anything to do with cars.

This distinction is significant because of its implications for third parties. If a convention of coordination exploits a cross-cutting asymmetry, *everyone* stands to be harmed by the existence of mavericks who break the convention. (Suppose the established convention is 'Priority to the right'. My friend tells me that *he* never bothers about this convention, but instead always tries to force the other driver to slow down. It is bound to occur to me that some day I might meet a fool like him approaching from my left.) In contrast, if a convention exploits an asymmetry that is *not* cross-cutting, there are at least some people who can never meet one another as opponents in games to which the convention applies. Such people may be more inclined to make light of one another's breaches of conventions.

To sum up, then, provided an established convention exploits a cross-cutting asymmetry, everyone has an interest in everyone else's keeping to it. This is true even if some people (or even if everyone) would prefer a different convention to have become established. This suggests that conventions of coordination are likely to acquire moral force: they are likely to become norms, or principles of natural law.

Conventions of property

The hawk–dove or chicken game is typical of the games from which conventions of property evolve. As a typical convention, consider the rule: 'If possessor, play "hawk"; if challenger, play "dove" '. This, like most conventions of property,[5] is asymmetrical. In most practical cases, the asymmetry between possessor and challenger is cross-cutting: everyone is the possessor in *some* conflicts. In some cases this cross-cutting is close to perfect – consider the convention of queueing, or the convention that a passenger on a train may reserve his seat by leaving his coat on it. In other cases it is not – consider the principle of prescriptive rights, which systematically favours those who have been most successful in holding on to valuable resources in the past, or who are lucky enough to have the right kind of ancestors. But for the argument that follows, all that matters is that conventions of property exploit asymmetries that are *to some degree* cross-cutting.

Suppose some individual follows the convention: 'If possessor, play "hawk"; if challenger, play "dove" '. Is it in his interests that his opponents follow it too? This clearly depends on the individual's role in a game. When he is the possessor it is in his interests that his opponent follows the convention: if someone commits himself to fighting, he wants his opponent to back down. Equally obviously, when an individual is the challenger, it is *not* in his interests that his opponent follows the convention: he is ready to back down in the face of aggression, but doesn't *want* to meet aggression. Similar conclusions apply to the division game and the war of attrition.

In all these games of property, strategies vary in their degrees of aggression – whether this is represented by the difference between 'dove' and 'hawk', by the amount of a disputed resource that is claimed, or by the length of time a player is prepared to fight before surrendering. Conventions prescribe appropriate degrees of aggression for each player. It is characteristic of all these games that each player prefers that his opponent should be less aggressive rather than more. (There are some cases in which a player may be indifferent about his opponent's degree of aggression, at least within some range; but there are no cases in which a player would positively prefer greater aggression by his opponent.) Thus if an individual follows a convention, he wants his opponent's behaviour to be no more aggressive than the convention prescribes.

This suggests that conventions of property are likely to be associated with norms forbidding excessive aggression: people will tend to believe that it is wrong for anyone to press a claim that is not supported by convention. In contrast, unconventional meekness – as prescribed, for example, by the Christian ethic of turning the other cheek – seems less likely to provoke moral censure.[6] Of course, this is not to say that we should expect to find much in the way of Christian meekness, since it is highly *imprudent* to be less aggressive than an established convention allows one to be.

Notice that a convention of property may become a generally accepted norm even though it cannot be justified in terms of any external standard of fairness. Having become a norm, a convention *becomes* a standard of fairness; but, on my account, it does not become a norm *because* it is seen to be fair. Equally, a person may believe that everyone ought to follow an established convention even though that convention systematically favours others at his expense. For example, suppose there is an established convention that each person retains possession of those things he has possessed in the past. The corresponding norm against over-aggression is the Old Testament one: 'Thou shalt not steal.' Clearly, this convention favours some people much more than others. Those who start out in life possessing relatively little would much prefer many other conventions – for example, a convention of equal division – to the one that has become established. Nevertheless, it is in each individual's interest to follow the established convention, given that almost everyone else does. And once a person has resolved to follow the convention, his interests are threatened by the existence of mavericks who are aggressive when the convention prescribes submission. Or in plainer English: provided I own *something*, thieves are a threat to me. So even if the conventions of property tend to favour others relative to me, I am not inclined to applaud theft.

Conventions of reciprocity

The extended exchange-visit or prisoner's dilemma game is typical of the games from which conventions of reciprocity evolve. As a typical convention, consider the tit-for-tat convention I called T_1 (Sections 6.2–6.3). Recall that this convention is defined for an extended game in which players occasionally make mistakes. T_1 is a symmetrical convention prescribing that each player should co-operate as long as his opponent co-operates, and should punish to a prescribed degree an opponent who defects in breach of the convention. It also prescribes that a player who defects by mistake should accept his punishment and not retaliate. Suppose that some individual A follows this convention. Is it in his interests that his opponents do the same?

Suppose that A follows the convention T_1 in a game against B, and suppose that A never makes a mistake. How will he want B to behave? One feature of T_1 is that, although the punishment prescribed for breaches of the convention is enough to deter deliberate defections, it is not enough to make full reparation to the injured party. This reflects the fact that T_1 is the most 'forgiving' tit-for-tat strategy that is capable of constituting a stable equilibrium (Section 6.3). Thus if A follows T_1 he will not want B to defect in breach of the convention; even if B were then to accept his punishment without retaliating, A would still be left worse off than if there had been no breach. But if B *does* defect, it is in A's interest that B should not retaliate when A punishes him. So if A follows T_1 without making mistakes, it is in his interest that B should do the same; and if B does make a mistake, it is in A's interest that B should continue the game in the way prescribed by T_1.

What if A tries to follow T_1 but defects by mistake? Suppose that in some round i, T_1 prescribes co-operation for A, but he defects; B co-operates. Then, following T_1, A will co-operate in round $i + 1$; and, irrespective of what B does in round $i + 1$; A will co-operate in round $i + 2$. (In other words, if B defects in round $i + 1$, A will accept this as a legitimate punishment and not retaliate.) If B follows T_1 he *will* defect in round $i + 1$; he will punish A for his defection. But A does not want to be punished; he would prefer it if B co-operated. So in this case, but only in this case, A would prefer B not to keep to the convention.

To sum up: if an individual follows a convention of reciprocity, he wants his opponents to be no less co-operative than the convention prescribes. This suggests that conventions of reciprocity are likely to be associated with norms forbidding non-co-operative behaviour in situations in which the convention calls for co-operation. In other words, people are likely to subscribe to an ethic of reciprocity, according to which each person ought to co-operate with those who are prepared to co-operate with him.

Earlier in this section I suggested that our sense of morality may sometimes motivate us to follow the dictates of natural law even when it is contrary to our interests to do so. Clashes between interest and morality seem particulary likely to occur in cases where public goods can be supplied only through the voluntary sacrifices of many individuals. From our experience of playing the public-good game in small groups – within the family, among neighbours and friends and workmates – we learn that there are established conventions of reciprocity and that it is generally in our interest to follow them. Around these conventions a system of morality grows up; we come to recognize a moral obligation to play our part in co-operative arrangements and learn to condemn those who try to take free rides on other people's efforts. When we play the public good game in large groups, however, we find that conventions of reciprocity are fragile. It is often *not* in our interests to be co-operative: free riding often pays. But we may still feel the force of the ethic of reciprocity. We may still believe that we *ought* to shoulder our share of the costs of co-operative arrangements – that if others are doing their part, we ought to do ours. It is because we subscribe to some such ethic, I suggest, that even within large groups public goods are sometimes supplied through voluntary contributions.[7]

8.A Appendix: reciprocity in Hobbes's theory of natural law

Hobbes's theory, as set out in *Leviathan* (1651), begins with the following definition:

> A LAW OF NATURE, *lex naturalis*, is a precept or general rule, found out by reason, by which a man is forbidden to do that, which is destructive of his life, or taketh away the means of preserving the same; and to omit that, by which he thinketh it may be best preserved. (Ch. 14)

For Hobbes, then, natural law is sheer prudence. Men are basically self-interested; natural laws are answers to the question, 'How best can I promote my self-interest?' or – since Hobbes always emphasizes the dangers men face from one another – 'How best can I ensure my survival in a dangerous world?'. My starting-point – which I think is broadly in line with Hume's – is not dissimilar to this. I have not gone so far as Hobbes in assuming individuals to be selfish; I have assumed only that they have *conflicting* interests (Section 2.3). But I have assumed that each individual is concerned only with promoting *his own* interests (whether selfish or not: my interest in my son's welfare is not selfish, but it is *my* interest). The conventions of coordination, property and reciprocity that I have called natural laws are grounded in each individual's pursuit of his own interests; they are answers to the question, 'How best can I promote my interests in a world in which other people are promoting theirs?'.

Notice, however, that Hobbes's natural laws are found out by reason. The idea seems to be that natural laws can be *deduced* by a chain of logic from a few self-evident first principles. This is in marked contrast to Hume's idea that natural laws *evolve* and are *learned by experience*. If natural laws can be found out by reason, then presumably there is a unique code of natural law that can be discovered by any rational person in any society. This leaves no room for the possibility that some natural laws might be conventions – rules that have evolved in particular forms in particular societies, but that might have evolved otherwise.

So much for what Hobbes *means* by natural law. What about its *content*? Hobbes formulates no fewer than nineteen laws of nature, but the core of his system seems to be contained in his first three laws. The first law of nature is that every man should 'seek peace, and follow it'; this is presented as part of a more comprehensive rule:

> it is a precept, or general rule of reason, *that every man, ought to endeav-our peace, as far as he has hope of obtaining it; and when he cannot obtain it, that he may seek, and use, all helps, and advantages of war.* (Hobbes, 1651, Ch. 14)

In the state of nature – that is, in a society without government – no man has any hope of obtaining peace; and so, in accordance with Hobbes's 'general rule of reason', there is a state of war of all against all: every man, Hobbes says, has a right to every thing. The second law of nature expands on the precept that every man ought to endeavour towards peace. This law is:

> that a man be willing, when others are so too, as far-forth, as for peace, and defence of himself he shall think it necessary, to lay down this right to all things; and be contented with so much liberty against other men, as he would allow other men against himself. (Hobbes, 1651, Ch. 14)

This requires that men be willing to make covenants with one another; if these covenants are to be more than empty words, there must be a third law of nature: *'that men perform their covenants made'*. This law is 'the fountain and original of JUSTICE' (Ch. 15). But in the state of nature this law has little force, because:

> If a covenant be made, wherein neither of the parties perform presently, but trust one another; in the condition of mere nature, which is a condition of war of every man against every man, upon any reasonable suspicion, it is void: but if there be a common power set over them both, with right and force sufficient to compel performance, it is not void. For he that performeth first, has no assurance the other will perform after . . . . And therefore he which performeth first, does but betray himself to his enemy; contrary to the right, he can never abandon, of defending his life, and means of living. (Hobbes, 1651, Ch. 14)

Hobbes is describing a problem whose structure seems rather like that of the prisoner's dilemma game – and particularly like the version of that game that I called the trading game (Section 6.1; see also Taylor, 1976, pp. 101–11). In the state of nature, two or more people may be able to benefit from some agreement – provided that all the parties to the agreement keep it. But each party is tempted to make the agreement and then break it, in the hope that the others will still keep to it. Since everyone knows that everyone else is tempted in this way, no one can trust anyone else to keep an agreement; and so agreements can never be made. This problem stands in the way of any escape from the war of all against all, since the only way to achieve peace – which everyone prefers to war – is by an agreement to cease fighting.

Contrary to my arguments in this book, Hobbes seems to be claiming that this problem has no solution *within the state of nature;* agreements can be made only if there is a 'common power' set over all individuals with sufficient force to compel them to keep agreements. This is why, according to Hobbes, everyone will agree to subject himself to some sovereign power, provided that everyone else does the same; once this agreement has been made, the state of nature is at an end.

For my point of view, however, what is most interesting about Hobbes's laws of nature is that their central principle seems to be reciprocity. Each person must 'endeavour peace, as far as he has hope of obtaining it'; as the second law of nature makes clear, this means that each must be prepared to make peace provided that everyone else makes peace too. Similarly, each person must keep his part of any agreement he has made, provided that the other parties to the agreement keep theirs. To aim for more than this – to refuse to make peace even though everyone else is willing, to break your side of an agreement even though you know the other side will be kept – is contrary to natural law. In other words, it is contrary to rational self-interest. As Hobbes puts it, 'justice [is] not contrary to reason' (1651, Ch. 15).

Hobbes takes the case of an agreement between two individuals, according to which one performs his part of the agreement before the other. (Compare Hume's case of the two farmers – see Section 6.1.) Suppose 'one of the parties has performed already'. Then:

there is the question whether it be against reason, that is, against the benefit of the other to perform, or not. And I say it is not against reason. For the manifestation whereof, we are to consider; first, that when a man doth a thing, which notwithstanding any thing can be foreseen, and reckoned on, tendeth to his own destruction, howsoever some accident which he could not expect, arriving may turn it to his benefit; yet such events do not make it reasonably or wisely done. Secondly, that in a condition of war, wherein every man to every man, for want of a common power to keep them all in awe, is an enemy, there is no man who can hope by his own strength, or wit, to defend himself from destruction, without the help of confederates; where every one expects the same defence by the confederation, that any one else does: and therefore he which declares he thinks it reason to deceive those that help him, can in reason expect no other means of safety, than what can be had from his own single power. He therefore that breaketh his covenant, and consequently declareth that he thinks he may with reason do so, cannot be received into any society, that unite themselves for peace and defence, but by the error of them that

receive him; nor when he is received, be retained in it, without seeing the danger of their error; which errors a man cannot reasonably
reckon upon as the means of his security.... (Hobbes, 1651, Ch. 15)

Hobbes's argument here seems rather like the game-theoretic arguments
I presented in Chapters 6 and 7, showing that strategies of reciprocity
can be stable equilibria. Hobbes is saying that in the state of nature
self-interest will lead each individual to follow the strategy: 'Keep agreements only with those who keep agreements with others.' (This seems
to amount to what I have called 'multilateral reciprocity' – compare the
mutual-aid game of Section 7.2.) It is in each individual's self-interest to
follow this strategy, provided everyone else does.

It seems that, after all, Hobbes recognizes that *some* agreements will
be made and kept in the state of nature. How else could men combine
into 'confederations' for self-defence? And Hobbes specifically mentions
the case of a 'covenant to pay a ransom ... to an enemy' which 'in the
condition of mere nature [is] obligatory' (1651, Ch. 14). These agreements work because self-interest leads everyone to follow a strategy of
reciprocity. However, Hobbes is extremely pessimistic about the *extent*
of co-operation that can be expected in the state of nature. Here I have
to confess that I cannot understand Hobbes's argument. He seems to be
saying that, although it is rational (i.e. in your self-interest) to perform
your part of an agreement if the other party has already performed, it is
not rational to perform first because you have no assurance that the other
party will perform after you. This seems inconsistent: if you know that
it is in the other party's interest to perform, why doesn't this give you
the assurance you need? Hobbes's picture of the state of nature seems
something like an extended prisoner's dilemma game in which everyone is following a strategy of cautious reciprocity; since no one is willing
to make the first move, no one ever co-operates. But if the analysis of
Section 6.4 is correct, this is not necessarily a stable equilibrium. In a
world of cautious reciprocators it may pay to be brave: it may be in each
individual's interest to make the first move. In other words, co-operation
can evolve in a Hobbesian state of nature.

9
Rights, Co-operation and Welfare

9.1 Sympathy and social welfare

If my argument so far is right, a rule is likely to acquire moral force if it satisfies two conditions:

1 Everyone (or almost everyone) in the relevant community follows the rule.
2 If any individual follows the rule, it is in his interest that his opponents – that is, the people with whom he deals – follow it too.

Any rule that is a convention necessarily satisfies a third condition:

3 Provided that his opponents follow the rule, it is in each individual's interest to follow it.

Notice that none of these conditions requires any comparison to be made between a world in which the rule is generally followed and one in which it is not. This leads to an implication that many will find surprising: a convention can acquire moral force without contributing to social welfare in any way.

Take, for example, those conventions of property that resolve disputes in favour of possessors. Such conventions, I have argued, are likely to become norms. Yet in many cases they maintain inequalities that seem arbitrary from any moral point of view (except, of course, a viewpoint that makes morality a matter of convention). The asymmetry between possessor and challenger tends to be prominent, unambiguous and cheat-proof, so we can easily understand how such a convention might have evolved; but there seems no good reason to expect that the distribution of property that it generates will be one that can be justified in terms of any coherent conception of social welfare.

It might be objected that although a convention favouring possessors is morally arbitrary, it is in everyone's interest that everyone follows *some convention or other*. Perhaps the established convention is not quite the best there could possibly be; but things would be much worse for everyone if there were no established convention at all. On this argument, conventions of property *do* contribute to social welfare, however arbitrary they may be. But is it true that conventions of property necessarily work to everyone's benefit?

The hawk–dove game provides a theoretical counter-example. Suppose there is an established convention that possessors play 'hawk' and that challengers play 'dove'. Then, using the utility indices I presented in Figure 4.1, possessors derive a utility of 2 from each game while challengers derive a utility of 0. So if a particular individual has a probability p of being the possessor in any game, the expected utility of each game for him is $2p$. What if instead there were no established convention at all? One way of representing such a state of affairs is as an equilibrium state of a *symmetrical* game. (Recall that this is how I modelled the Hobbesian state of nature.) The symmetrical hawk–dove game has a unique and stable equilibrium in which the probability that any player will play 'dove' is 0.67; this gives each individual an expected utility of 0.67 (Section 4.2). More pessimistically, we might represent the absence of any established convention by assuming that everyone chooses strategies entirely at random. If the probability that any player will play 'dove' is 0.5, the expected utility for each player is 0.25. In either event, a player with a sufficiently low – but still non-zero – value of p would be better off without the convention. In other words, a person who possesses relatively little might be better off taking his chances in a state of nature. Nevertheless, the convention that favours possessors may acquire moral force for *everyone* in the community, including those who would be better off without it.

This conclusion may be surprising, but the form of my argument is not new. Lewis argues that conventions of coordination[1] often become norms. He writes that if other people

> see me fail to conform [to a convention of coordination], not only have I gone against their expectations; they will probably be in a position to infer that I have knowingly acted contrary to my own preferences, and contrary to their preferences and their reasonable expectations. They will be surprised, and they will tend to explain my conduct discreditably. (1969, p. 99)

This is essentially the same kind of argument as I presented in Chapter 8; notice how it appeals to the fact that a convention of coordination satisfies the three conditions I have listed. However, the kinds of rules that Lewis considers can be said to serve everyone's interests. Lewis defines conventions as solutions (of a certain kind) to 'coordination problems'. These are games whose structure approximates to that of a pure coordination game. The players' main concern is to coordinate their strategies in some way or other; in *which* way they coordinate their strategies is a matter of relatively little importance to them (Lewis, 1969, pp. 5–24). Thus although individuals may have preferences between alternative conventions, each has a stronger interest that some convention becomes established rather than none. In this sense, at least, an established convention serves everyone's interests.

A similar argument can be found in Ullman-Margalit's *The Emergence of Norms* (1977, p. 88). Ullman-Margalit follows Lewis's argument very closely – as far as conventions of coordination are concerned. But, significantly, she is unwilling to apply to other kinds of games the same logic as she applies to coordination problems. She recognizes that rules of property can correspond with stable equilibrium strategies in games of conflict,[2] and that these rules can become norms; but her explanation of *how* these rules become 'norms of partiality' seems entirely separate from her earlier account of the evolution of 'coordination norms'. If I read her correctly, norms of partiality are supposed to come about because they fortify a discriminatory status quo and in doing so promote the interests of those who are favoured in that status quo (Ullman-Margalit, 1977, Ch. 4, especially pp. 173–97). The implication is that when a convention of property becomes a norm, those who are not favoured by that convention are somehow being hoodwinked into approving it.

There seems no good reason, however, to confine Lewis's argument to conventions of coordination. Lewis's explanation of how these conventions become norms does not depend on his assumption that they work to everyone's advantage. It may be true that we all benefit from the existence of certain established conventions, but this is not *why* we believe we ought to follow them. So we should not be surprised if we find that other conventions, which do not work to everyone's advantage, also become norms.

In arguing that conventions can acquire moral force without working in the interests of society as a whole I am making something of a break with the arguments of Hume. Hume claims that conventions of property ultimately work to everyone's benefit:

> 'Tis impossible to separate the good from the ill. Property must be stable, and must be fix'd by general rules. Tho' in one instance the public be a sufferer, this momentary ill is amply compensated by the steady prosecution of the rule, and by the peace and order, which it establishes in society. And even every individual person must find himself a gainer, on ballancing the account; since, without justice, society must immediately dissolve, and every one must fall into that savage and solitary condition, which is infinitely worse than the worst situation that can possibly be suppos'd in society. (1740, Book 3, Part 2, Section 2)

I have already explained why I cannot accept that this optimistic conclusion is necessarily true: some people may be better off in a state of nature than in a society with rules of property that discriminate against them.

The claim that conventions of property work to everyone's benefit plays an important part in Hume's account of how these conventions become norms – or, in Hume's words, of why we annex the idea of virtue to justice. For Hume the rules of justice are what I have called conventions of property. These conventions evolve spontaneously in a state of nature in which each individual pursues his own interests. The original motive for individuals to follow these conventions is simple prudence:

> To the imposition then, and observance of these rules, both in general, and in every particular instance, they are at first mov'd only by a regard to interest; and this motive, on the first formation of society, is sufficiently strong and forcible.

But these conventions come to have moral force:

> But when society has become numerous, and has encreas'd to a tribe or nation, this interest is more remote; nor do men so readily perceive, that disorder and confusion follow upon every breach of these rules, as in a more narrow and contracted society. But tho' in our own actions we may frequently lose sight of that interest, which we have in maintaining order, and may follow a lesser and more present interest, we never fail to observe the prejudice we receive, either mediately or immediately, from the injustice of others; as not being in that case either blinded by passion, or byass'd by any contrary temptation.

Nay when the injustice is so distant from us, as no way to affect our interest, it still displeases us; because we consider it as prejudicial to human society, and pernicious to every one that approaches the person guilty of it. We partake of their uneasiness by *sympathy*; and as every thing, which gives uneasiness in human actions, upon the general survey, is call'd Vice, and whatever produces satisfaction, in the same manner, is denominated Virtue; this is the reason why the sense of moral good and evil follows upon justice and injustice. And tho' this sense, in the present case, be deriv'd only from contemplating the actions of others, yet we fail not to extend it to our own actions. The *general rule* reaches beyond those instances, from which it arose; while at the same time we naturally *sympathize* with others in the sentiments they entertain of us. (Hume, 1740, Book 3, Part 2, Section 2)

I have quoted this passage at length because it so closely parallels my own argument about how conventions become norms. When other people breach conventions in their dealings with us, we are harmed; and we resent this. This, I take it, is the prejudice we receive 'immediately' from the injustice of others. When other people breach conventions in dealings in which we are not involved, our interests are still endangered, because we may have to deal with these people in the future. This is perhaps what Hume means when he speaks of the prejudice we receive 'mediately'.[3] And we feel uneasy about being the focus of other people's resentment: we 'naturally sympathize with them in the sentiments they entertain of us'. Our disapproval of other people's breaches of conventions, and our uneasiness about our own breaches, are universalized in our acceptance of the general rule that *all* breaches are to be disapproved of: conventions ought to be kept.

Hume's argument diverges from mine, however, in stressing the role of *sympathy*. According to Hume, we are displeased by breaches of conventions even in cases in which our interests are completely unaffected; and our displeasure stems from sympathy. Whether this claim is compatible with my own argument depends on how we suppose sympathy works.

One conception of sympathy is endorsed by Hume when he says that the happiness or misery of any human being, or indeed of any animal capable of these feelings, can affect us *'when brought near to us, and represented in lively colours'* (1740, Book 3, Part 2, Section 1; my italic). The idea here is that the extent of our sympathy with another person is usually a product of the relationship between him and us: his happiness or misery has to be *brought near to us* if it is to engage our sympathies. Thus, other things being equal, we tend to sympathize most strongly with those people whose situations are most like our own: these are the people with whom we can most easily identify. Now suppose that I always follow a particular convention. For example, suppose that I never pick pockets. This respect for established rules of property may be a matter of simple prudence: I am not particularly dextrous, and afraid of being caught. But whatever the reason for my keeping to the convention, I have no *experience* of the pickpocket's satisfaction at successfully completing a job of work. In contrast, I do have experience of the fear of having my pocket picked; I may also have experience of feeling anger and resentment after being robbed in this way. Thus, I suggest, I shall be inclined to sympathize less with pickpockets than with their victims. More generally, if I follow a convention I shall be inclined to sympathize less with those who breach it than with those who are harmed by these breaches. Thus, to use Hume's words, we can be displeased by injustice because of a natural tendency to sympathize with the uneasiness of those who are the victims of injustice.

So far there is no contradiction with the argument of this book. But, according to Hume, we sympathize with the victims of injustice because we consider injustice 'prejudicial to human society'. His position is made more clear in his summing-up of the passage I have just quoted:

> *Thus self-interest is the original motive to the* establishment *of justice: but a* sympathy *with public interest is the source of the* moral approbation, *which attends that virtue.* (1740, Book 3, Part 2, Section 2)

Notice that Hume is talking about sympathy *with public interest*. The idea here seems to be that we sympathize impartially with everyone's pleasures and pains; because principles of justice work in the public interest, the balance of our sympathies come down on the side of justice. On this view of sympathy, conventions can acquire moral force only if they contribute to the overall welfare of society.

It is at this point that I part company with Hume. The idea that we sympathize on the basis of some kind of cost–benefit analysis seems psychologically implausible. No doubt we are *capable* of imagining ourselves into the position of what Adam Smith (1759, Part 3, Ch. 3) called an 'impartial spectator', sympathizing equally with everyone in society; but, as Smith himself recognized,[4] this is not how our sympathies *naturally* work.

To this it might be objected that the concept of a moral judgement requires a degree of impartiality; however partial our sympathies may be, our moral judgements must be universalizable. Or, as Hume put it, it is a convention of language that we 'fix on some *steady* and *general* points of view' when we make moral judgements (cf. Section 8.3). I accept this; but we can be impartial without being impartially *sympathetic*. A judge who impartially upholds the law of property need not (and, I think, will not) always decide cases in the way that would be dictated by an equal sympathy for every member of society; but he is nevertheless impartial. Similarly, if I am prepared to condemn all breaches of a convention, including my own, my condemnation is sufficiently steady and general to be recognizable as moral; I need not believe that the convention works for the overall welfare of society.

Some readers may still think that conventions are too arbitrary to form the basis for a system of morality; moral judgements, it might be argued, should follow from the impartial application of a few simple and general moral principles. To answer this objection, I shall try to show that the morality that grows up around conventions – the morality of natural law – *does* have a unifying principle.

9.2   The principle of co-operation

In this book I have argued that certain kinds of conventions tend to evolve spontaneously in human society, and that these conventions come to have the moral status of principles of justice, of natural law. It is tempting to suppose that if the members of a society subscribe to a common moral code, then that code must serve some social purpose. There must be *some* sense, we are tempted to say, in which this code is good for society. But this is a mistake. As I have argued in Section 9.1, conventions can acquire moral force without contributing to the overall welfare of society. So if there is a unifying principle behind natural law, it is not a principle of social welfare.

Nevertheless it *is* possible to extract a general principle from my argument about how conventions acquire moral force. Recall that, according to my argument, a convention is likely to acquire moral force if it satisfies two conditions: first, that almost everyone in the relevant community follows it; and second, that it is in each individual's interest that the people with whom he deals follow the rule, provided that he follows it too (Section 9.1). (The first condition ensures that everyone *expects* everyone else to follow the convention; the second condition ensures that everyone *wants* everyone else to follow it.) So the moral rules that grow up around conventions are likely to be instances of the following principle:

> *The principle of co-operation.*[5] Let *R* be any strategy that could be chosen in a game that is played repeatedly in some community. Let this strategy be such that if any individual follows *R*, it is in his interest that his opponents should do so too. Then each individual has a moral obligation to follow *R*, provided that everyone else[6] does the same.

Let me make it clear that I am not claiming that this principle constitutes the *whole* of our morality. I am claiming only that there is a strong tendency for us to subscribe to moral rules that are instances of this principle; to put this another way, we are inclined to give this principle *some* moral weight.

It does, I believe, appeal to some common moral intuitions. Suppose that almost everyone in the community follows *R*. Then if I play a game against you, it is reasonable for me to expect that you will play *R*. For me to play *R* is for me to act in a way that I can reasonably expect to be in your interests (since if you do play *R*, my playing *R* will be in your interests). Equally, for you to play *R* is for you to act in a way that you can reasonably expect to be in my interests. Then if I play *R* but you do not, I have acted in the way best calculated to accommodate you, but you have failed to reciprocate. The moral intuition behind the principle of co-operation is that in such a case I have a legitimate complaint against you. Take, for example, the crossroads game. Suppose it is the general practice at crossroads to give priority to the vehicle approaching from the right. Suppose you always follow this practice. Then, given the way other drivers can be expected to behave, you are behaving in the way that is best calculated to benefit them. I eccentrically choose to adopt the strategy of never giving way to anyone, and in doing so put your life at risk. Then you have grounds for complaint against me.

The morality that grows up around conventions, then, is a morality of *co-operation*. It is also a morality of *rights*. If everyone else in my community is following *R*, I am obliged to do the same. Notice that this obligation arises out of my relationship with other individuals: I am obliged to benefit them because they are benefiting me. My obligation, then, is *to particular other people*. Corresponding with my obligation to follow *R* is everyone else's *right* that I should do so; each other person is entitled to demand that I meet my obligation to him. This is quite different from the sort of obligation imposed by a morality of maximizing social welfare, or of maximizing the sum of happiness in the world – which are obligations to no one in particular.

Any system of morality that rests on an idea of co-operation must incorporate some reference point from which benefit or disbenefit is to be measured. The idea is that if I benefit you, I am entitled to demand that you benefit me in return; but benefit is a comparative concept.[7] When I say that I have benefited you, I am saying that I have made you better off than you would have been in some other state of affairs: this state of affairs is the reference point. What, then, is the reference point for the principle of co-operation that underlies natural law? The reference point is the status quo.

Why do I say this? Notice that the principle of co-operation obliges an individual to follow a strategy R only if everyone else is doing so. Thus there can be a general obligation for everyone to follow R only in a state of affairs in which R is being generally followed. In other words, to suppose that there is such a general obligation is to suppose that the status quo is one in which everyone follows R. Now the idea behind the principle of co-operation is that if any individual *unilaterally* defects from the established practice of following R he will disadvantage his opponents; an individual who chooses *not* to disadvantage his opponents in this way is entitled to expect in return that his opponents will not disadvantage him. Here disadvantage is being measured relative to the state of affairs in which everyone follows R; and this is the status quo.

To recognize that natural law is based on a principle of mutual advantage, and that the reference point for measuring advantage is the status quo, is to recognize that rights and obligations are matters of convention. In a community in which everyone follows some rule R, everyone may have a moral right to expect everyone else to follow this rule; and yet it may be equally true that if everyone followed a different rule S, everyone would have a moral right to expect everyone else to follow S.

Many readers, I imagine, will object strongly to this idea. Moral theories are usually constructed so that the question, 'What rights and obligations do individuals have?' has a unique answer. Take, for example, the theory that morality is concerned with the maximization of some conception of social welfare. Following Sen (1979), I shall call this kind of theory 'welfarist'; the classical utilitarian position, that the sum of happiness should be maximized, is a special case of welfarism. For a welfarist, rights and obligations can be justified only as means for achieving the end of maximum social welfare. Welfare, unlike benefit or advantage, is *not* a comparative concept; so once the concept of social welfare is defined, the problem of how to maximize it will normally have a unique solution.

Or take Rawls's (1972) theory of justice. For Rawls, justice is a matter of mutual advantage, but advantage is defined in relation to a fixed 'initial arrangement' in which what Rawls calls 'social primary goods' – including income and wealth – are distributed equally (Rawls, 1972, p. 62). Principles of justice are those principles that would secure the unanimous agreement of individuals in this position of initial equality. Now, of course, this is not enough to ensure a unique set of principles. (There may be a choice between alternative sets of principles, all of which make everyone better off than in the initial position; some individuals may benefit more from one set of principles, others from another.) Rawls recognizes this problem but, significantly, responds by designing the initial position so that a unique set of principles of justice *will* be generated (Rawls, 1972, pp. 139–40). The device that ensures this is the 'veil of ignorance': no one is allowed to know his or her identity, and so no one can know which principles would work out most to his or her advantage.

As a final example, take Nozick's (1974) entitlement theory of justice. Nozick simply *assumes* the existence of a unique code of natural law. He provides no real justification for this assumption beyond an appeal to the authority of Locke – while remarking that Locke 'does not provide anything like a satisfactory explanation of the status and basis of the law of nature' either (Nozick, 1974, p. 9). For Locke, natural law is a system of moral rights and duties that embodies the will of God, as interpreted by natural reason – that is, without the aid of divine revelation (Locke, 1690, Book 2, Ch. 2). It is not clear whether Nozick shares Locke's deism; certainly God plays no explicit part in Nozick's theory. It seems that for Nozick it is a matter of simple moral intuition that individuals have certain clearly defined rights.

Against this background, the claim that rights and obligations are matters of convention will be controversial. Let me therefore repeat what I have said several times before. It is no part of my argument that the morality that evolves in human society is the morality that we *ought* to follow. I am not presenting a moral argument; I am trying to explain how we come to have some of the moral beliefs we do. My claim is that human beings tend to use the status quo as a moral reference point. Whether they ought to do so is another matter, and (at least for those of us who accept Hume's Law) one that can never be resolved by an appeal to reason.

It is, therefore, open to anyone to say that he or she refuses to accept the moral legitimacy of claims based on what I have called natural law. He or she may say: 'The only right thing to do is ...; if this means violating what some people regard as their moral rights, then that's just too bad.

I don't accept that these so-called rights have any claim on my respect.' A consistent welfarist, for example, would say that the right thing for a government to do is whatever maximizes social welfare. In his rejection of claims based on natural law, the welfarist would (I imagine) be emboldened by the reflection that, after all, these 'laws' are only conventions. He may even be tempted to think about moral engineering. If people's moral beliefs are based on conventions, they can be changed. Rather than accept the convention that happens to have become established, we can work out which of the many possible conventions would maximize social welfare, and then require everyone to follow it. At first, no doubt, some people will resist the change, claiming that they have been cheated out of their entitlements; but with time these ideas of rights and obligations will die out and be replaced by new ones that are more compatible with the maximization of welfare.

The analysis of this book provides no moral counter-argument to such a committed welfarist. (Nor does it provide a counter-argument to someone who is committed to a Rawlsian or a Nozickian theory of justice.) However, it does provide some warnings. Established conventions *can* be overturned – consider the success of the metric system – but history is littered with failed attempts to reform conventions. The same generation of rationalistic Frenchmen and Frenchwomen who introduced the metric system attempted to reform the calendar; but we all still use the old irrational one. Successive Irish governments have made great efforts to re-establish the Gaelic language, but they have been unable to prevent the overwhelming majority of the Irish people from speaking and writing in English. The convention that gold is money has lasted for thousands of years and is still resistant to attempts to reform the international monetary system.

Consider the convention that conflicts are resolved in favour of possessors. This may have no rational foundation; from a welfarist point of view it may be morally perverse. But is it in the power of any government to eradicate it? Think of all the situations in which this convention is used to resolve disputes, and of how it can spread by analogy from one situation to another (Section 5.3). Think how many disputes are settled outside the influence of the legal system – between neighbours and workmates, in clubs and associations, on the roads, in school playgrounds, in youth gangs, …. How is any government going to change the way people behave in *these* situations? Think also of the way the convention favouring possessors is used to settle international disputes. (Think how the political map of Europe has been determined by the positions reached by the Soviet and American armies in 1945.) How can any one government renounce this convention in its own dealings with other governments?

If, as I have argued, the conventions by which people resolve disputes come to have the status of moral rights and obligations, any government that tries to overturn these conventions must expect its actions to be viewed as morally wrong – as illegitimate invasions of individuals' rights. The consistent welfarist must be prepared to accept the blame his policies will attract from the members of the society whose welfare he is seeking to promote. Recalling Bernard Williams's analogy between utilitarian theory and colonial administration (see Section 1.4), one is reminded of Rudyard Kipling's account of the white man's burden.[8]

However, the viewpoint of the colonial administrator, seeking to promote the welfare of a society without being constrained by its prevailing morality, is a peculiar one: there is no reason why we must adopt it. There is no reason why we must justify our moral beliefs by showing that they are beliefs that would be shared by an impartially benevolent observer, looking on society from some distant vantage point. We are entitled to make moral judgements from *where we are* – as members of a society in which certain ideas of obligations and rights have become established and accepted by us as part of our morality. In Sen's language, these ideas may be basic value judgements for us (cf. Section 8.3), just as the welfarist's judgements are basic for him. We cannot give any ultimate justification for our adherence to a morality of co-operation; but neither can the welfarist justify his welfarism.

For most of us, I suggest, morality cannot be reduced to welfarism. Whatever political principles we may profess, most of us believe that we each have rights that cannot be legitimately overridden merely to increase the overall welfare of society. When what we take to be our rights or legitimate expectations are under threat, we feel entitled to ask: 'But *why* must I sacrifice my expectations for the good of society?' This question is not a stupid one. It does not reveal a failure to grasp the logic of moral reasoning. It is a real moral question. When the chips are down – when it is *our* expectations that are at stake – this is a question that we *do* ask. As Rawls (1972, pp. 175–9) puts it, it is a general fact of moral psychology that we are inclined to conceive of society as a system of co-operation through which *our* interests, as well as everyone else's, are to be advanced; we are not psychologically equipped to take the welfarist's view of society in which our interests are subsumed in some social whole.

If the argument of this book is correct, at least some of what we take to be our rights are grounded in nothing more than convention; in accepting them as morally significant we are using the status quo as a moral reference point. This is an unmistakably conservative idea. There is no claim, however, that the status quo is *better*, all things considered, than any other possible state of society. To suppose that some claim of this kind is being made is to interpret a conservative theory as a species of welfarism; the theory has nothing to say about the overall welfare of society, or about how one possible state of society should be compared with another. The significance of the status quo is simply that, as James Buchanan (1975, p. 78) has put it, we start from here, and not from some place else.

Many readers, I suspect, will still balk at such conservatism, and will look for some other way of rationalizing their moral convictions. I wish them luck, but I suspect that the task is hopeless. Certain moral beliefs, I have argued, have a natural tendency to evolve. We cannot easily shake these beliefs off. Nor are we inclined to try, since they are *our* beliefs: they are part of our moral view of the world. However much we might wish to deny it, our morality is in important respects the morality of spontaneous order; and the morality of spontaneous order is conservative.

Afterword

When I started work on the second edition of *The Economics of Rights, Co-operation and Welfare* (*ERCW*), I had a plan of updating it by inserting new chapters, while keeping the original text intact. But the new chapters kept growing longer, and eventually I realized that the mixture of old and new material would not work. To keep the new material under control, I have restricted myself to a commentary on the content of *ERCW* in the light of subsequent developments in evolutionary game theory, and of what seem to me to be the most substantial criticisms that have been made of its arguments. I have resisted the temptation to use this Afterword as an opportunity to show how the arguments in *ERCW* can be applied in new areas, or to discuss further topics, however closely related to *ERCW*. My concern here is with what *ERCW* says, and whether it is right. I give most attention to those elements of *ERCW* that remain most controversial: the emphasis on the role of 'prominence' (or 'salience')[1] in determining which conventions emerge, the argument that inefficient conventions can be favoured by the forces of social evolution, and the claim that certain kinds of convention tend to acquire moral force for the people who follow them, even if, viewed from outside, those conventions appear morally arbitrary.

A.1 Evolution

To the present-day reader, the evolutionary game theory presented in Chapter 2 and used in the rest of the book may sometimes seem idiosyncratic. This should not be surprising: when I finished writing the book in 1985, evolutionary game theory hardly existed as a technique of economics. Subsequent work in this branch of theory has generated new conventions of analysis and terminology. In this section, I explain how the theory used in *ERCW* relates to modern evolutionary game theory.

In the theory I present in Chapter 2, the most fundamental concept is *utility*. Re-reading this chapter in 2004, I feel dissatisfied with its discussion of utility; but I still do not know how to improve it.

In conventional game theory, the concept of utility is built into the definition of a game. For each combination of strategies that the players of a game might choose, there has to be a utility score for each player; unless such numbers exist, there is no game in the formal sense. Utility is taken to be measurable on a cardinal scale (mathematically: it is unique up to an affine transformation); and it is assumed that each player seeks to maximize the expected value of his utility. When John von Neumann and Oskar Morgenstern (1947) first proposed their theory of games, economists were highly sceptical about the cardinality of utility (although, perhaps mistakenly, most of them were confident about the existence of *ordinal* utility). In order to convince their readers that cardinal utility was a meaningful concept, von Neumann and Morgenstern proved that if a person has preferences over gambles which satisfy certain conditions of rational coherence, then those preferences can be *represented* as maximizing the expected value of some function. On this interpretation, 'utility' is not any particular kind of thing (like wealth or pleasure) which people are assumed to set out to achieve. Instead, it is a way of describing coherent preferences. Provided we are prepared to endorse von Neumann and Morgenstern's axioms as principles of ideal rationality, we have an interpretation of utility that is suitable for use in the kind of game theory that these authors were developing: the theory of ideally rational play in games. But evolutionary game theory is intended to be an empirical theory, not an *a priori* one. It is intended to explain how games are actually played.

There is a lot of evidence that actual behaviour is not consistent with the theory of expected utility. The observed deviations from that theory are not just random, but are systematic and predictable. In Chapter 2 I describe this body of evidence as 'growing', and it has indeed grown enormously since 1985. There are now many theories of decision-making which try to explain these observations. Expected utility theory is just one of a whole array of rival theories, each of which explains some but not all of the evidence. The strongest case that can be made for expected utility theory as an empirical theory is that it is simple and tractable, and that its predictions are often a reasonably good first approximation to a much more complex reality.[2]

Most evolutionary game theory, as applied in economics, rests on some variant of expected utility theory: the outcomes of evolutionary games are defined in terms of cardinal utility, and the process of evolution is assumed to favour those strategies with the highest values of expected utility. Effectively, I take this approach too, although instead of talking about the *expected* value of utility in each play of a game, I talk about the *average* value of utility over many repetitions of a game. I cannot pretend that the argument I offer in Section 2.3 in support of this approach is particularly strong. Rather, I take some pride in the caution with which this argument is presented, and in its recognition of the difficulties of justifying expected utility theory in an evolutionary context.[3] Still, one has to start somewhere. For the arguments presented in *ERCW*, the finer issues of choice under uncertainty are not central.

The evolutionary content of the theory I use is contained in the idea that individuals *learn by experience*. What I take this to mean is explained in Chapter 2. The basic idea is that individuals play (what they take to be) the same game many times, that each individual has preferences over sequences of outcomes of the game, and that these preferences generate a measure of long run 'success' (the average of the utility payoffs received). Players are said to 'gravitate' towards those strategies that are most successful in the long term.

The gravitational forces involved are not described very precisely, but the basic idea is clear enough. Individuals, while consciously seeking success, do so by trial and error rather than through the use of forward-looking Bayesian rationality of the kind assumed in classical decision theory. Although Chapter 2 is imprecise about the mechanisms by which people learn, it presents a very specific model of the long-run implications of this learning. The central theoretical concept is *evolutionary stability*. Lying behind the equilibrium analysis is an account of the dynamic process which leads to equilibrium; this process is represented in the phase diagrams used in Chapters 2 and 3. Implicitly, what is being assumed is a property that game theorists now call *payoff monotonicity*: within any population at any given time, and comparing across strategies, the rate of growth of the frequency with which a strategy is played is greater, the greater the expected utility of that strategy. Thus, in a game in which there are only two pure strategies R and S for players in a given role, the frequency with which strategy R is played in the population will increase, stay constant, or fall over time depending on whether the expected utility of playing R is greater than, equal to, or less than that of playing S. This gives the kind of dynamics represented by the phase diagrams.

Evolutionary game theorists now commonly use a specific model of the dynamics of evolutionary processes.[4] This model, *replicator dynamics*, satisfies payoff monotonicity but assumes some additional mathematical structure. In this model, the rate of growth of the frequency with which any given strategy is played is proportional to the difference between the expected utility of that strategy and the weighted average of the expected utilities of all strategies (each strategy being weighted by the frequency with which it is played).

There is a close connection between replicator dynamics and the concept of evolutionary stability used in *ERCW*. Consider a population of players of a game in which there are n different strategies. For any point in time t, we can define a probability distribution $p(t)$ which specifies the frequency with which each strategy is played in the population. Taking some time t_0 and a given distribution $p(t_0)$ as our starting point, we can calculate the expected utility derived from playing each strategy at t_0. Using the model of replicator dynamics, we can then calculate the rate at which the frequency of each of strategy is changing. And so we can calculate the probability distribution $p(t_1)$ for a later point in time, recalculate the rates of change, and so on. In this way we can plot the path of $p(t)$ from t_0 onwards. It is natural to define an *equilibrium* as a distribution p^* such that, if the distribution at any time is p^*, it will remain p^* for ever. We can define an equilibrium distribution p^* to be *stable* if, starting from any distribution which is sufficiently close to p^*, $p(t)$ approaches p^* as time progresses. If we wanted to predict the long-run evolution of a population governed by replicator dynamics, a natural first step would be to look for stable equilibria. It turns out that any probability mix of strategies which is evolutionarily stable, in the sense defined in Section 2.6, is also a stable equilibrium of replicator dynamics.

So the *mathematical* analysis of evolutionary processes in *ERCW* – the analysis that is embodied in the phase diagrams and in the concept of evolutionary stability – is consistent with what has now become a standard modelling strategy of evolutionary game theory. However, *ERCW* uses other modes of analysis too. It does so because social evolutionary processes are subject to influences that are not represented in those now-standard models.

Replicator dynamics was originally developed for use in biology, with *relative fitness* in place of utility. Roughly, the fitness of any given type of organism is the rate at which its genes replicate themselves. For many purposes, it is sufficient to measure the fitness of a type of organism by its *expected reproductive success* – that is, for a random individual of that type, the expected number of descendants that reach maturity in the next generation. Thus, the relative 'success' of a type of organism just *is* the tendency for its frequency in the population to increase. In a sufficiently simple biological model, the equations of replicator dynamics are theorems whose truth can be proved by deduction from the biological assumptions.

These theorems do not translate smoothly to models of trial-and-error learning. If success is measured in terms of utility, and if utility is defined in terms of individuals' preferences, it is not a matter of definition that more successful strategies grow in frequency at the expense of less successful ones. What is necessarily true in a model of trial-and-error learning is roughly this: a strategy increases in frequency to the extent that it has whatever properties favour its adoption by individuals who are learning by trial and error. It seems unexceptionable to assume that, *other things being equal*, strategies which offer higher expected utility are more likely to be adopted. Replicator dynamics, then, captures the workings of *one* significant element of trial-and-error learning. But there is much more to learning than this.

A.2 Salience

ERCW differs from most current work in evolutionary game theory in treating salience as a significant factor in trial-and-error learning. I still think that I was right to put salience at the centre of the analysis. In this section, I explain why.

However successful a strategy might be, it cannot be learned unless the people who are to learn it first *recognize* it as a possible strategy. This immediately suggests that the rate of change in the frequency of a strategy may depend, not only on the expected utility of that strategy, but also on its salience to potential learners – on its possession of whatever characteristics lead to its being recognized.

To illustrate the significance of salience in trial-and-error learning, consider the following game, which I shall call the narrow road game. (This game belongs to the same general family of coordination problems as the crossroads game analysed in Chapter 3, but is rather simpler.) The game is played recurrently and anonymously by pairs of individuals drawn at random from a large population.[5] In any instance of the game, two cars are approaching each other on a road which is only just wide enough to allow them to pass. Initially, each car is in the middle of the road. Each driver has to choose whether to steer to the left or to steer to the right. If both steer left, or if both steer right, the payoff to each of them is one unit of utility. If one steers left and one steers right, the payoff to each of them is zero. This is a classic example of the kind of game in which we might expect to see the evolution of a convention. What might that convention be?

In thinking about the alternative conventions that might evolve in this game, most people immediately think of the rules 'keep left' and 'keep right'. But these are not the only possible rules that can lead to coordination. Think of the variant of the narrow road game that is played by pedestrians who approach each other on footpaths or in the corridors of buildings. How do they avoid collisions? From what I must admit are fairly casual observations, I have come to the conclusion that British pedestrians do not consistently follow either the 'keep left' or the 'keep right' rule. In practice, they usually follow what I shall call the rule of *heading away*. If you are following this rule and are approaching someone, you project forward the directions in which the two of you are heading, and assess which of the two ways of passing would involve the least divergence from those trajectories. You then steer in that direction, 'heading away' from the other person's path. Both in judging the direction in which a person is heading, and in signalling your own direction, you probably make use of subtle eye and body language, some of which may be unconscious.

Clearly, the narrow road game can admit a vast range of alternative conventions. But to keep things simple, let us confine attention to just two possible conventions: the keep left rule and the head away rule. Suppose that, for players who understand either of these rules, that rule's prescriptions are never ambiguous. Suppose also that, in any randomly-selected instance of the game, the probability that the head away rule prescribes passing on the left is 0.5. Now let us start from an arbitrary frequency distribution over the two relevant strategies, and think about how behaviour will evolve. Suppose that initially, 51 per cent of drivers always keep left, while 49 per cent always head away. Expected utility is slightly higher for the keeping-left drivers, because they are slightly more likely to meet drivers who behave as they do. (In fact, expected utility is 0.755 for the drivers who keep left and 0.745 for those who head away.) If we simply assume (utility-based) replicator dynamics, we will predict a gradual increase in the frequency of keeping left. At first, the rate of increase will be slow, but it will gather pace as the advantage of keeping left increases. Sooner or later, everyone will keep left.

But should we accept these predictions of replicator dynamics without further question? Imagine the state of affairs I took as my starting point. Think of a driver who sees another car coming towards him, and who is deciding which way to steer. Some drivers (51 per cent of the population) conceptualize this problem as a choice between 'left' and 'right'. From their experience, they know that other drivers are more likely to steer left than right, but they keep coming across drivers who unaccountably steer right. Other drivers (49 per cent of the population) conceptualize the problem as a choice between 'heading away' from the other car, and 'heading in' towards it. From their experience, they know that other drivers are more likely to head away than to head in, but they keep coming across drivers who unaccountably head in. Notice that, *in terms of his own conceptualization of the game*, each driver is already choosing the strategy which, of those available to him, has proved the most successful. If the heading-in drivers are to learn to keep left, as the replicator model predicts, they have to understand the game in a new way.

At first sight, it is tempting to think that this is just a matter of time. Since the keeping-left drivers are already following the more successful strategy, they have no reason to switch to the other rule, even if they come to recognize it as a possibility. So, one might think, switching will be a one-way street. But that is to ignore all the random variation that underlies the aggregate picture. For example, suppose that over time there is some turnover of the population of players of the game. At random intervals, some individuals leave the population (they stop driving, leave the area, die, or whatever) and others join it. The new entrants begin with no experience of the game – or at least, none of this particular game, played in this particular place – from which to extrapolate. They have to make the best sense they can of their early observations. How they interpret their experience of the game will depend on whether they think in terms of left and right, or in terms of heading away and heading in. Suppose that the distinction between heading away and heading in is more likely to occur to new entrants than the distinction between left and right. Then new drivers will tend to learn to head away, even if initially the keep left rule is slightly more common among experienced drivers. And if this effect is strong enough, it will cause a gradual increase in the frequency of the head away rule in the population as a whole. Contrary to the predictions of utility-based replicator dynamics, the path of evolution may lead to the head away rule becoming the established convention.

So, if we are to understand the dynamics of learning by experience, it is not enough to take account of the relative payoffs of different strategies. We also have to take account of their relative salience, since the salience of a strategy affects its susceptibility to being learned. Salience is likely to be particularly significant in influencing the relative rates of change of the frequencies of alternative strategies when differences in expected utility are hard to detect. This is typically the case in the early stages of the evolution of conventions, before any of the potential conventions has many adherents; it is also true of situations (like that in the example of the narrow road) in which two or more potential conventions are beginning to establish themselves, but none is yet the clear front runner.

It would be a mistake to think that salience matters only because individuals are imperfectly rational. Learning by experience is possible only for actors who are capable of distinguishing a few salient patterns against a background of (what they interpret as) random variation. If some agent was so perfectly rational that he recognized all possible patterns and privileged none of them, he would be incapable of inductive learning. Imagine a driver who has played the narrow road game 1,000 times, and on every occasion the other driver has steered left. It may seem obvious that the rational inference for him to draw is that the next driver he meets will very probably steer left. But although that inference is obvious *for us*, as ordinarily rational human beings, it is not accessible to the perfectly rational agent. For us, the fact that all 1,000 observations fit the pattern 'always left' is a remarkable fact, which calls for some explanation beyond pure chance. But, from the perspective of the perfectly rational agent, we are merely betraying our lack of imagination, the poverty of our notion of 'pattern'. For him, *every* sequence of 1,000 instances of 'left' or 'right' has some pattern that can be projected forward. In fact, every such sequence fits an infinite number of different projectible patterns. Thus, no particular sequence of observations can give the perfectly rational agent any special reason to doubt that what he is observing is random variation. Inductive learning works by privileging a small number of salient patterns and by being alert for evidence which shows those particular patterns. If this account of inductive learning is right, our dependence on salience is not a sign of our imperfect rationality, but an essential part of the mechanism by which we learn.[6]

A.3 Language

In Chapter 3, my central example of a coordination problem was the case of two drivers on collision courses at a crossroads. I argued that if the resulting crossroads game was played recurrently, some convention would emerge, assigning one driver priority over the other. I also offered some explanation of why certain kinds of convention are more likely to emerge than others. Thomas Schelling's concept of salience (or, as he calls it, prominence) played an important part in this account. To illustrate how ideas of salience can help people to coordinate, I discussed some classic coordination games such as the game in which players have to name either 'heads' or 'tails', and the one in which they have to name a place to meet in New York City. Then, in the final section of the chapter,

I claimed that some much more fundamental social practices, including money and language, are conventions in the same sense that the rules we use at crossroads are.

Some readers have thought this move from driving practices to languages too glib. They have objected that the crossroads game, as I have imagined it, is played by individuals who already belong to a specific society, sharing a common stock of linguistic concepts and of historical, geographical and cultural references. The same is true of Schelling's coordination games. It seems that I am explaining some conventions by assuming others. Does this make my theory circular?

I think not. It is an essential feature of all evolutionary explanations that complexity arises gradually. To understand how some complex entity has come into existence, we have to understand how it has grown out of something else that is almost equally complex. This explanatory strategy is not circular, because it allows the slightly more complex to grow out of the slightly less. Ultimately, the highly complex can be traced back to the very simple; but for most explanatory purposes, it is not necessary to go so far back. If we want to explain a set of conventions as complex as those governing driving behaviour, we must expect the explanation to take many other conventions and regularities as given.

Still, a critic may ask whether it is coherent to assume that people who lack a common language have common concepts of salience.[7] In responding to this objection, I must make it clear that I am not proposing a theory of the emergence of the first human languages. My claim is that languages – by which I mean intelligible systems of inter-personal communication, whether based on sounds, inscriptions, gestures, or anything else – can emerge as conventions among modern human beings in much the same way that conventions of priority at crossroads can. (I say 'modern' human beings to mark that I am assuming a population of individuals with what we now take to be normal human reasoning abilities; I am taking no position on the question of whether such abilities would be possible for beings who had no language at all.) The process by which a new language emerges in a population need not involve the public use of any pre-existing common language; but (I maintain) it must involve common concepts of salience.

First, let me explain why common concepts of salience are essential. As a model of the emergence of a language, I borrow an example from David Lewis's *Convention* (1969). Lewis analyses what he calls *signalling problems*. A signalling problem is a particular type of coordination problem, in which two individuals A and B can both benefit if B's choice of action is predictably conditional on which of a set of arbitrary actions

A takes. (To use one of Lewis's examples: B is backing a truck into a narrow opening, and A is standing behind, guiding him. They would both bene-fit if there was a signalling convention, such as: If A gives a beckoning gesture, B reverses; if A holds up both hands, palms outwards, B stops.) Lewis argues that signalling conventions are not only resolutions of coordination problems, but also rudimentary languages. I agree.

Now suppose we try to model the emergence of a signalling conven-tion for the reversing game, under the (in this case, highly artificial) assumptions that the game is played recurrently between As drawn at random from one population and Bs drawn at random from another, and that there is no pre-existing language common to As and Bs. Sup-pose that A can gesture independently with each arm, each of which can be pointed *up, down, left* or *right*. This gives us $4 \times 4 = 16$ possible gestures. Suppose that, in any given instance of the game, A observes either that it is *safe* for the truck to reverse further, or that it is *unsafe*. Let us define a strategy for A as any partition of the set of sixteen ges-tures into two non-empty subsets, the *safe* gestures and the *unsafe* ones; according to the strategy, one of the *safe* gestures (let us say, chosen at random) is to be made if the *safe* case obtains, and one of the *unsafe* gestures otherwise. This gives us $2^{16} - 2 = 65,534$ alternative strategies for A.[8] A strategy for B consists of an action to be performed in the event of each gesture. If we assume that there are two alternative actions for B, *reverse* and *stop*, a strategy for B consists of one of those actions for each of the sixteen possible gestures. This gives us $2^{16} = 65,536$ alternative strategies for B.[9] For each of A's strategies, there is a unique best reply by B – the strategy which plays *reverse* to every *safe* gesture and *stop* to every *unsafe* one. Each of these pairs of strategies is a strict Nash equilbrium (and therefore a convention). So we have a $65,534 \times 65,536$ game with 65,534 alternative conventions.

If we do not appeal to salience, we have a model in which each person recognizes that he has a set of 65,534 or 65,536 alternative strategies, and tries to learn by trial and error which of these is the most successful. If everyone starts out by choosing strategies at random, and if each person observes only the outcomes of the games in which he participates, how long will it take for a convention to emerge? It is enough to say: a very, very long time. I conclude that any adequate theory of the evolution of signalling systems in the real world will need to assume that the senders and the receivers of the signals come to the game with prior – and, cru-cially, *shared* – ways of thinking which privilege some possible signalling conventions relative to the rest. In other words, there must be common concepts of salience with respect to potential signals.

But this is not to say that a common *language* is necessary. There may be aspects of salience that are common to all human beings, irrespective of their culture. Two sets of natural facts provide obvious sources for cross-cultural concepts of salience: the biological similarities between human beings, and the regularities in the world to which they have to adapt.

The most basic properties of our ways of perceiving the world and of our ways of responding to it are induced by the biological constitution of the human species. There is good evidence that the human brain is organized so as to privilege some ways of classifying experience over others. Some of the best evidence of this comes from experiments that have been carried out on very young babies, only a few days old. Many of these experiments use a *habituation* method. A baby is repeatedly presented with the same stimulus, and its state of alertness is continuously monitored (for example, by recording the rate at which it sucks at a teat). As the baby becomes habituated to – or, we might say, bored with – the stimulus, its alertness decays. Then the stimulus is changed in some way. If this causes an increase in the baby's alertness, we can infer that the baby is treating the new stimulus as something different from the old one – something new, something worth attending to. Conversely, if there is no change in alertness, we can infer that the baby is treating the new stimulus as just another instance of the old one. In this way, it is possible to investigate some of the classification systems that are built into the human brain.

Here is an example of what has been discovered. If a baby has been habituated to seeing a simple shape, and then is shown the mirror image of that shape reflected around a vertical axis, it treats the new shape as another instance of the old one; but if the shape is rotated through ninety degrees, the baby reacts as if it is seeing something new. Also, when shown complex shapes that are symmetrical around some axis, babies become habituated to those shapes more rapidly if the axis is vertical than if it is horizontal or diagonal. The implication is that babies find the vertically-symmetrical shapes easier to 'read': it seems that we are born with a prior expectation of finding vertical symmetry in the world. It is easy to see how these principles of classification help to adapt human beings to the world in which they live. For most human purposes, two objects that appear to be identical except for left–right orientation are likely to have similar properties; they may even be the same object, merely seen from different viewpoints. And it is a fact of biology that many of the living things we are likely to encounter are roughly symmetrical about a vertical axis.[10] Ultimately, the special significance of the vertical axis reflects the importance of gravity in our world.

Quite apart from similarities in our *perceptions* of experience, there are many biologically-determined similarities in human responses to external stimuli. For example, hunger and repleteness, anger and fear, sexual arousal and its absence are all associated with observable physiological responses that are very difficult either to fake or to suppress. Because these responses are involuntary, they cannot be thought of as any kind of language; but they provide a basic repertoire of reference points whose salience is not culturally specific. Some of these responses are even shared by other species; such cross-species similarities have surely been significant in enabling human beings to understand dogs sufficiently to work with them.

Still other concepts of salience are the product of learning. In learning from experience, human beings develop classification systems that are useful to them in coping with the world in which they live. To the extent that people in different cultures are subject to the same natural forces, there must be some tendency for convergence among the conceptual schemes that they use to organize their experiences.

For all these reasons, common concepts of salience need not depend on a common language or a common culture. There need be no circularity, then, in appealing to some such common concepts as part of an explanation of the emergence of a language, and in claiming that a signalling system can emerge through a process that does not require the public use of a pre-existing language. If this conclusion is correct, we might expect to find examples of signals that have emerged in this way. I think we can.

In the middle of the eighteenth century, the English navigator James Cook commanded three great voyages of exploration to parts of the world that no Europeans had visited before. Exceptionally humane by the standards of his time, Cook made great efforts to cultivate friendly relations with the native populations of the lands he visited. For the most part these efforts were remarkably successful. How was this possible, when, at first contact, the natives and the Europeans had no common spoken language?[11]

It seems that much of the communication was carried out by gestures, and that each party was able to find gestures that were intelligible to the other. Here is one typical incident, which occurred in 1769. Cook's ship has anchored off the coast of Tierra del Fuego. So far, there has been no contact with the native Fuegians. Cook records in his journal, in a typically matter-of-fact way, that 'after dinner I went on shore, accompanied by Mr Banks and Dr Solander [the naturalists of the first voyage], to look for a watering place, and speak to the natives, several of whom had come in sight'. How, we may wonder, is Cook expecting to *speak* to the natives?

The party of Europeans lands at one end of a bay. Thirty or forty native Fuegians appear at the other end of the bay, and then retreat. Banks and Solander advance, holding out trinkets and coloured ribbon, intended as gifts. Two Fuegians then step forward, sit down, stand up again, display large sticks, gesture with them, and then ostentatiously throw them away. The Europeans interpret these gestures as signalling the renunciation of violence. Soon the two groups are exchanging what are apparently mutually intelligible gestures of friendly greeting (if 'uncouth' to European sensibilities – it seems that penis gestures were somehow involved on the Fuegian side), and the Fuegians are being entertained to bread and beef on board ship.

Episodes such as this suggest that human beings from cultures that have been isolated from one another for thousands of years can communicate simple messages quite effectively by means of signals. The signals used are not arbitrary. Rather, they are stylized forms of purposive actions (the use of sticks as weapons, the giving up of valuable possessions), or of natural expressions of affective states (sexual arousal). We might say that the original purposive actions or expressions are *natural signals*: they communicate information about the actor's beliefs, intentions or emotions, even though they are not carried out with the intention of communicating anything. When people *are* trying to communicate, natural signals provide cues whose salience does not depend on any pre-existing common language. Such cues are seeds from which languages can grow.

Cook's contacts with previously unknown cultures are exceptional situations. But we do not need to look to such distant times or exotic locations to find examples of the spontaneous emergence of signalling systems which do not seem to owe anything to spoken language. For example, at most road junctions in Britain, traffic on one road has official priority over other traffic, and this is signalled by 'Give Way' markers on the other roads. But if drivers always insisted on their rights at road junctions, the system would become gridlocked. Fortunately, there is a general understanding that major-road drivers occasionally allow minor-road drivers to enter the flow of traffic in front of them. For this practice to work smoothly, a minor-road driver has to be able to work out when a major-road driver is intending to give way to her; and she has to be able to respond in a matter of split seconds. How does a major-road driver signal 'I am giving way'? Often, this is done by the motoring equivalent of a gesture – a slight reduction of speed, so that the gap between the signalling driver and the vehicle in front becomes just a little wider than normal. What we see here is an early stage in the evolution of a signalling system from a natural signal.

There is another signal for 'I am giving way', commonly understood among road users: a flash of one's headlights. According to the British Highway Code, a flash of headlights is solely a warning signal; because of the dangerous ambiguity of using the same signal for 'I'm giving way' and 'Look out! I'm approaching!', the 'give way' usage is officially proscribed, but is widely used all the same. In yet another context – and even more the subject of official disapproval – a flash of headlights signals something like 'You fool!' Or, again, it may mean 'Drive carefully, you are approaching some danger', or 'You have forgotten to switch your lights on', or 'Thank you'. It seems that the headlight flash, having become an established warning signal, has gradually taken on multiple meanings. I see no reason to think that the emergence of signalling systems like these depends on the use of spoken language.

A.4 Power

Some readers of *ERCW* have doubted its claims about the importance of salience in determining which of a set of possible conventions becomes established. They may accept that salience might work as a tie-breaker when each player is indifferent about which convention comes about. But when different conventions lead to different distributions of payoffs between players, the idea that salience can determine which of them comes about strikes many people as implausible and even fanciful. Surely (it is said), salience is too insubstantial a factor to resolve conflicts of interest. If social practices favour some people at the expense of others, isn't the obvious explanation that those who are favoured have more power?[12]

The idea that conflicts are resolved, not by convention, but according to the relative power of the contestants, can be found in much writing in the social contract tradition. In one major line of contractarian thought, a principle of social organization is deemed to be just if rational and self-interested individuals, bargaining in some hypothetical and pre-social state of nature, would have agreed to it. If this method is to yield a determinate theory of justice, we need to be able to identify the outcome of rational bargaining from a given starting point. In contractarian theory, it is usual to assume the truth of some theory of bargaining which makes the outcome depend only on the relative power of the parties involved, and then to construct the initial bargaining position so that the distribution of power is equal or fair. If, instead, the outcome of rational bargaining depends on shared conceptions of salience, it may not be possible to define an initial bargaining position in which there are no 'arbitrary' (that is, historically or culturally contingent) asymmetries between individuals. And then the contractarian approach, as usually understood, will fail.[13]

I believe that the argument presented in *ERCW* stands up well. Before trying to justify this claim, however, I must emphasize that *ERCW* does not claim that relative power has *no* bearing on the outcomes of games of bargaining and conflict. Such a claim would be implausible. What is claimed is that, holding constant the relative power of the participants, salience has some influence on outcomes. *ERCW* explores the role of salience by investigating various simple two-person games of conflict in which the players are equal in power. In these controlled settings, the issue reduces to whether each game supports a range of alternative conventions, some of which favour one player and some the other, or whether each game has a unique solution in which the two players benefit equally.

To explore how the arguments in *ERCW* relate to the arguments of those of who are sceptical about salience, I focus on the division game. Recall that this is a game between two players A and B who are in dispute about the division of one unit of some resource. The players independently and simultaneously submit *claims* c_A and c_B; a claim can be any number from 0 to 1. If $c_A + c_B \leq 1$, the claims are *compatible*, and each player's utility is equal to his claim. Otherwise, the claims are in *conflict*, and each player's utility is -1. This game is a variant of the *Nash demand game*, which has been much discussed in game theory.[14] Since the positions of the two players are entirely symmetrical as far as strategy choices and payoffs are concerned, there is complete equality of power.

The analysis of the asymmetrical form of this game (presented in Section 4.6) assumes that A and B are distinguished by some difference of labelling: for example, A is the 'possessor' (the resource in dispute is currently in his possession) and B is the 'challenger'. This asymmetry has no significance for the payoffs of the game, but it is recognized by both players. I show that this game has a continuum of evolutionarily stable equilibria. Each equilibrium is defined by a value of c in the range $0 \leq c \leq 1$; for each such value of c, the equilibrium takes the form $c_A = c, c_B = 1 - c$. Thus, how much each player claims is a matter of convention. I then argue that salience may help to determine which convention emerges. If this is right, the outcome of the game can depend on salience rather than relative power.

To my knowledge, no one disputes that this result is correct for the division game. However, a critic may reasonably ask whether I have stacked the cards by using this particular model. Is this model sufficiently representative of real bargaining problems?

Theorists who are sceptical about the role of salience in bargaining often argue that the Nash demand game is a very special case. They appeal to a variant of this game, the *smoothed* Nash demand game. A version of that game can be constructed by making a small amendment to the division game. The amendment (or 'smoothing') is that the players are not completely sure how much of the resource there is to divide between them. In each game, the amount of the resource (or 'size of the pie') is $1 + \varepsilon$, where ε is a continuously distributed random variable with a mean and median of zero. The variance of ε is usually assumed to be small, so that the players are *almost* certain about the size of the pie. The assumption that the players do not know the exact size of the pie is a theoretically convenient way of modelling a much more general idea: that in most of the bargaining games of real life, even the most experienced players can never be completely sure about the dividing line between those combinations of strategies that will lead to conflict and those that will not.

Because of the size of the pie is uncertain, even a player who can predict his opponent's claim with complete confidence has to fine-tune his own claim according to his willingness to take risks. Suppose player A is sure that B's claim will have some particular value c'_B. Then if A claims $1 - c'_B$, there is a 50–50 chance that the two claims will be in conflict. The probability of conflict varies continuously with the size of A's claim; the more A claims, the higher that probability. But, of course, the more A claims, the more she receives if the claims are compatible. Thus, if she is to find the value of c_A which maximizes her expected utility given the value of c'_B, she has to find an optimal balance between these two effects. (To keep things simple, I assume that the distribution of ε is such that there is a uniquely optimal value of c_A for each possible value of c'_B.)

Let us define A's *safety margin* as $m_A = 1 - c'_B - c_A$, where c'_B is A's expectation of the value of c_B. (For the purposes of the analysis, I assume that A feels sure that B's claim will be c'_B.) That is, A's safety margin is the amount by which, in the event that $\varepsilon = 0$, her claim is less than the amount of the resource that would be left after B made the claim that A expects her to make. Similarly, we can define B's safety margin as $m_B = 1 - c'_A - c_B$, where c'_A is B's expectation of the value of c_A.

Now consider what safety margin is optimal for A, given the value of c'_B. By the definition of 'safety margin', A's claim is $c_A = 1 - c'_B - m_A$. A expects B to claim c'_B. So A expects the sum of the two claims to be $1 - m_A$. And so the probability of conflict, as viewed by A, is $pr[1 - m_A > 1 + \varepsilon]$, or $pr[\varepsilon < -m_A]$. Notice that the probability of conflict depends only on the distribution of ε and on A's safety margin; it is independent of c'_B. However, what A stands to lose from conflict is the value of her own claim. For a given safety margin, A's claim is lower the higher is c'_B; so the more B is expected to claim, the less A stands to lose. It follows from this that the optimal safety margin for A falls as c'_B increases. A symmetrical argument shows that the optimal safety margin for B falls as c'_A increases.

Now for the punch line. If each player's expectation of the other is correct, as must be the case in equilibrium, we have $c'_A = c_A$ and $c'_B = c_B$. Thus $m_A = m_B = 1 - c_A - c_B$: *the players' safety margins must be equal.* But we know that the optimal safety margin for each player is less, the more the other player claims. Thus, since the game is completely symmetrical with respect to the two players, there can be an equilibrium only if the two players' claims are equal. Further: if the variance of ε is small, optimal safety margins are small, and so each player's equilibrium claim must be close to 0.5. In the smoothed game, then, equality of power implies equality of payoffs. It seems that no space is left in which salience could work.[15]

So the smoothed and the unsmoothed versions of the division game lead to very different conclusions about equilibrium. Which model should we prefer? On the face of it, it seems that we should prefer the smoothed game. In life, there is always *some* uncertainty about everything; to ignore uncertainty, as we do if we use the unsmoothed game as our model, is to suppress a significant feature of real bargaining. Ken Binmore (1998, pp. 103–04) uses this argument to conclude that the multiplicity of equilibria in the unsmoothed game is 'spurious'.

Certainly, the analysis of smoothed bargaining games gives us an important insight into how relative power can impact on bargaining. It suggests that, *other things being equal*, there is a tendency for bargaining problems to be resolved in ways which reflect the balance of power. But, even if we accept the smoothed division game as a valid model of many real-world conflicts, we may still ask how useful the *equilibrium* of that game is as a model of real-world behaviour. To answer that question, we need to consider the strength of the forces which pull players towards equilibrium.

As I argued in Section A.2 using the example of the narrow road game, the dynamics of learning by experience are influenced by salience as well as by utility. The conventional model of replicator dynamics, which predicts convergence on evolutionarily stable equilibria, takes account only of the effects of utility. If these effects are sufficiently weak, they may be outweighed by the effects of salience.

Consider the process which leads to equilibrium in the smoothed division game. Since I need a numerical example, I take the case in which

ε has a normal distribution with a standard deviation of 0.01. Imagine that at some point in time, the state of the population is one in which challengers always claim $c_B = 0.1$ and possessors always claim $c_A = 0.873$. Since the sum of these claims, 0.973, is close to 1, we can guess that each player's claim is fairly close to the value that is optimal for her, given the claim that her opponent can be expected to make. In fact, in this example, the possessors' claim is exactly optimal, given the challengers' claim. But the challengers, who stand to lose less from conflict, are incurring a less-than-optimal degree of risk. So we might expect that over time, challengers' claims will increase slightly. But if this happens, the best reply by possessors must fall slightly. And so on: small increases in challengers' claims induce small decreases in possessors' claims, which induce further small increases in challengers' claims. There is a creeping process of mutual adjustment which comes to an end only when possessors' and challengers' claims are equal.

But we need to ask how quickly and reliably this adjustment process will work. If the claims of possessors and challengers are not even approximately matched, the gains to be made by adjustment will be easy to see. Thus, we should expect relatively quick convergence to some state of affairs in which claims are approximately matched. This part of the adjustment process is modelled by the dynamics of the unsmoothed division game. But once claims have adjusted in this way, the gains to be made by subsequent adjustments will typically be very small, and will be difficult to detect against the background noise created by random variation. The adjustment process can be expected to slow down dramatically.

Take the numerical example I presented two paragraphs back. Initially, possessors claim 0.873 and challengers claim 0.1. The challengers' claim is sub-optimal, but by how much? Taking the possessors' claim as given, it turns out that the optimal claim by challengers is 0.110; this gives an expected utility of 0.105. The sub-optimal claim of 0.1 yields an expected utility of 0.100, 5 per cent less than the optimum. This 5 per cent deficit is an expectation; an individual challenger can discover this value only by experimenting with different claims and observing how often each of these claims is followed by conflict. So, once claims are approximately matched, the utility-based forces pulling towards the 50–50 division are relatively weak. Relatively weak but systematic and offsetting biases in the learning process might be sufficient to bring the adjustment process to a halt.

As I argued in Section A.2, some regularities may be easier to learn than others, because of their salience – because they correspond with patterns that people are predisposed to look for. It may be easier for a player of the division game to learn to claim 0.1 than to learn to claim 0.11. If the optimum really is 0.11, and if expected utility is not very sensitive to differences in claims, a player might be satisfied when she has learned that the optimum is somewhere near 0.1. To adapt one of Schelling's (1960, pp. 70–1) metaphors, it is as if the space of possible agreements is not a perfectly smooth plane, but has 'grooves' at those terms of agreement that the bargainers recognize as salient – for example, prices that can be expressed in round numbers, or shares that can be expressed in simple fractions. Schelling suggests that, when thinking about whether or not to make concessions, bargainers 'dig in their heels' at these grooves. My suggestion is that salient regularities may exert friction in the processes by which players learn to optimize. So it is *not* fanciful to suggest that the rules of property that tend to emerge in human societies reflect facts about salience as well as facts about power.

What about the specific hypotheses about salience that Hume used to explain property conventions, and that are discussed in Chapter 5? Since writing *ERCW*, I have run experiments to test these hypotheses, using coordination games rather like the one presented in Figure 5.2. The results suggest that people do use principles of closeness and accession, as well as equality, when assigning objects of one type to objects of another (Mehta, Starmer and Sugden, 1994a, 1994b). I stand by the argument of *ERCW*: salience *does* matter in bargaining games.

A.5   Competition between conventions

Theorists who explain social order as the outcome of spontaneous social evolution often suggest that the process of evolution is benign – that it tends to select conventions and norms whose overall effects are to the benefit of the people who follow them. The most famous expression of this idea is probably Adam Smith's metaphor of the *invisible hand*. Smith's theory of morality and his theory of the market rest on a common set of ideas: that human beings are naturally endowed with certain 'propensities' and 'sentiments', that these propensities and sentiments, if allowed to operate freely in a social environment of 'natural liberty', generate complex forms of social order, and that these forms of social order tend to promote everyone's interests. In the modern literature of the evolution of norms, something of the same optimism can be found in Brian Skyrms's (1996) analysis of 'correlated convention', which I shall discuss later in this section, and in Binmore's (1998) account of 'fairness norms'.[16] Although Smith's theory of moral sentiments was one of my inspirations, *ERCW* is more sceptical about the efficiency properties of spontaneous order.

ERCW claims that evolutionary selection does *not* directly favour efficient conventions. Rather, it favours those conventions that give the best results to whoever follows them *in the environment in which a convention first begins to emerge*. Conventions that are favoured in this way are not necessarily efficient (see especially Sections 3.2 and 3.3). In this section, I look again at that conclusion in the light of subsequent work in game theory.

In the current literature of game theory, the issue of whether evolutionary selection favours efficiency is often posed in relation to the *stag hunt* game. The story behind this game is loosely adapted from Jean-Jacques Rousseau's *Discourse on Inequality* (1755, p. 36). In a state of nature, two people are hunting in a forest. Each of them, acting independently, can hunt for hares; this will yield each a modest return. Alternatively, they can hunt for deer. If both work according to a concerted deer-hunting plan, they will both do better than by separately hunting hares. But the plan requires them to work out of sight of one another in different parts of the forest. If one of them sticks to the plan while the other defects to hunt hares, the first person will get nothing. The payoffs of this symmetrical game are shown in Figure A.1.

It is easy to think of modern examples of this kind of game. Keeping to the spirit of Rousseau's story, think of two people who meet in anonymous circumstances, who can both benefit by acting together in some way which requires each to trust the other. For each of them there is a less good, but still satisfactory option which does not involve any interaction with the other. For example: you and I are passengers who happen to meet in an airport departure lounge. Each of us has a heavy bag. Each of us wants to make a brief trip out of the lounge – I to a cafe, you to a shop. The public address system announces that unattended baggage will be removed. I can take my bag with me to the cafe, which will be inconvenient, or I can suggest we take turns to look after each other's

		Opponent's strategy	
		Hare	Deer
Player's strategy	Hare	2	2
	Deer	0	3

Figure A.1   The stag hunt game

bag. That will be better for me, so long as you don't wander off after I have gone.

As far as game theory is concerned, the essential features of the stag hunt game are these. There are two conventions. In one convention, *hare* is played with probability 1; in the other, *deer* is played with probability 1. In any instance of the game, both players do better if both act according to the *deer* convention than if both act according to the *hare* convention. But if a player's opponent is equally likely to play according to either convention, the first player does better to play *hare*. In the language of game theory, *deer* is *payoff-dominant* while *hare* is *risk-dominant*.[17]

Which of these conventions is more likely to become established? Using the analysis introduced in Section 2.4, let p be the probability that any individual, selected at random from the population to play the game, plays *hare*. If $p > \frac{1}{3}$, the expected utility from playing *hare* is greater than that from playing *deer*; if $p < \frac{1}{3}$, the opposite is true. So if, at any time, the value of p is greater than $\frac{1}{3}$, it will tend to rise towards 1, while if it is less than $\frac{1}{3}$ it will tend to fall towards 0. Thus, the *hare* convention has a larger zone of attraction than the *deer* convention. This suggests that, other things being equal, *hare* is more likely to emerge from the evolutionary process – even though *deer* is more efficient.

Rather than asking which convention is more likely to evolve from an arbitrary initial position, we might want to ask a different question: how likely it is that each convention, if established, will be displaced by the other? Do inefficient conventions tend to be displaced by efficient ones? Or do risk-dominated conventions tend to be displaced by risk-dominant ones?

One way of approaching this question is due to Peyton Young (1993), who assumes that, with very low probability, players make independent random errors. In a model with this kind of error mechanism, and under the assumption that individuals play those strategies that are optimal relative to the recently-observed behaviour of potential opponents, there can be transitions from one equilibrium to another if enough individuals simultaneously make the same error. In an equilibrium in which everyone (when not making errors) plays *deer*, a collection of simultaneous errors which resulted in more than a third of the population playing *hare* would make *hare* optimal, and so induce a transition to the *hare* equilibrium. Conversely, in a *hare*-playing equilibrium, a collection of simultaneous errors which resulted in more than two-thirds of the population playing *deer* would induce a transition to the *deer* equilibrium. Since the first kind of transition requires fewer errors, it is more likely to occur. More generally, risk-dominated conventions (such as *deer*) are more vulnerable to errors than risk-dominant ones (such as *hare*). The implication is that 'in the long run' the risk-dominant equilibrium will be observed more frequently. In fact, if the probability of error is sufficiently small, the risk-dominant equilibrium will be observed 'almost always'.

The difficulty with this argument is that, although it tells us about what will happen in the long run, the long run may be very long indeed. While it is true that transitions from risk-dominated to risk-dominant conventions are much more likely than transitions in the opposite direction, it is also true that, in populations of any size, transitions in either direction are, to all intents and purposes, impossible. For example, suppose we have a population of n individuals and a probability of error ε. Suppose each individual plays the stag hunt game once per day. If everyone plays *deer* except when making errors, and if errors are independent between individuals and between days, what is the expected length of time before there is a day on which at least $n/3$ people play *hare*? Let us set $\varepsilon = 0.05$ (for each person, one error every twenty games), which seems rather high. Then, if $n = 8$, the answer is 173 days. If $n = 20$, it is 81 years. If $n = 29$, it is 3,400 years. Even if the population size is that of a small village, we can expect to wait billions of years. The implication, I suggest, is that a theory of uncorrelated errors is not going to explain how, in reality, one convention supplants another.

We have a better chance of understanding how conventions displace one another if we allow the same game to be played at different locations in some social space. 'Space' and 'location' can be interpreted in terms of any dimension that is salient enough to be perceived as potentially significant by the players of the game. For example, think of the conventions which govern the use of the English language. These differ across geographical space; they differ according to the age, social class and ethnicity of the people who are communicating with one another; they differ according to the social environment in which the communication takes place (the same person may use one set of expressions in the office and another in the bar); and so on. Once we recognize the existence of social space, we can think about how different conventions for playing the same game can persist alongside one another. And, more to the present purpose, we can investigate the processes by which one convention encroaches on another.

For a given game, I define *social space* as the set of locations in which that game can be played. A given individual can play different strategies depending on the location in which the game is played. Variation in behaviour across space is treated as resulting from the ways in which individuals condition their choices on location.[18]

Here is a simple spatial model of the stag hunt game. Space is represented by a circle. One point on the circle is the location 0; other points are defined by their distance from 0 in a clockwise direction, measured in 'degrees'; the distance round the circle is 360. It helps to use a form of arithmetic in which, for example, $359 + 3 = 2$ (starting 359 degrees clockwise from zero and going another 3 degrees clockwise takes us to a point 2 degrees clockwise of zero). There is a population of potential players. Each instance of the game is played between two individuals, picked at random from that population, and takes place at some location, picked at random from the points on the circle. Now for the crucial assumption: players do not know with complete accuracy the location of the game they are playing. If the game's location is x, each player receives an independent *signal* $x + \varepsilon$, where ε is a random variable. To keep things simple, I assume that ε has a rectangular distribution on the interval $[-1, 1]$. Intuitively, the idea is that each player conditions his behaviour on his perception of the social location at which he is playing. Because the perceptions of different individuals are not perfectly correlated, behaviour at one location is influenced by behaviour at nearby locations.

A *strategy* for the game is a rule which assigns some probability mix of *hare* and *deer* to each possible signal. It is immediately obvious that there are at least two conventions. In one of these, *hare* is played with probability 1 at all signals; in the other, *deer* is played with probability 1 at all signals. But can there be a convention which results in *hare* being played at some locations and *deer* at others?

Give or take a few technical qualifications, the answer provided by the model is: No. It turns out that, in equilibrium, if *hare* is played with probability 1 at all signals in some interval $(x^* - 1, x^* + 1)$, then it is played with probability 1 at all signals. To see why, suppose that *hare* is played with probability 1 at these signals. To stack the cards as far as possible against *hare*-playing, suppose that *deer* is played with probability 1 at every other signal.

Consider some player who receives a signal $x^* + b$. Conditional on this signal, what is the probability that her opponent will play *hare*? Let this probability (which, by virtue of the symmetries of the model, is independent of x^*) be denoted by $p(b)$. It should be clear that $p(b)$ is at a maximum when $b = 0$; in fact, $p(0) = \frac{3}{4}$. If the signal is outside the interval $(x^* - 3, x^* + 3)$, then $p(b) = 0$. (This follows from the fact that the absolute value of the difference between the player's signal and the opponent's signal cannot be greater than 2.) Within the interval $(x^* - 3, x^* + 3)$, $p(b)$ falls as $|b|$ increases. Crucially, it turns out that $p(1) = p(-1) = \frac{1}{2}$. That is, if the player's signal is exactly on the borderline between the set of signals at which her opponent plays *hare* and the set of signals at which he plays *deer*, the opponent is equally likely to play either strategy. Given the symmetries of the model, this should not be surprising. However, it has a very significant implication. Recall that *hare* is uniquely optimal for a player if the probability that her opponent plays *hare* is greater than $\frac{1}{3}$. That is, *hare* is uniquely optimal if $p(b) > \frac{1}{3}$. So *hare* is strictly the better strategy, not only at all signals in the interval $(x^* - 1, x^* + 1)$, but also at some signals outside this interval. In fact, the signals at which *hare* and *deer* give the same expected utility are $x^* - 1.37$ and $x^* + 1.37$.

Recapitulating, we started out by assuming an equilibrium in which *hare* is played with probability 1 at all signals in the interval $(x^* - 1, x^* + 1)$. We have proved that, if such an equilibrium exists, *hare* is uniquely optimal – and therefore played with probability 1 – at all signals in the larger interval $(x^* - 1.37, x^* + 1.37)$. But then we can repeat the argument. If, in equilibrium, *hare* is played with probability 1 at all signals in the interval $(x^* - 1.37, x^* + 1.37)$, *hare* is uniquely optimal – and therefore played with probability 1 – at all signals in the still larger interval $(x^* - 1.37 - 1.37, x^* + 1.37 + 1.37)$. And so on. So the original assumption implies that *hare* is played with probability 1 at *all* signals.

The intuition behind this result is simple. If a (not too small) *deer*-playing region of social space adjoins a (not too small) *hare*-playing region, there must be areas at the border between the two regions in which the two strategies are played with approximately equal probability. But, because *hare* is risk-dominant, it is the optimal strategy to play in these areas. So, as players gravitate towards more successful strategies, the *hare*-playing region will expand and the *deer*-playing region will contract. The implication is that, if even a small region of *hare*-playing becomes established, it will expand until *deer*-playing is eliminated everywhere. In other words, the *deer* convention is much more vulnerable to invasion than the *hare* convention.

Of course, a *hare*-playing invasion of the *deer* convention still requires there to be simultaneous deviations from the convention in some region of social space. For the reasons I explained earlier, a mechanism of uncorrelated error is unlikely to generate the preconditions for a successful invasion within any realistic time scale. But we do not need to have a specific theory of deviations to see that risk-dominant conventions are favoured in the evolutionary selection process. It is sufficient to recognize that there are all sorts of reasons why correlated deviations might occur on a local scale. Here is one historical example. During the nineteenth century, the use of the Welsh language suffered a catastrophic decline in large parts of south Wales. There are many explanations for this decline, but one was the rapid development of the south Wales coalfield, which induced large-scale immigration of English-speaking workers. The use of English may have spread outwards from the areas of social space domin-ated by those immigrants. Since many more Welsh speakers had English as a second language than the other way round, English-speaking might be thought of as the risk-dominant convention.

This abstract spatial model should not be interpreted too literally. The creeping process by which, in the model, *hare*-playing regions encroach on *deer*-playing ones is similar to the process by which the Nash bargain-ing solution comes about in the model of the smoothed division game. In Section A.4 I argued that the utility-based forces behind such processes may be relatively weak, and can be opposed by other forces, particularly those associated with salience. The same applies in the present case. For example, if *deer* is more salient or easier to learn than *hare*, this may out-weigh the advantage that *hare* has by virtue of risk dominance. And, just as there can be grooves on the surface of potential bargains, so there can be grooves on the surface of social space. Thus, if a *deer*-playing region has sufficiently salient boundaries, it may be able to survive, even if it is surrounded by *hare*-playing regions. Still, the model suggests that the utility-based forces of social evolution favour risk dominance rather than payoff dominance.

Many people find this conclusion hard to accept. A common objection goes something like this. Consider two groups of players of the stag hunt game. For many natural ways of defining such 'groups', it is plausible to assume that, within each group, individuals are on average more likely to play against opponents from their own group than against opponents from the other. If one group follows the *deer* convention while the other follows *hare*, the *deer*-playing group may do better on average. So (it is said) we might expect the *deer*-playing group to grow relative to the *hare*-playing one.

Skyrms (1996, pp. 58–9) offers an analogy from biology in support of his analysis of 'correlated convention'. In its biological form, this theory is due to William Hamilton (1964); I have adapted it to apply to the stag hunt game. Consider a population of some territorial animal species, dispersed over some area. Suppose there is a recurrent process by which pairs of these animals play a game with the same structure as the stag hunt game, but with payoffs measured in terms of reproductive success. These pairings are not completely random; the closer two animals' territories are, the more likely those animals are to meet. Suppose that almost all of these animals are genetically programmed to play *hare*, but there is a small geographical cluster of animals who are programmed to play *deer*. If the cluster is not too small, *deer*-players whose territories are near the centre of the cluster will play almost all their games against other *deer*-players. For *deer*-players closer to the boundary, the probability of meeting other *deer*-players will be less. Averaging over all the *deer*-players, let q be the proportion of their games that are played against other *deer*-players. Then the average payoff to the *deer*-players is $3q$. If $q > \frac{2}{3}$, which is entirely consistent with the assumptions of the model, then, on average, *deer*-players have greater reproductive success than *hare*-players. Suppose this condition holds. It follows from the meaning of 'reproductive success' that the *deer*-playing population will grow in relative size. If this population change leads to a reallocation of territories, the *deer*-players now occupying a larger area but remaining geographically clustered, we should expect the value of q to rise slightly (since a smaller proportion of the *deer*-playing population will have territories close to the edge of the cluster). So the inequality $q > \frac{2}{3}$ will still be satisfied, and the process will continue until the population is entirely composed of *deer*-players.

In Hamilton's model, then, evolutionary selection favours payoff dominance rather than risk dominance. My spatial model has exactly the opposite implication. Which should we believe?

It seems to me that Hamilton's model, however valid in biology, does not apply to social evolution. The crucial disanalogy concerns the interpretation of payoffs. If payoffs are measures of reproductive success, it is a tautology that groups with higher average success grow more quickly. But in the context of social evolution, payoffs are measures of success in terms of what individuals want. The process by which successful strategies come to be played more frequently is one of trial-and-error learning. Given that *deer* is relatively successful, on average, for people in one region of geographical or social space, we must ask why that fact should be expected to induce individuals *in a different region* to adopt it. The logic of trial-and-error learning is that people tend to adopt the strategies that are good for them in whatever social environment they inhabit. Although *deer* is a very successful strategy for people lucky enough to be well inside a *deer*-playing area, it is less successful than *hare* everywhere else – including locations inside, but near the edge of, the *deer*-playing area. Under these circumstances, as my spatial model shows, trial-and-error learning leads to selection in favour of *hare*.

My hunch is that, in order for the forces of social evolution to favour *deer*, *hare*-playing and *deer*-playing must be alternative characteristics of organized groups of interacting individuals (for example, firms, clubs or political parties), and these groups must compete to attract and retain members. In such cases, groups are analogous with biological organisms: they can live and die, and their survival prospects may depend on their efficiency.[19] In contrast, the methods of analysis used in *ERCW* are more applicable to environments in which conventions compete for the allegiance of individuals *as individuals*, and in which the survival of the individuals themselves is not in question. (Take the example of Welsh and English. The expansion of the English language in Wales was not the result of different birth and death rates in two distinct ethnic groups. Rather, the practice of English-speaking spread from one ethnic group to another.)

In environments of this latter kind, the qualities of conventions that are favoured by evolutionary selection are much more like risk-dominance than payoff dominance. Or, to put this another way: when thinking about which conventions are favoured, we need to consider situations in which no convention is universally followed. A given convention has an evolutionary advantage to the extent that, in such situations (and especially in the ones that are most likely to occur) people tend to gravitate towards using it. How well people do by following it in situations in which everyone follows it is of little significance.

The reader may ask how this conclusion squares with the claims made in Chapter 6 about the tendency for conventions of reciprocity to evolve in the iterated (or 'extended') prisoner's dilemma. In that particular game, according to *ERCW*, evolutionary selection favours efficient strategies. But *ERCW* does not claim that reciprocity emerges in this game *because* it is an efficient convention. To the contrary, Chapter 7 expresses doubts about how far the optimistic results of Chapter 6 can be generalized to other games in which there is a conflict between individual and group interest. In fact, one of the arguments deployed in Chapter 6 appeals to what would now be called risk dominance. Section 6.4 begins by considering a stripped-down version of the iterated prisoner's dilemma in which there are only two strategies, *brave reciprocity* (B) and *unconditional defection* (N). Each of these is a convention. It is shown that, unless games can be expected to end after very few rounds, the frequency of B-playing which makes the two strategies equally successful is quite low – much less than 0.5. This result is interpreted as suggesting that evolutionary selection favours B relative to N. In the language of modern game theory, the result is that B risk-dominates N. Of course, it is also true that B is payoff-dominant; but it is the risk dominance and not the payoff dominance which gives B its evolutionary advantage.

A.6   The evolution of reciprocity

In Sections A.2 and A.4, I have argued that we need to take account of the *strength* of the forces that are represented in models of replicator dynamics, and not merely of the *direction* in which they pull. The weaker these forces are, the less confident we can be in the predictions of a model which ignores other factors which impact on the processes by which players learn. I have claimed that *ERCW* recognizes this general principle, at least implicitly, in its treatment of salience. I must now confess that there is an argument in *ERCW* which neglects this principle.

Chapter 6 analyses a number of variants of the iterated prisoner's dilemma game. The central claim of the chapter is that in these games, evolution tends to favour strategies of *brave reciprocity* – that is, strategies by which a player co-operates with an opponent who co-operates, defects against an opponent who defects, and is willing to experiment with co-operation without waiting for the opponent to co-operate first. The strategy of tit-for-tat (co-operate in the first round, then in every subsequent round, do whatever the opponent did in the previous round) is one example of such a strategy. Chapter 6 develops two distinct lines of argument in support of this claim.

The first argument, presented in Sections 6.2 and 6.3, is that a class of sophisticated tit-for-tat strategies are stable equilibria if mistakes are made with low probability.[20] These strategies work by instituting an indefinitely long chain of potential punishments. We start with a *first-order* rule (co-operation by both players in all rounds of the iterated prisoner's dilemma) which players are normally expected to follow. Then we add a *second-order* rule which prescribes what happens if anyone deviates from the first-order rule: this requires that all the players take particular actions of reparation (in the case of the deviator) or punishment (in the case of the others) which impose costs on the deviator. Then we add a *third-order* rule which prescribes how players are to be punished if they break a second-order rule, and so on. Any such strategy must specify exactly what punishments are imposed for breaches of the rules. For example, the strategy T_1 is defined so that all breaches of its rules are punished by one round of defection.

I now think that, in my discussion of these strategies, I was guilty of the error of applying formal models of replicator dynamics to situations in which selection pressures are weak. For example, imagine a population of players of the iterated prisoner's dilemma game in which everyone follows the sophisticated tit-for-tat strategy T_1. Except when mistakes are made, everyone co-operates in every round; but if a player defects by mistake, he is punished. Could this population be invaded by the sucker's strategy S of co-operating in all rounds, irrespective of what the opponent does? In the absence of mistakes, S does just as well as T_1 against any mix of S and T_1. The only forces to prevent drift towards S arise from the fact that T_1 does slightly better than S against a T_1-playing opponent who, in some round r, defects by mistake. (In this situation, the S-player fails to punish the opponent in round $r + 1$, and then is punished in round $r + 2$ for not punishing.) If mistakes are rare, the net cost of playing S rather than T_1, averaged over all games, may be very small. In other words, the selection pressure against S may be very weak. It might easily be outweighed by other factors which systematically favour S. (For example, S is a much simpler strategy than T_1, and so may be more salient, and easier to learn.) Thus, although it can be proved that sophisticated tit-for-tat strategies are evolutionarily stable, that proof does not give us much reason to expect that real evolutionary processes will select such strategies.[21]

However, *ERCW* offers another argument in support of the claim that evolution favours brave reciprocity. This argument is presented in Section 6.4. The main idea is that there can be strategies of *cautious reciprocity*, which do not initiate co-operation, but which reciprocate co-operation if an opponent initiates it. One example of such a strategy is C_1, which is just like T_1 except that it defects in the first round and then, if the opponent co-operates in the first round, responds by co-operating in both the second and third rounds (that is, making reparation for its initial defection). Such strategies are at no disadvantage in a population in which almost everyone plays the 'nasty' strategy of defecting in every round, and so can spread through the population by random drift. The presence of these strategies opens the way for invasion by strategies of brave reciprocity. The formal model presented in Section 6.4 now seems to me to be excessively simplified; but I think the conclusion that evolution favours brave reciprocity is correct.

Here is what now seems to me to be a better argument. Consider any strategy Q for the iterated prisoner's dilemma. One question we can ask about Q is how it responds to an opponent who, *playing against Q*, co-operates in every round. If, against such an opponent, Q co-operates in every round (including the first), Q *replicates co-operation.* Another question we can ask is how Q responds to an opponent who, playing against Q, defects in every round. If, against such an opponent, Q defects in every round (including the first), Q *replicates defection.* And we can ask: what sequence of moves is the best reply to Q? If the uniquely best reply is to co-operate in every round, Q *rewards co-operation.* If the uniquely best reply is to defect in every round, Q *rewards defection.* Using these definitions, we can define four broad (but not exhaustive) classes of strategies. First, there are strategies that both replicate and reward defection: the nasty strategy N is an example. Second, there are strategies that both replicate and reward co-operation: this class includes all strategies of brave reciprocity. Third, there are strategies that replicate defection but reward co-operation: this class includes all strategies of cautious reciprocity. Finally, there are strategies that replicate co-operation but reward defection: the sucker's strategy S is an example.

Now consider any population in which the only strategies that are played are ones that replicate and reward defection. In such a population, co-operative moves are never played. Any such population is in a state of weakly stable equilibrium, since every strategy that is being played is a best reply to every other. Let us call this an *equilibrium of defection.* The opposite polar case is a population in which the only strategies that are played are ones that replicate and reward co-operation. Such a population, in which no one ever defects, is also in a state of weakly stable equilibrium: this is an *equilibrium of co-operation.*

How might the pattern of play in the game tip from one type of equilibrium to the other? First, suppose we start from an equilibrium of defection. Random drift can lead to the emergence of strategies which replicate defection but reward co-operation. Initially, this development will have no observable effects: the only moves actually played will still be defections. However, if the proportion of this type of strategy reaches a critical size, there can be an invasion by strategies which both replicate and reward co-operation. This is the process that I described in Section 6.4; the strategies that invade are strategies of brave reciprocity.

What I did not say (because, as far as I recall, it had not occurred to me) is that there can be tipping in the opposite direction too. Suppose we start from an equilibrium of co-operation. Then random drift can lead to the emergence of strategies (such as the sucker's strategy) which replicate co-operation but reward defection. Initially, there will be no observable effects: only co-operative moves will actually be played. But if the proportion of this type of strategy reaches a critical size, there can be invasion by strategies which both replicate and reward defection.

In the long run, then, we might expect to find periods of apparent stability, during which almost all moves are co-operative or almost all moves are defections, punctuated by brief episodes of transition from one state to the other.[22] However, the two processes of tipping are not quite symmetrical with one another. Because of this asymmetry, transitions in one direction can come about much more easily than transitions in the other.

In each of the two transitions, random drift allows the growth of what might be called *sleeper* strategies – strategies that induce behaviour that at first is indistinguishable from that of the *incumbent* strategies they displace, but which favour certain kinds of potential invaders if and when they appear. The existence of the sleeper strategies provides the conditions that allow the invaders to succeed. So far, so symmetrical. Now for the asymmetry.

When the initial equilibrium is one of defection, the invaders' early success comes from their ability *to establish patterns of mutual co-operation with the sleepers*. In this way, the invaders reward the sleepers relative to the incumbents; because of this, growth in the frequency of the invading strategies will at first be predominantly at the expense of the incumbents. Since the early stages of the invasion are possible only in the presence of a critical mass of sleepers, this factor helps to make invasion a self-reinforcing process. In contrast, when the initial equilibrium is one of co-operation, the invaders' early success comes from their ability *to defect against the sleepers*. In this way, the invaders penalize the sleepers relative to the incumbents; because of this, growth in the frequency of the invading strategy will be predominantly at the expense of those strategies whose continued existence is essential for the success of the invasion. This creates a tendency for invasions to collapse. Thus, equilibria of co-operation are less vulnerable to invasion than are equilibria of defection.

One general lesson to be learned from this kind of analysis is that evolutionary processes do not necessarily converge to states of equilibrium from which no further changes take place. Instead, there may be continual change. Random drift of the frequencies of different strategies can lead to sudden, unpredictable transitions between one weakly stable equilibrium and another, or to would-be transitions which begin and then fail. In the case of the iterated prisoner's dilemma, there seems to be a general tendency for strategies of brave reciprocity to predominate over the long run, but suckers and nasties will never disappear

altogether. Indeed, occasional invasions by nasties, preying on fluctu-
ating populations of suckers, are part of the mechanism which sustains
reciprocity.

A.7   Normative expectations and punishment

In Chapter 8 of *ERCW*, I introduce the idea that 'other people's expectations matter to us'. I present this hypothesis in terms of what I claim are
two natural and primitive human sentiments: resentment, and unease
at being the object of resentment. Section 8.4 hints at the possibility of
a theory in which the desire to avoid being the object of resentment can
motivate non-selfish behaviour. In particular, it is suggested that such
a theory might explain why people sometimes follow established conventions even in the exceptional cases in which doing so is contrary to
self-interest, and how practices of reciprocity can be sustained in environments in which self-interested individuals would take free rides. Since
writing *ERCW*, I have fleshed out these ideas in the form of a simple
theory of *normative expectations* (Sugden, 1998 and 2000).

To keep things simple, I present this theory in relation to a game
between two players; but it can easily be extended to larger games. The
theory is formulated in terms of an equilibrium concept, *normative expectations equilibrium*, for a special type of game. It can be interpreted as
a theory of equilibrium states in an evolutionary process of trial-and-
error learning, given the assumption that the game is played recurrently
and anonymously by pairs of individuals drawn at random from a large
population.

The game itself has players A and B. A chooses a strategy from some set
$\{R_1, \ldots, R_m\}$; B chooses from $\{S_1, \ldots, S_n\}$. A distinction is made between
two kinds of payoff. Following an emerging convention in game theory,
I shall call the more fundamental of these kinds *material payoffs*. Like the
utility payoffs of standard game theory, material payoffs are measured
on a cardinal scale of real numbers. The interpretation is that a player's
material payoffs provide information about what he wants to achieve
from the game, after abstracting from any attitudes he has towards interaction with the other player. In thinking about the theory, it may help to
think of material payoffs simply as amounts of some resource that both
players prefer to have more of rather than less. If A chooses strategy R_i
and B chooses S_j, A's material payoff is denoted by $u(i, j)$ and B's by $v(j, i)$.
Let $p = (p_1, \ldots, p_m)$ be any probability distribution over A's strategies, and
let $q = (q_1, \ldots, q_n)$ be any probability distribution over B's. To simplify
notation, let $u(i, q)$ be the expected value of $u(i, j)$ if A chooses strategy

R_i and B chooses according to q; let $u(p, j)$ be the expected value of $u(i, j)$ if A chooses according to p and B chooses S_j; let $u(p, q)$ be the expected value of $u(i, j)$ if A chooses according to p and B chooses according to q; and let $v(q, j)$, $v(i, q)$ and $v(q, p)$ be defined symmetrically.

So far, the only difference from standard game theory has been the substitution of the term 'material payoff' for 'utility'. But, in contrast to standard game theory, normative expectations theory does not assume that players are motivated solely by the objective of maximizing material payoff (or utility). Players' motivations are represented by *subjective payoffs*, which take account not only of material payoffs but also of the players' attitudes to their mutual interaction. Formally, subjective payoffs depend both on material payoffs and on beliefs.

The aim of the theory is to provide a criterion for identifying which (p, q) pairs are equilibria of the game. Given that we are interpreting the theory in evolutionary terms, a (p, q) pair is to be interpreted as a *population state*, that is, as a description of the behaviour of the population of potential players at some given moment; p and q describe the behaviour that can be expected of a randomly-selected individual in the roles of A and B respectively.

Suppose that the current population state is (p, q), and that, in a particular instance of the game, A chooses to play strategy R_k. I define the *impact* of A's action on B as $v(q, k) - v(q, p)$. Similarly, if B chooses strategy S_k, the impact of her action on A is defined by $u(p, k) - u(p, q)$. Looking at the first of these definitions, $v(q, k)$ is the expected value of B's material payoff, given that she chooses her strategy according to q and that A chooses R_k; $v(q, p)$ is the expected value of B's material payoff when B does not know which strategy A will actually choose. Thus, the impact of A's action on B is the net increase in expected material payoff for B as a result of A's choosing R_k rather than acting according to p. B's impact on A can be interpreted similarly.

Now imagine that the population state (p, q) has persisted for a sufficiently long time for players to learn to expect their opponents to act according to p and q; and suppose A chooses to play strategy R_k. Then the impact of this choice, as I have defined it, is not just a measure of the net effect of A's action on B's material payoffs, as assessed by an all-seeing game theorist. It is also a measure of the net effect that A *can expect* his action to have on B. And B *can expect* that A can expect his action to have this effect on her. If the impact of A's action on B is negative, A is worsening B's position, relative to her prior expectations; and both players can see that this is the case. This is likely to arouse resentment in B. This suggests a simple method of modelling the idea that players are averse to being the object of resentment: we can assume that, other things being equal, each player prefers that the impact of his chosen strategy is non-negative, and that among negative impacts, less negative impacts are preferred.

Such preferences can be represented by subjective payoffs. Let $U(k; p, q)$ be the subjective payoff to A from choosing strategy R_k in population state (p, q); and let $V(k; q, p)$ be defined symmetrically. As a simple model of resentment-avoidance, I assume

$$U(k; p, q) = f[u(k, q), v(q, k) - v(q, p)] \tag{A.1}$$

and

$$V(k; q, p) = g[v(k, p), u(p, k) - u(p, q)], \tag{A.2}$$

where $f(., .)$ and $g(., .)$ are finitely-valued functions. I assume that each of these functions is increasing in its first argument, strictly increasing in its second argument when this is negative, and constant with respect to changes in the second argument when this is positive. In other words, I assume that each player seeks to maximize his own expected material payoff and to minimize any negative impact on his opponent.

A population state (p, q) is a *normative expectations equilibrium* if, evaluated in terms of expected *subjective* payoffs, p is a best reply to q and vice versa.[23] Thus, the amendment to standard game theory is to substitute subjective payoff for utility as a determinant of behaviour. Formally, subjective payoff (as defined by equations A.1 and A.2) varies with probabilities while, in standard game theory, the utility of any given combination of pure strategies is independent of probabilities.[24]

To illustrate the implications of this theory, I return to an example that I discussed in Section A.3: behaviour at road junctions with 'give way' markers. Here is a simple game-theoretic model of the situation. We are dealing with a recurrent interaction between players in two roles, the major-road driver (A) and the minor-road driver (B). A has a choice between two strategies: *maintain speed* and *give way*. If we assume that A's slowing down is sufficiently obvious as to leave B in no doubt that he is giving way to her, B does not need to make a decision until A has signalled his intentions. Effectively, there is no decision for B to make: she should move out into the major road if and only if A slows down. So let us call this strategy *sensible* and ignore any other possible actions by B. Figure A.2 presents material payoffs for a highly simplified version of this game. The idea behind these payoffs is that, by choosing *give*

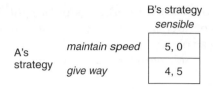

Figure A.2   The courtesy game

way rather than *maintain speed*, A incurs a small cost and confers a larger benefit on B.

If the numbers in Figure A.2 were utilities in the normal game-theoretic sense, the game would be trivial: B would have no decision to make, and A would clearly do best by choosing *maintain speed*. But if we apply normative expectations theory, there is more to the game than this. Suppose that, whenever A's impact on B is negative, the subjective payoff to A is the sum of (i) his material payoff and (ii) his impact on B, multiplied by some positive constant α; when A's impact on B is zero or positive, his subjective payoff is simply his material payoff. (The value of α measures how strongly A desires to avoid provoking resentment.) Let p be the probability that, in the population as a whole, individuals in the role of A choose *give way*. Now consider a particular game. B's expected material payoff is $5p$. If A chooses *maintain speed*, his expected subjective payoff is $5 - 5p\alpha$; if he chooses *yield*, it is 4. Thus, *maintain speed* is the better strategy in terms of subjective payoffs if $p\alpha < \frac{1}{5}$, while *give way* is better if that inequality is reversed. Clearly, $p = 0$ (the population state in which As always play *maintain speed*) is a normative expectations equilibrium, irrespective of the value of α. (If A is expected to *maintain speed*, his doing so does not provoke resentment.) But if $\alpha > \frac{1}{5}$, there is another normative expectations equilibrium, at $p = 1$: each A is expected to *give way* and, given this expectation, chooses to *give way* rather than provoke resentment.

As this example shows, there can be normative expectations equilibria in which individuals act contrary to their interests (in the 'material' sense). Such equilibria are maintained by self-reinforcing expectations: if a pattern of acting contrary to self-interest becomes established in a population, other people's expectations of that behaviour can induce conformity to the pattern.

Normative expectations theory, like the analysis in *ERCW* on which it is based, does not deal explicitly with resentment as a motivating force. I now see that as a limitation. Resentment is a primitive motivation for acts of punishment and revenge. In state-of-nature interactions, taking revenge tends to be costly: like other forms of fighting, it hurts both parties. Thus, acts of revenge are instances of non-selfish behaviour. Just as unease at being an object of resentment can motivate non-selfish acts which benefit others, so resentment can motivate non-selfish acts which harm others.

There is growing evidence that acts of revenge play an important part in maintaining practices of reciprocity.[25] In Chapter 7, I argued that conventions of reciprocity, if maintained only by self-interest, tend to be fragile when the group of potential co-operators is at all large. The instability of such conventions arises from the difficulty of punishing individual free riders without bringing down the whole edifice of co-operation. Co-operative practices are somewhat more stable if people have some degree of non-selfish motivation to reciprocate other people's co-operative acts. However, even if many people are motivated in this way, co-operation is liable to unravel in the presence of a small minority of determined free riders. In contrast, if some people are motivated to punish free riders *individually* in ways that do not compromise the larger scheme of co-operation, free riding can be deterred more easily. Thus, non-selfish motivations of negative reciprocity – motivations which prompt acts of punishment and revenge – may be more important in stabilizing co-operative practices than are the more attractive motivations of positive reciprocity on which *ERCW* focuses.

Even so, the analysis of resentment in *ERCW* provides a starting point for thinking about the conditions which prompt acts of revenge. It suggests the hypothesis that the revenge-taker is motivated to harm individuals who have gone against his interests and expectations, and hence that acts of revenge occur in response to disruptions of established expectations.

A.8   Resentment and morality

In *ERCW*, I argue that there is a general tendency for certain kinds of behavioural rule – specifically, rules of co-ordination, of property and of reciprocity – to emerge and to reproduce themselves in human populations. Within the populations in which they operate, these rules are not merely shared expectations about how in fact people behave. They are also perceived as having moral force: each person has the perception that he *ought* to follow these rules, and that he is *entitled* to expect other people to follow them too.

On my analysis, as presented in Section 9.1, a behavioural rule R is likely to acquire moral force within a population if it has the following three characteristics. First, almost everyone in the population follows R. Second, for any individual who follows R, it is in his interest that the people with whom he interacts follow R too. Third, if almost everyone with whom some individual interacts follow R, it is in that individual's interest to follow R too. Yet, as *ERCW* makes clear throughout, a rule may have all three of these characteristics and yet give worse results for everyone than some alternative rule. And a rule which has these characteristics may favour some people at the expense of others in ways which, when viewed from outside, seem morally arbitrary. Many readers have been unpersuaded by my argument that such undesirable or arbitrary rules come to be perceived as moral.

That argument postulates a natural human propensity to feel resentment when other people act in ways which frustrate one's expectations. It then shows that, if some rule R has the three characteristics, people who follow R feel resentment towards people who don't. Since resentment implies disapproval, deviations from R are generally disapproved. But (the argument concludes) morality as a social phenomenon just *is* rule-governed approval and disapproval. Some critics think that this argument conflates moral disapproval and a non-moral, psychological reaction to the stimulus of frustrated expectations. For example, Jane Mansbridge (1998, pp. 162–6) distinguishes between irritation and anger on the one hand and resentment on the other. Resentment, she says, differs from irritation and anger in having moral content. If your expectations are frustrated as a result of someone else's breach of a convention, you may feel irritation or anger; but you feel resentment only if you already perceive that convention as moral or fair. Similarly, Bruno Verbeek (1998, chapter 1) identifies what he calls 'co-operative virtues' – virtues associated with doing your part in a fair co-operative scheme or tacit agreement. He argues that resentment about breaches of conventions is aroused only when those breaches take the form of failures to act according to the co-operative virtues. Thus, according to both Mansbridge and Verbeek, what I claim to be an explanation of morality depends on smuggled-in moral premises. What is at issue here is whether resentment, as I have characterized it, occurs as a primitive psychological response to the frustration of expectations, or whether it occurs only in the presence of certain moral judgements.

One of the difficulties in discussing natural sentiments is that the language we use to describe them often seems to have cognitive content. Because of this, it is easy to make the mistake of thinking that the sentiment itself cannot occur without the corresponding cognition. Take the relatively straightforward case of fear. There can be no doubt that fear is a natural emotion that is experienced by many animals. It may be plausible to suppose that humans are the only animals with a *concept* of fear and with a language within which that concept can be expressed, but fear itself is surely prior to the concept of fear. What fear feels like for us is probably not very different from what it feels like for our closer relatives among the mammals: the concept provides us with a way of *classifying* the feeling, not a different way of experiencing it. Even so, we may be inclined to say that the concept of fear, as used in human language, is not just a description of a feeling, but also includes the cognition that there is something to be feared. For example, suppose I am looking over the edge of a high cliff. Between me and the edge of the cliff is an unobtrusive fence which I know to be safe. Even so, I feel a sense of unease, an urge to move back. This *feels like* other sensations that are clear cases of fear, and just as in those other cases, I feel an urge to move away from the source of the sensation. The difference is that on the cliff top I do not have the cognition of danger which is typically associated with the sensation. Am I experiencing fear? That seems to me to be a question of semantics, not of psychological substance. Whether we call it 'fear' or not, there is a fear-like sensation which is common to situations in which there is a perception of a real danger and situations like the cliff top.

What Mansbridge and Verbeek say about resentment is analogous to the claim that the cliff-top experience isn't real fear. Consider one of Mansbridge's examples. It is Jane's first day at high school. She comes in black socks, but finds that everyone else is wearing white ones. She wants to fit in, but all the socks she owns are black. After a week of being the only student not wearing white socks, she throws away all her old black ones and buys ten pairs of white. When she goes back to school in her new socks, she finds that her fellow-student Katie has started wearing black socks. Does Jane feel resentment towards Katie? Katie's behaviour is contrary to established expectations. If there is a possibility that Katie's behaviour will set a new fashion, her action harms Jane. On my analysis, we should expect Jane to feel resentment. According to Mansbridge, Jane doesn't feel resentment, she feels only irritation. What is the difference? Irritation, like resentment, is an emotion with negative 'valence': it is a form of pain rather than of pleasure. Like resentment, it involves a negative attitude towards another person who is perceived as the origin of the pain. The difference, it seems, is that Jane does not have the cognition that Katie has breached a moral rule. In other words, Jane's irritation *feels like* resentment, but it isn't *really* resentment because it isn't associated with the appropriate cognition.

My response is that 'resentment' is just the word I use to describe a certain complex of feelings. These feelings combine disappointment at the frustration of an expectation and anger and hostility towards the person who is perceived as having frustrated them. As it happens, these feelings are often associated with certain beliefs about morality, but the feelings can and do exist without those beliefs. The regular association between the feelings and the moral beliefs can be explained by the nature of the feelings and the conditions that tend to generate them.

A critic may still be suspicious about my claim that *disapproval* is a component of resentment. Is there some slippage between 'anger', which seems non-normative, and 'disapproval'? For example, if I bang my head against a low doorway, I suffer the pain of a disappointed expectation. If I am in a bad mood, my emotional response may feel very much like anger; I may even experience an incoherent desire to direct this anger against something; but, it seems, there is no disapproval. So does Jane *disapprove* of Katie's choice of socks, rather than merely being angry about it?

My understanding of approval and disapproval is broadly in line with Adam Smith's analysis in his *Theory of Moral Sentiments*. On Smith's account, we approve of an another person's sentiments just to the extent that (in Smith's words) we 'go along' with them – just to the extent that, as we perceive it, our emotional response to whatever has stimulated the other person's response is (or, in some versions of the argument, would have been) similar to the other person's:

> To approve of the passions of another, therefore, as suitable to their objects, is the same thing as to observe that we entirely sympath-ize with them; and not to approve of them as such, is the same thing as to observe that we do not entirely sympathize with them. (1759, p. 16)

For Smith, 'sympathy' is a psychological concept: we sympathize with other person's sentiment when we have *fellow-feeling* for it – when the affective state of the other person, as imagined by us, induces in us a (usually weak) affective state of the same kind.[26] So approval is ultimately a matter of the psychology of fellow-feeling: there is no added moral ingredient. If Jane is eager to fit in, she will not have fellow-feeling for Katie's desire to be different; and if so, her attitude *will* be disapproval.

Finally, the critic may be sceptical about whether, *in fact*, the psychology of resentment is as I have described it. As a partial answer to such scepticism, I offer some speculations about the biological functions that resentment might serve. On my account, a core feature of resentment is a feeling of hostility towards other people who frustrate one's own expectations. What does it mean to have a feeling of hostility towards someone? I suggest: to have some primitive desire to attack or harm him. Conversely, to feel unease about being the object of another person's resentment is to be inhibited against acts which are likely to prompt in the other person a desire to attack or harm us. If we are looking for a biological function of resentment, we need to think about how this particular combination of desire and inhibition might enhance fitness.

The kind of reason that allows us to reflect on our desires and to think consciously about how best to satisfy them seems to be a relatively recent development in evolutionary history, and to be a characteristic of, at most, only a few species. In contrast, many of the desires themselves date much further back in evolutionary time, and are common to a much larger group of species. Desires, then, must initially have evolved to work independently of reason, as direct prompts to action. Reason is perhaps best seen as a parallel system of decision-making, which is capable of using desires as data, but which has not completely supplanted the original mechanism for determining our actions. To understand the evolutionary origins of particular desires, we need to look for fitness-enhancing properties of the actions for which those desires are the direct prompts.

Consider what *general* desires and aversions would be adaptive for an animal which is social and which recurrently plays mixed-motive games – games in which the interests of the players are neither completely opposed nor completely aligned – with individuals of the same species. Here, I use the concept of a game in the biological sense, with payoffs measured in terms of fitness; these games might be understood as conflicts over scarce and fitness-enhancing resources – food, territories, mates, and so on. Such conflicts are the biological correlates of games such as the crossroads game, the war of attrition, and chicken.

In games like these, it is fitness-enhancing to adapt one's behaviour to what can be expected of the other player. Typically, it pays to be aggressive against an opponent who is likely to back down in the face of aggression, but to back down against an opponent who is not himself likely to back down. In such a world, clearly, an ability to recognize and project patterns in the behaviour of other individuals will be adaptive. But recognition is not enough: one has to have the *desire* to act aggressively in situations in which aggression is likely to pay; and one must have a corresponding *aversion* to acting aggressively when it is not. Thus, we might expect one of the triggers of aggression to be the sense that there is something desirable to be had, that someone else is frustrating one's attempts to get it, and this is a kind of situation in which individuals in one's own position usually get what they want. Conversely, we might expect fear and unease to be triggered by the contemplation of acts of aggression in the sorts of situation in which such acts are usually met by counter-aggression, and in which individuals in one's own position usually fail to get what they want. Once emotions of aggression and submission have become triggered by negatively-correlated stimuli (that is, so that one person's aggression dovetails with another's submission), this set of triggers will have evolutionary stability: everyone's acting on these emotions creates the environment to which such behaviour is well-adapted.

I suggest that this kind of mix of desires for, and inhibitions against, aggression is sufficiently like our human experience of resentment to make it at least credible that resentment is a primitive human emotion.[27] Biologically and conceptually, resentment may be prior to morality.

A.9   The view from where we stand

ERCW maintains a sharp distinction between, on the one hand, the social psychology of morality and, on the other, ethics – the study of questions about what we ought and ought not to do. I repeatedly say that *ERCW* is not a contribution to ethics. It does not claim to say anything about what rules of morality people *ought* to accept. Instead, it tries to explain how people come to accept some of the moral rules that they do. It may be surprising and unwelcome that the moral practices that emerge out of recurrent social interaction can be inefficient, and that they can favour some people at the expense of others in apparently arbitrary ways. But if that's true, it's true. It's not my fault as a social theorist if the world is not as the reader might wish it to be.

In the final section of the book, however, I take a few cautious steps into the terrain of ethics. I define the following *principle of co-operation*: 'Let *R* be any strategy that could be chosen [by each player] in a game that is played repeatedly in some community. Let this strategy be such that if any individual follows *R*, it is in his interest that his opponents should do so too. Then each individual has a moral obligation to follow *R*, provided that everyone else does the same.' I argue that this principle is the common core of the moral rules that tend to grow up around conventions. I then look at this principle from the viewpoint of an ethical theorist.

Viewed in this perspective, the principle of co-operation has two strik-ing properties. First, it makes no reference to any idea of social welfare or, more generally, to any idea of the good of the community or the good of the world. It refers to each person's *interest*, but there is no aggregation of the interests of different individuals. In this sense, it is contractarian in spirit: it expresses a moral view in which social life is a seen as co-operation between individuals for mutual advantage, rather than as a way of pursuing some unified conception of goodness. Second, the principle makes our obligations to one another matters of conven-tion. There might be two strategies, say *R* and *S*, such that each individual has an obligation to follow *R* if everyone else does, but just as much of an obligation to follow *S* if that is what everyone else does. The prin-ciple has nothing to say about how to compare a state of affairs in which everyone follows *R* with one in which everyone follows *S*. Nor does it ever demand of an individual that she acts contrary to a strategy that is generally followed in her society.

One way of summarizing these properties is to say that the morality expressed in the principle of co-operation is constructed *from where we stand*. Each of us is required to take some account of how the world looks from the viewpoint of each other person, as well as of how it looks from our own; but we are not required to think about what is good in some universal sense. Nor are we required to think about how the world would be if we all followed conventions other than the ones we actually follow. Morality is construed in terms of mutual advantage, but the reference point from which advantage is measured is the status quo.

The idea that the moral viewpoint is just wherever we stand is foreign to most of the main currents of ethical thought. In *ERCW*, I emphas-ized the ways in which this idea is in conflict with utilitarianism and welfarism. Eighteen years on, utilitarianism and its derivatives are less popular than they were; but the prevailing views in ethical theory still maintain that, when we make moral judgements, we do so from a standpoint outside our particular lives and outside our particular societies.

One version of this idea, deriving from the Kantian philosophical tra-dition, is well expressed in the work of Thomas Nagel. The title of one Nagel's books, *The View from Nowhere* (1986), encapsulates the idea. Nagel maintains that there are *objective* or *agent-neutral* reasons for action – reasons that apply universally to anyone in a given situation. Thus, when we think ethically, we can transform the agent-centred question 'What shall I do?' into the agent-neutral form 'What should this person do?' (p. 141). By imaginatively standing outside ourselves, by taking the view from nowhere, we can bring our motivations into line with objective reasons.

A different attempt to find a neutral standpoint is characteristic of modern work in the Aristotelian tradition. Here, the guiding idea is that, through reflection about the human condition, it is possible to discover the true nature of human good (or 'well-being', or 'flourishing'). This concept of goodness is supposed to apply to all human beings, independently of their subjective perceptions and independently of the particular societies in which they live. Modern versions of this approach often end up with an 'objective list' of the components of human flourishing, leaving some room for subjective judgement in mixing and matching these components (see, for example, Griffin, 1986 and Nussbaum, 2000).

In the final pages of *ERCW*, I express my own conviction that a coherent conception of morality does *not* require a neutral standpoint. That is still my conviction. I recognize the meaningfulness of asking what would be best for the world, as seen from the viewpoint of an impartially benevolent observer; but I do not see how an answer to that question tells any of us what he or she ought to do. In reply to the advocates of the Kantian and Aristotelian approaches, I have space to say only that I am not persuaded of the existence either of objective reasons or of objective lists of the elements of human flourishing. I share Hume's sense that, when we try to explain how people come to have whatever moral beliefs they do, we find that the best available explanations do not require hypotheses about objective reasons or moral truths. Our moral beliefs are not (as our sense perceptions are) imperfect tools for enquiring into a reality that exists beyond our perceptions. If we are to think ethically, we have to find a way of asking what we ought to do that does not trade on the illusion that there are sources of moral authority outside our own sentiments and perceptions.[28]

ERCW offers a theory about the kinds of moral beliefs that are likely to emerge in human societies. If that theory is correct, some of those beliefs are grounded in nothing more than convention. I do not claim that, when we think as moral agents rather than as social theorists, we *must* endorse this conventional morality. But I do claim that we *can* endorse it sincerely and clear-sightedly.

Notes

1 Spontaneous Order

1 Spontaneous order is the central theme of Hayek's three-volume work *Law, Legislation and Liberty* (1979). In *The Constitution of Liberty* (1960, p. 160), Hayek attributes the phrase 'spontaneous order' to Polanyi.

2 Some economists (e.g. Becker, 1974) have tried to explain voluntary contributions to the supply of public goods in terms of conventional economic theory: each individual is assumed to choose the contribution that maximizes his own utility, taking other people's contributions as given. It is claimed that such a theory is consistent with the observation that *some* voluntary contributions are made – even though the theory also predicts that public goods will be supplied in less-than-efficient amounts. I have argued that the evidence of voluntary contributions to public goods cannot plausibly be explained in this way (Sugden, 1982, 1985; see also Margolis, 1982, pp. 19–21).

3 This shrewd analogy is due to Williams (1973, p. 138).

2 Games

1 This piece of terminology is due to Gibbard (1973).

2 A somewhat similar conception of utility has been developed by Camacho (1982).

3 This work is summarized by Maynard Smith (1982). I shall be saying more about the biological literature in Chapter 4.

4 Axelrod uses only condition (2.1) and not (2.2) to define his concept of a 'collectively stable strategy'. In the language I shall be using, what Axelrod calls a collectively stable strategy is an equilibrium strategy, but not necessarily a stable one.

5 This assumption, which makes the position of each individual symmetrical with that of every other, is convenient but not strictly necessary. All that is required for the argument that follows is that in any game each individual has *some* (i.e. some non-zero) probability of being A and *some* probability of being B.

6 Lewis (1969, p. 22) uses the concept of a 'proper equilibrium', which he defines as a situation in which each player's strategy is his *unique* best reply to his opponent's strategy (or opponents' strategies). This is sufficient but not necessary for stability on my definition.

3 Coordination

1 Nozick (1974, p. 18) offers an alternative reading of these passages from Locke. Nozick argues, as I do, that the use of money is a convention that

could have evolved spontaneously, but he claims that Locke believed that the 'invention of money' was the result of 'express agreement'. I think Nozick is taking Locke's use of the concept of agreement too literally; Locke does, after all, say that this agreement is 'tacit' and 'without compact'.

2 Schotter (1981, Ch. 2) presents a model of the evolution of market-day conventions.

4 Property

1 It would be anachronistic not to follow Hobbes in speaking of 'men' rather than 'persons'.

2 Most versions of the teenagers' game are probably better modelled by the 'war of attrition' game presented in Section 4.3.

3 The assumption that utility is lost at a constant rate through time is not really necessary, although it allows the analysis to be simplified slightly. All that is necessary is that utility is lost continuously until one player surrenders. To generalize the argument in the text, a pure strategy should be interpreted as an 'acceptable penalty' (i.e. the maximum loss of utility a player will sustain before surrendering) rather than as a persistence time (cf. Norman *et al.*, 1977).

4 More formally, let $f(t)$ be the probability density function for persistence times in a given strategy. Then $S(t) = f(t)/[1 - \int_0^t f(t)\,dt]$.

5 I have avoided using differential calculus so as to make the argument comprehensible to as many readers as possible. This result could have been derived more elegantly by taking limits as $\delta t \to 0$.

6 This result corresponds with one in the theory of 'rent-seeking': if individuals can compete for access to economic rents, free entry to the competition will ensure that in the long run the value of the rents is entirely dissipated (cf. Tullock, 1967 and Krueger, 1974).

7 A slightly different game can be constructed by assuming instead that where the claims sum to less than 1, the unclaimed portion of the resource is divided equally between the players. The analysis of this game is very similar to that of the division game.

8 In Schelling's game, when players' claims are incompatible, each simply receives nothing.

9 In more mathematical language, the claims that are assigned a non-zero probability are the *support* of the relevant strategy.

10 This paper develops an idea first put forward by Parker and Rubinstein (1981).

11 Throughout this paragraph and the next, the terms 'challenger' and 'possessor' should be read as shorthand for 'self-styled challenger' and 'self-styled possessor'.

12 This case should be distinguished from the one discussed in Section 3.2, in which a game has two stable equilibria but an asymmetry in the utility scores makes one of these more likely to evolve than the other.

13 In order to prove the stability of this equilibrium, it is necessary to assume that there is some very small probability that players make mistakes. Compare the discussion in Section 7.3 and in the appendix to Chapter 7.

14 Much recent discussion of commitment and credibility has been within the framework set up by Selten's (1978) famous paper on the 'chain-store paradox' (see, for example, Milgrom and Roberts, 1982). My model differs from Selten's in two important respects. First, Selten's paradox arises because his game has a fixed and finite number of rounds; thus there is a last round in which commitments cannot be credible (since after the last round reputations can have no value). My notion of long-run equilibrium presupposes that there is never a 'last round': reputations always have value. Second, the structure of Selten's chain-store game is such that only one player (the chain-store owner) is able to make a commitment. In my model *all* players have the same opportunities to make commitments.

5   Possession

1 This, at any rate, is how the problem was perceived by governments. The idea that private individuals might be claimants does not seem to have been considered at all seriously.
2 In this respect my analysis of the war of attrition differs from the analysis to be found in the biological literature (see Section 4.7).
3 This is not to say there is no scope at all. There is, for example, room for debate about what counts as part of a nation's land mass. In particular, the status of small uninhabited islands, such as Rockall in the North Atlantic, is open to rival interpretations.

6   Reciprocity

1 Here I am assuming that my act of restraint is independent of yours. More precisely, suppose that I play this game repeatedly against different opponents. Then the utility I derive from a sequence of games depends only on the number of times I show restraint and the number of times my opponents do; it doesn't matter whether I show restraint in the same games as my opponents do.
2 This use of words is a little unfortunate. The state of affairs in which one player chooses 'co-operate' while the other chooses 'defect' has to be called a state of unilateral co-operation – which sounds like a contradiction in terms. Similarly the state in which both players choose 'co-operate' has to be called a state of mutual co-operation – which sounds like a tautology. Nevertheless I shall follow the established convention and call the two strategies in the exchange-visit game 'co-operate' and 'defect'.
3 Strictly speaking, the exchange-visit game is a special case of the prisoner's dilemma game. The classic prisoner's dilemma game is a symmetrical two-person game in which each player chooses 'co-operate' or 'defect'. Using Taylor's (1976, p. 5) notation, let w be the utility score for each player if they both defect, let x be the score for each player if they both co-operate, let y be the score for a player who defects when his opponent co-operates, and let z be the score for a player who co-operates when his opponent defects. The classic game is defined by setting $y > x > w > z$; the condition $2x > y + z$ is sometimes added (e.g. Rapoport and Chammah, 1965,

p. 34; Axelrod, 1981). I have effectively imposed the stronger condition $x + w = y + z$.

4 My analysis of equilibrium strategies in the extended prisoner's dilemma game is not original; it derives from (among others) Taylor (1976) and Axelrod (1981). But I believe that my analysis of stability *is* original.

5 Axelrod (1981) uses a similar argument to show that a community of nasties can be invaded by a small 'cluster' of individuals playing tit-for-tat.

6 The utility scores shown in Figure 6.3 are calculated on the assumption that the probability of mistakes is insignificantly small.

7 Strictly speaking, if players occasionally make mistakes there is a slight risk associated with being a cautious reciprocator in a world of nasties. Suppose your opponent is nasty, but accidentally co-operates in the first round. If you are a cautious reciprocator you will respond by co-operating in the second round, whereas the best reply is to defect. But provided that $pq > 0$ – that there are *some* brave reciprocators around – and provided that the probability of mistakes is sufficiently small, C_1 will yield more expected utility than N.

8 Using Taylor's (1976) notation, Axelrod's game is defined by $w = 1, x = 3$, $y = 5$ and $z = 0$. These values satisfy the two conditions for a classic prisoner's dilemma game, namely $y > x > w > z$ and $2x > y + z$. My game also satisfies these conditions (compare note 3).

9 Axelrod did, in fact, organize a simulation of evolutionary processes, and the most successful strategy was again tit-for-tat. However, it seems that Axelrod conducted this experiment by using the strategies that had been submitted for – and therefore designed for – the round-robin tournament. A better test would be to see how tit-for-tat fared in a competition in which people were invited to enter strategies for a tournament carried out under explicitly evolutionary rules.

7 Free Riders

1 The classic prisoner's dilemma game is described in note 3 to Chapter 6. This would be exactly equivalent to the snowdrift game if we set $w = 0$, $x = v - c_2$, $y = v$ and $z = v - c_1$ and then imposed the restrictions $c_1 > v > c_2 > 0$ and $c_1 > 2c_2$.

2 A strategy corresponding to T_1 (i.e. 'Play "dove" if your opponent is in good standing, or if you are not; otherwise play "hawk" ') can be defined for the hawk–dove game. But with the particular utility values I used in presenting the hawk–dove game, this strategy turns out *not* to be a stable equilibrium, however close the value of π is to 1. My version of the hawk–dove game is equivalent to the snowdrift game with $v = 4$, $c_1 = 2, c_2 = 1$; this gives $\max [c_2/v, c_2/(c_1 - c_2)] = 1$.

3 Here I am assuming the probability of mistakes to be insignificantly small.

4 Mackie (1980, pp. 88–9) offers two different interpretations of Hume's rowing example. On one interpretation the rowers' problem is merely to coordinate their strokes (perhaps each rower has one oar): this is a pure coordination game. On Mackie's other interpretation it is a prisoner's dilemma game in which the players adopt tit-for-tat strategies.

5 The idea that the voluntary supply of public goods can be modelled by the chicken game has been developed by Taylor and Ward (1982); as I pointed out in Section 7.3, the snowdrift game is a form of the chicken game.

6 To simplify the presentation, I shall ignore the possibility that v might be *exactly* equal to one of $c_1 \ldots, c_n$.
7 Models in which public goods are supplied in this kind of way have been presented by, among others, Taylor (1976, Ch. 3) and Guttman (1978).
8 This idea is developed by Nozick, (1974, Ch. 2).
9 Lifeboat services could no doubt be organized on the club principle, provided lifeboatmen were prepared to be sufficiently ruthless and rescue only those who had paid subscriptions. But given the principles on which the lifeboat service actually operates, its life-saving activities are to the benefit of anyone who goes near the sea.

8 Natural Law

1 The problem of wishful thinking is explored by Elster (1983).
2 Hobbes's fifth law of nature 'is COMPLAISANCE; that is to say, *that every man strive to accommodate himself to the rest*' (1651, Ch. 15). Hobbes's argument is that a man who wishes to survive and prosper among other men ought, as a matter of prudence, to cultivate a complaisant or sociable character. If this argument is correct, we should expect some tendency for biological natural selection to favour the same character traits.
3 See Hume (1740, Book 3, Part 1, Section 1) for a statement of this 'law'.
4 The idea that moral judgements are universalizable is developed by Hare (1952). It will be clear from what follows that I do not accept Hare's (1982) more recent argument that universalizability entails some kind of utilitarianism.
5 In the division game there is one symmetrical convention – that of equal division. But all the other conventions in this game, and all the conventions in the hawk–dove and war of attrition games, are asymmetrical.
6 An individual who benefits from the fact that a particular convention has become established might perhaps resent such meekness because of its tendency to undermine the convention; but as long as the convention is secure, the existence of a meek minority works to everyone else's benefit.
7 I have developed this idea more fully in a recent paper (Sugden, 1984). As I emphasize in that paper, the ethic of reciprocity is not to be confused with the principle – often called Kantian – that in games with a prisoner's dilemma structure each individual has an unconditional moral obligation to play the co-operative strategy (cf. Laffont, 1975; Collard, 1978; Harsanyi, 1980). A principle of reciprocity obliges a person to co-operate only if others co-operate too.

9 Rights, Co-operation and Welfare

1 Lewis calls these simply 'conventions'; his definition of convention excludes the rules I have called conventions of property and conventions of reciprocity (see Section 2.8).
2 The game that she takes as her paradigm has the same structure as the banknote game I presented in Chapter 2: there are two players and two alternative conventions, one favouring one player and one the other.

3   An alternative reading is that every breach of a convention tends to weaken it. On *this* reading, we receive 'mediate' prejudice from acts of injustice only if the rules of justice work to our advantage in the long run.

4   In the *Theory of Moral Sentiments* Smith argues against the view that our approval of principles of justice is grounded in sympathy with public interest: 'The concern which we take in the fortune and happiness of individuals does not, in common cases, arise from that which we take in the fortune and happiness of society' (1759, Book 2, Section 2, Ch. 3).

5   This principle is a close relative of the 'principle of fairness' formulated by Hart (1955). It also has some similarities with the principle of reciprocity that I have presented in a recent paper (Sugden, 1984).

6   Or, if we are concerned with practical morality, *almost* everyone else. Such a qualification is theoretically awkward, but unavoidable.

7   This point is made by Buchanan (1985, p. 63).

8   'Take up the white man's burden / And reap his old reward / The blame of those ye better / The hate of those ye guard.'

Afterword

1   *ERCW* follows Schelling (1960) in using the word 'prominence' for the property of being noticeable or sticking out. The synonym 'salience', which seems to have been introduced by Lewis (1969), has now become standard in game theory; I use the latter term in this Afterword.

2   Camerer (1995) and Starmer (2000) survey the evidence.

3   I discuss these difficulties in Sugden (2001).

4   The evolutionary game theory sketched out in the following paragraphs is explained in more detail by Binmore (1992, pp. 414–34) and Weibull (1995). The model of replicator dynamics is due to Taylor and Jonker (1978).

5   In *ERCW* I use the term 'repeated game' for a game that is played recurrently by different sets of individuals drawn from a population and 'extended game' for a game which is made up of a sequence of identical 'rounds'. The former would now more usually be called a *recurrent* game and the latter an *iterated* game (the rounds of which are *stage games*). In this Afterword, I follow current usage.

6   My account of how inductive reasoning works, and of why perfectly rational agents with no sense of salience would be unable to make inductive inferences, is inspired by Goodman (1954). Lewis (1969, pp. 36–42) explains why shared perceptions of salience are an essential part of the process by which conventions are learned. For more on these issues, see Goyal and Janssen (1996), Schlicht (1998, 2000), and Cubitt and Sugden (2003).

7   Skyrms (1996) asks this question in relation to Lewis's (1969) analysis of language as convention, which provides the starting point for my own analysis. Cubitt and Sugden (2003) defend Lewis's theory against Skyrms's critique.

8   A set of sixteen elements has 2^{16} distinct subsets. One of these is empty and the other contains all sixteen elements.

9   I have been surprised by how many sophisticated readers have disbelieved the analogous claim, made in Section 2.1, that if chess ended after Black's first move, there would be 20^{20} alternative strategies for Black. Don't I mean

20 × 20? No: there are 20×20 possible *positions* after Black's first move, but 20^{20} possible *strategies* for Black.

10   My minimal knowledge of experimental child psychology is gleaned from Mehler and Dupoux (1994) and Kellman and Arterberry (2000). The particular results about symmetry are due to Bornstein and Krinsky (1985).

11   The source of my information about Cook's voyages is Hough (1994).

12   Barry (1989, pp. 168–73, 346–7) is one such sceptic. His criticism is directed at Hume's analysis of property conventions, which is the starting point for Chapter 5 of *ERCW*. Barry thinks this theory 'fanciful', and puts it down to youthful attention-seeking on Hume's part. Although Barry seems to suggest that property conventions have been selected for their efficiency, he argues that bargaining problems are resolved by relative power (pp. 12–24).

13   I say more about this problem in Sugden (1990).

14   In the usual version of the Nash demand game, each player gets a utility of zero in the event of conflict. My version allows there to be a stable equilbrium in which the whole of the resource is taken by one of the players. In *ERCW*, I attribute this game to Schelling, but it was first analysed by Nash (1950).

15   This result can be generalized. In a wide class of 'smoothed' bargaining games, equilibrium is possible only if the utility outcomes for the two players are very close to the 'Nash bargaining solution' of the unsmoothed game. The Nash bargaining solution can be interpreted as reflecting relative power. Binmore (1992, pp. 299–304) gives an accessible treatment of this body of theory.

16   For Binmore, fairness norms are normative principles which evolve spontaneously and which allow groups to resolve the problem of selecting between alternative conventions; the norms that are favoured in the evolutionary process are ones which allow groups to coordinate on *efficient* conventions (p. 422).

17   These concepts were introduced to game theory by Harsanyi and Selten (1988).

18   The spatial model I present in the following paragraphs is developed with more generality in Sugden (1995). It is adapted from a model proposed by Ellison (1993), but uses a different concept of space. In Ellison's model, as in most spatial game-theoretic models, people (rather than, as in my model, games) have locations. Each person is assumed to play the relevant game only with her closest neighbours, but to do so anonymously. Thus, variation in behaviour across space comes about through inter-personal variations in behaviour.

19   When there is this kind of inter-group competition, there may be selection in favour of more efficient rather than less efficient *conventions*. But we should not expect selection in favour of strategies which (like co-operation in the one-off prisoner's dilemma) are not evolutionarily stable – however efficient they may be. In groups in which such strategies are played, average payoffs are relatively high, but individuals who deviate unilaterally do even better.

20   This result is an instance of what game theorists call the Folk Theorem. For an explanation of this theorem, see Binmore (1992, pp. 369–79).

21   Binmore, Gale and Samuelson (1995) draw a similar conclusion in relation to evolutionarily stable equilibrium in the ultimatum game.

22   Exactly this pattern has been found in simulations of the iterated prisoner's dilemma reported by Hoffman (1999). Hoffman uses a simulation method

based on a genetic algorithm; this allows a very large number of potential strategies to be represented in a tractable model.

23 It can be shown that a normative expectations equilibrium exists for every game if, in addition to the assumptions I have already stated, $f(.,.)$ and $g(.,.)$ are continuous and weakly concave (Sugden, 2000).

24 Games in which subjective payoffs depend on probabilities are *psychological games*, a type of game invented by Geanakoplos, Pearce and Stacchetti (1989). One of the best-known applications of psychological game theory is Rabin's (1993) theory of fairness. In Rabin's theory, player A is defined to be more or less 'kind' to player B according to how far A forgoes his own material payoff to benefit B. Players' subjective payoffs have the property that each player desires to be kind to an opponent who is kind, and unkind to one who is unkind. This is a very different motivation from that of not frustrating other people's expectations. For example, in the courtesy game (Figure A.2), Rabin's theory implies that *maintain speed* is the unique equilibrium strategy.

25 Much of this evidence comes from the experimental research of Fehr and his associates, who explain the desire to punish by assuming that individuals are averse to *inequality*, particularly when inequality favours others rather than themselves. (For an overview of this research, see Fehr and Fischbacher, 2002.) I think it is psychologically more credible, and more consistent with the evidence, to explain the desire to punish in terms of resentment at the frustration of expectations.

26 In Sugden (2004) I reconstruct Smith's theory of fellow-feeling and argue that its main hypotheses are consistent with what is now known about the psychology and neurology of sympathy and empathy.

27 It might be objected that aggression and resentment are not quite the same thing: aggression in the pursuit of gain is forward-looking, while resentment can motivate costly acts of backward-looking revenge. How does a desire for revenge enhance fitness? One possible answer is that it doesn't, but is an unavoidable by-product of biologically feasible mechanisms of aggression. Frank (1988) offers a more sophisticated answer in terms of the strategic value of commitment. Because anger is associated both with some loss of rational control and with visible physiological signals that are not easy to fake, anger can signal that a person is committed to aggression if some desire is not satisfied. Following through on that commitment is revenge.

28 For me, the possibility and value of such an approach to ethics is confirmed by the work of Bernard Williams (e.g. Williams, 1981) – which is not to say that Williams sympathizes with the conservatism of *ERCW*.

References

Allais, M. (1953) 'Le comportement de l'homme rationnel devant le risque; critique des postulats et axiomes de l'ecole Americaine'. *Econometrica*, **21**, 503–46.

Arrow, K. J. (1963) 'Uncertainty and the welfare economics of medical care'. *American Economic Review*, **53**, 941–73.

Arrow, K. J. (1967) 'Values and collective decision-making'. In Laslett, P. and Runciman, W. G. (eds), *Philosophy, Politics and Society*. London: Blackwell.

Arrow, K. J. and Debreu, G. (1954) 'Existence of an equilibrium for a competitive economy'. *Econometrica*, **22**, 265–90.

Axelrod, R. (1981) 'The emergence of cooperation among egoists'. *American Political Science Review*, **75**, 306–18.

Bacharach, M. (1976) *Economics and the Theory of Games*. London: Macmillan.

Barry, Brian (1989) *Theories of Justice*. London: Harvester-Wheatsheaf.

Becker, G. S. (1974) 'A theory of social interactions'. *Journal of Political Economy*, **82**, 1063–93.

Bell, F. (1907) *At the Works: A Study of a Manufacturing Town*. London: Edward Arnold.

Binmore, Ken (1992) *Fun and Games: A Text on Game Theory*. Lexington, Mass.: D. C. Heath.

Binmore, Ken (1994) *Game Theory and the Social Contract, Volume I: Playing Fair*. Cambridge, Mass.: MIT Press.

Binmore, Ken (1998) *Game Theory and the Social Contract, Volume 2: Just Playing*. Cambridge, Mass.: MIT Press.

Binmore, Ken, Gale, John and Samuelson, Larry (1995) 'Learning to be imperfect: the ultimatum game'. *Games and Economic Behavior*, **8**, 56–90.

Bishop, D. T. and Cannings, C. (1978) 'A generalized war of attrition'. *Journal of Theoretical Biology*, **70**, 85–124.

Bishop, D. T., Cannings, C. and Maynard Smith, J. (1978) 'The war of attrition with random rewards'. *Journal of Theoretical Biology*, **74**, 377–88.

Bornstein, M. H. and Krinsky, S. J. (1985) 'Perception of symmetry in infancy: the salience of vertical symmetry and the perception of pattern wholes'. *Journal of Experimental Child Psychology*, **39**, 1–19.

Buchanan, A. (1985) *Ethics, Efficiency, and the Market*. Oxford: Clarendon Press.

Buchanan, J. M. (1965) 'An economic theory of clubs'. *Economica*, **32**, 1–14.

Buchanan, J. M. (1975) *The Limits of Liberty*. Chicago: University of Chicago Press.

Camacho, A. (1982) *Societies and Social Decision Functions*. Dordrecht: Reidel.

Camerer, Colin (1995) 'Individual decision making'. In Kagel, John and Roth, Alvin (eds), *Handbook of Experimental Economics*. Princeton: Princeton University Press.

Collard, D. A. (1978) *Altruism and Economy*. Oxford: Martin Robertson.

Cubitt, Robin and Sugden, Robert (2003) 'Common knowledge, salience and convention: a reconstruction of David Lewis's game theory'. *Economics and Philosophy*, **19**, 175–210.

Dawkins, R. (1980) 'Good strategy or evolutionarily stable strategy?'. In Barlow, G. W. and Silverberg, J. (eds), *Sociobiology: Beyond Nature/Nurture*. Boulder: Westview Press.

Ellison, Glenn (1993) 'Learning, local interaction, and coordination'. *Econometrica*, **61**, 1047–71.

Elster, J. (1983) *Sour Grapes: Studies in the Subversion of Rationality*. Cambridge: Cambridge University Press.

Fehr, Ernst and Fischbacher, Urs (2002) 'Why social preferences matter: the impact of non-selfish motives on competition, cooperation and incentives'. *Economic Journal*, **112**, C1–C33.

Frank, Robert H. (1988) *Passions within Reason*. New York: Norton.

Friedman, M. (1962) *Capitalism and Freedom*. Chicago: University of Chicago Press.

Geanakoplos, John, Pearce, David and Stacchetti, Ennio (1989) 'Psychological games and sequential rationality'. *Games and Economic Behavior*, **1**, 60–79.

Gibbard, A. (1973) 'Manipulation of voting schemes: a general result'. *Econometrica*, **41**, 587–601.

Goodman, Nelson (1954) *Fact, Fiction, and Forecast*. Cambridge, Mass.: Harvard University Press.

Goyal, Sanjeev and Janssen, Maarten (1996) 'Can we rationally learn to coordinate?' *Theory and Decision*, **40**, 29–49.

Griffin, James (1986) *Well-being: Its Meaning, Measurement and Moral Importance*. Oxford: Oxford University Press.

Guttman, J. M. (1978) 'Understanding collective action: matching behavior'. *American Economic Review*, **68**, Papers and Proceedings, 251–5.

Hamilton, William D. (1964) 'The genetical evolution of social behavior'. *Journal of Theoretical Biology*, **7**, 1–52.

Hammerstein, P. and Parker, G. A. (1982) 'The asymmetric war of attrition'. *Journal of Theoretical Biology*, **96**, 647–82.

Hardin, G. (1968) 'The tragedy of the commons'. *Science*, **162**, 1243–8.

Hare, R. M. (1952) *The Language of Morals*. Oxford: Oxford University Press.

Hare, R. M. (1982) 'Ethical theory and Utilitarianism'. In Sen, A. K. and Williams, B. (eds), *Utilitarianism and Beyond*. Cambridge: Cambridge University Press.

Harsanyi, John C. (1955) 'Cardinal welfare, individualistic ethics and interpersonal comparisons of utility'. *Journal of Political Economy*, **63**, 309–21.

Harsanyi, John C. (1980) 'Rule utilitarianism, rights, obligations and the theory of rational behavior'. *Theory and Decision*, **12**, 115–33.

Harsanyi, John C. and Selten, Reinhard (1988) *A General Theory of Equilibrium Selection in Games*. Cambridge, Mass.: MIT Press.

Hart, H. L. A. (1955) 'Are there any natural rights?' *Philosophical Review*, **64**, 175–91.

Hayek, F. A. (1960) *The Constitution of Liberty*. London: Routledge and Kegan Paul.

Hayek, F. A. (1979) *Law, Legislation and Liberty*. London: Routledge and Kegan Paul. (In three volumes, Vol. 1 published 1973, Vol. 2 published 1976, Vol. 3 published 1979).

Hobbes, T. (1651) *Leviathan*, edited by M. Oakeshott. London: Macmillan, 1962.

Hoffman, Robert (1999) 'The independent localisations of interaction and learning in the repeated prisoner's dilemma'. *Theory and Decision*, **47**, 57–72.

Hough, Richard (1994) *Captain James Cook: A Biography*. London: Hodder and Stoughton.

Hume, David (1740) *A Treatise of Human Nautre*, edited by L. A. Selby-Bigge (2nd edition). Oxford: Clarendon Press, 1978.

Hume, David (1759) *Enquiries concerning Human Understanding and Concerning the Principles of Morals*. Oxford: Oxford University Press, 1975.

Johnson, N. (1981) *Voluntary Social Services*. Oxford: Basil Blackwell.

Kahneman, D. and Tversky, A. (1979) 'Prospect theory: an analysis of decision under risk'. *Econometrica*, **47**, 263–91.

Kellman, Philip J. and Arterberry, Martha E. (2000) *The Cradle of Knowledge* (Cambridge, Mass.: MIT Press).

Keynes, J. M. (1936) *The General Theory of Employment, Interest and Money*. London: Macmillan.

Kramer, R. M. (1981) *Voluntary Agencies in the Welfare State*. Berkeley: University of California Press.

Krueger, A. O. (1974) 'The political economy of the rent-seeking society'. *American Economic Review*, **64**, 291–303.

Laffont, J.-J. (1975) 'Macroeconomic constraints, economic efficiency and ethics: an introduction to Kantian economics'. *Economica*, **42**, 430–7.

Lewis, D. K. (1969) *Convention: A Philosophical Study*. Cambridge, Mass.: Harvard University Press.

Locke, J. (1690) *Two Treatises of Government*, edited by P. Laslett. Cambridge: Cambridge University Press, 1960.

Loomes, Graham and Sugden, Robert (1982) 'Regret theory: an alternative theory of rational choice under uncertainty'. *Economic Journal*, **92**, 805–24.

Mackie, J. L. (1980) *Hume's Moral Theory*. London: Routledge and Kegan Paul.

Mansbridge, Jane (1998) 'Starting with nothing: on the impossibility of grounding norms solely in self-interest'. In Ben-Ner, Avner and Putterman, Louis (eds), *Economics, Values, and Organization*. Cambridge: Cambridge University Press.

Margolis, H. (1982) *Selfishness, Altruism and Rationality*. Cambridge: Cambridge University Press.

Maynard Smith, J. (1974) 'The theory of games and the evolution of animal conflicts'. *Journal of Theoretical Biology*, **47**, 209–21.

Maynard Smith, J. (1982) *Evolution and the Theory of Games*. Cambridge: Cambridge University Press.

Maynard Smith, J. and Parker, G. A. (1976) 'The logic of asymmetric contests'. *Animal Behaviour*, **24**, 159–75.

Maynard Smith, J. and Price, G. R. (1973) 'The logic of animal conflicts'. *Nature*, **246**, 15–18.

Mehler, Jacques and Dupoux, Emmanuel (1994) *What Infants Know: The New Cognitive Science of Early Development*. Oxford: Blackwell; first published in French in 1990.

Mehta, Judith, Starmer, Chris and Sugden, Robert (1994a) 'Focal points in games with multiple equilibria: an experimental investigation'. *Theory and Decision*, **36**, 163–85.

Mehta, Judith, Starmer, Chris and Sugden, Robert (1994b) 'The nature of salience: an experimental investigation of pure coordination games'. *American Economic Review*, **84**, 658–73.

Milgrom, P. and Roberts, J. (1982) 'Predation, reputation and entry deterrence'. *Journal of Economic Theory*, **27**, 280–312.

Morgenstern, O. (1979) 'Some reflections on utility'. In Allais, M. and Hagen, O. (eds), *Expected Utility Hypotheses and the Allais Paradox*. Dordrecht: Reidel.

Nagel, Thomas (1986) *The View from Nowhere*. Oxford: Oxford University Press.

Nash, John (1950) 'The bargaining problem'. *Econometrica*, **18**, 155–62.

Neumann, J. von and Morgenstern, O. (1947) *Theory of Games and Economic Behavior* (2nd edition). Princeton: Princeton University Press.

Norman, R., Taylor, P. and Robertson, R. (1977) 'Stable equilibrium strategies and penalty functions in a game of attrition'. *Journal of Theoretical Biology*, **65**, 571–8.

Nozick, R. (1974) *Anarchy, State and Utopia*. New York: Basic Books.

Nussbaum, Martha (2000) *Women and Human Development: The Capabilities Approach*. Cambridge: Cambridge University Press.

Parker, G. A. and Rubinstein, D. I. (1981) 'Role assessment, reserve strategy, and acquisition of information in asymmetrical animal conflicts'. *Animal Behaviour*, **29**, 135–62.

Rabin, Matthew (1993) 'Incorporating fairness into game theory and economics'. *American Economic Review*, **83**, 1281–302.

Rapoport, A. (1967) 'Exploiter, Leader, Hero and Martyr: the four archetypes of the 2 × 2 game'. *Behavioral Science*, **12**, 81–4.

Rapoport, A. and Chammah, A. M. (1965) *Prisoner's Dilemma: A Study in Conflict and Cooperation*. Ann Arbor: University of Michigan Press.

Rousseau, Jean-Jacques (1755) *Discourse on the Origin and Foundations of Inequality among Men*. New York: Norton, 1988.

Rawls, J. (1972) *A Theory of Justice*. Oxford: Oxford University Press.

Samuelson, P. (1954) 'The pure theory of public expenditure'. *Review of Economics and Statistics*, **36**, 387–9.

Schelling, T. (1960) *The Strategy of Conflict*. Cambridge, Mass.: Harvard University Press.

Schlicht, Ekkehart (1998) *On Custom in the Economy*. Oxford: Oxford University Press.

Schlicht, Ekkehart (2000) 'Aestheticism in the theory of custom'. *Journal des Economistes et des Etudes Humaines*, **10**, 33–51.

Schoemaker, P. (1982) 'The expected utility model: its variants, purposes, evidence and limitations'. *Journal of Economic Literature*, **20**, 529–63.

Schotter, A. (1981) *The Economic Theory of Social Institutions*. Cambridge: Cambridge University Press.

Selten, Reinhard (1975) 'Reexamination of the perfectness concept for equilibrium points in extensive games'. *International Journal of Game Theory*, **4**, 25–55.

Selten, Reinhard (1978) 'The chain store paradox'. *Theory and Decision*, **9**, 127–59.

Selten, Reinhard (1980) 'A note on evolutionarily stable strategies in asymmetric animal conflicts'. *Journal of Theoretical Biology*, **84**, 93–101.

Sen, A. K. (1970) *Collective Choice and Social Welfare*. Edinburgh: Oliver and Boyd.

Sen, A. K. (1977) 'Rational fools: a critique of the behavioural foundations of economic theory'. *Philosophy and Public Affairs*, **6**, 317–44.

Sen, A. K. (1979) 'Personal utilities and public judgements: or what's wrong with welfare economics?' *Economic Journal*, **89**, 537–58.

Shubik, M. (1971) 'The Dollar Auction game: A paradox in noncooperative behavior and escalation'. *Journal of Conflict Resolution*, **15**, 109–11.

Skyrms, Brian (1996) *Evolution of the Social Contract*. Cambridge: Cambridge University Press.

Slovic, P. and Tversky, A. (1974) 'Who accepts Savage's axiom?' *Behavioral Science*, **19**, 368–73.

Smith, A. (1759) *The Theory of Moral Sentiments*, edited by D. D. Raphael and A. L. Macfie. Oxford: Clarendon Press, 1976.

Smith, A. (1776) *An Inquiry into the Nature and Causes of the Wealth of Nations*, edited by R. H. Campbell, A. S. Skinner and W. B. Todd. Oxford: Clarendon Press, 1976.

Starmer, Chris (2000) 'Developments in non-expected utility theory: the hunt for a descriptive theory of choice under risk'. *Journal of Economic Literature*, **38**, 332–82.

Sugden, Robert (1982) 'On the economics of philanthropy'. *Economic Journal*, **92**, 341–50.

Sugden, Robert (1984) 'Reciprocity: the supply of public goods through voluntary contributions'. *Economic Journal*, **94**, 772–87.

Sugden, Robert (1985) 'Consistent conjectures and voluntary contributions to public goods: why the conventional theory does not work'. *Journal of Public Economics*, **27**, 117–24.

Sugden, Robert (1990) 'Contractarianism and norms'. *Ethics*, **100**, 768–86.

Sugden, Robert (1995) 'The coexistence of conventions'. *Journal of Economic Behavior and Organization*, **28**, 241–56.

Sugden, Robert (1998) 'Normative expectations: the simultaneous evolution of institutions and norms'. In Ben-Ner, Avner and Putterman, Louis (eds), *Economics, Values, and Organization*. Cambridge: Cambridge University Press.

Sugden, Robert (2000) 'The motivating power of expectations'. In Nida-Rümelin, Julian and Spohn, Wolfgang (eds), *Rationality, Rules and Structure*. Dordrecht: Kluwer.

Sugden, Robert (2001) 'The evolutionary turn in game theory'. *Journal of Economic Methodology*, **8**, 113–30.

Sugden, Robert (2004) 'Fellow-feeling'. Forthcoming in Gui, Benedetto and Sugden, Robert (eds), *Economics and Social Interaction*. Cambridge: Cambridge University Press.

Taylor, M. (1976) *Anarchy and Cooperation*. London: John Wiley and Sons.

Taylor, M. and Ward, H. (1982) 'Chickens, whales and lumpy goods: alternative models of public-goods provision'. *Political Studies*, **30**, 350–70.

Taylor, Peter and Jonker, Leo (1978) 'Evolutionarily stable strategies and game dynamics'. *Mathematical Biosciences*, **40**, 145–56.

Tullock, G. (1967) 'The welfare costs of tariffs, monopolies and theft'. *Western Economic Journal*, **5**, 224–32.

Ullman-Margalit, E. (1977) *The Emergence of Norms*. Oxford: Clarendon Press.

Verbeek, Bruno (1998) *The Virtues of Cooperation*. Doctoral dissertation, University of Amsterdam.

Walmsley, L. (1932) *Three Fevers*. London: Collins.

Weibull, Jörgen (1995) *Evolutionary Game Theory*. Cambridge, Mass.: MIT Press.

Williams, Bernard (1973) 'A critique of utilitarianism'. In Smart, J. J. C. and Williams, Bernard *Utilitarianism: For and Against*. Cambridge: Cambridge University Press.

Williams, Bernard (1981) *Moral Luck*. Cambridge: Cambridge University Press.

Young, H. Peyton (1993) 'The evolution of conventions'. *Econometrica*, **61**, 57–84.

Young, H. Peyton (1998) *Individual Strategy and Social Structure: An Evolutionary Theory of Institutions*. Princeton, N.J.: Princeton University Press.

Index